CHRIS BONINGTON'S
EVEREST

*To my fellow expeditioners*

# CHRIS BONINGTON'S
# EVEREST

## Chris Bonington

RAGGED MOUNTAIN PRESS / McGRAW-HILL

*Camden, Maine • New York • Chicago • San Francisco • Lisbon • London
• Madrid Mexico City • Milan • New Delhi • San Juan • Seoul • Singapore
• Sydney • Toronto*

# Contents

'I was determined not to loose sight of the foundations of my love of climbing, the moments of being out in front, on rock or snow, picking out a route, or of sitting on a belay gazing at the mountains stretched below and around.'

# Introduction

M Y CALVES ACHED. MY NOSE ITCHED and I longed to scratch it. We'd been standing for what seemed hours. It was the Coronation Parade at RAF Hednesford in the Midlands, where I was doing my basic training as a National Serviceman. We were called to attention and the Camp Commander announced that on this auspicious day news had just arrived that Mount Everest had been climbed. Although I had discovered climbing two years before and it had become the all-absorbing drive of my life, Everest seemed too distant, unattainable, almost irrelevant. I little more than noted the fact that it had been climbed and continued planning in my mind my next sortie to Snowdonia.

In 1953 I had never been abroad, but since starting to climb I had hitchhiked from the chalk cliffs of Beachy Head to the wild empty spaces of the northwest Highlands of Scotland. These filled the horizons of my ambition, pushing my standard up a notch, going to new crags, putting up new routes. My bible was W.H. Murray's *Mountaineering in Scotland*. I hadn't read any alpine or Himalayan books at this time. Everest was to come into my life much later.

My early career was anything but successful. I had a provisional place at University College, London to study history but failed my English A Level, couldn't face taking my A levels again, so left school to do my National Service in the RAF, with an eye to getting into RAF Mountain Rescue. I decided to make the RAF my career, but at Cranwell proved a hopeless pilot. I made a career move into the army, went to Sandhurst and was commissioned into the Royal Tank Regiment. Not the best choice, perhaps, for someone whose commanding officer described him as the least mechanically minded person he had ever encountered.

This did get me abroad, however, and took me a little closer to the Alps for the next step forward in my mountaineering apprenticeship. My regiment was stationed on the flat plains of Münster, Westphalia, a long train journey from the Alps. My first visit to the Western Alps in 1957 was a baptism of fire. I'd arranged to climb with Hamish MacInnes, already a well-known and very experienced mountaineer, whom I'd met in Glen Coe just after I had left school. Since there were no more experienced climbers around, he had taken me up Raven's Gully, a test piece of the time, making the first winter ascent. His plans for 1957 were no less ambitious – we were going to attempt the North Wall of the Eiger as my first alpine climb. At this time it had only had 12 ascents, none of them by Britons. We didn't get

*The South Face of Nuptse from Lobuche was a bit of a shock. The summit is the third bump from the left and on our first ascent we eventually reached it by the couloir to the immediate left.*

*Chris on the ridge leading up into the South Face of Nuptse. The windproofs are finely woven cotton and the boots — made for North American hunters — are rubber. They had a vapour barrier which made them warm but not much good for climbing.*

far, bivouacking below the Difficult Crack at the start of the real difficulties, and retreating, much to my relief, in the face of threatening weather. We went on to make a first ascent in the Mont Blanc massif. The following year Hamish and I climbed together again, basing ourselves in a little hut near Montenvers, above Chamonix, and it was with Hamish on the South West Pillar of the Dru that I first met Don Whillans.

Shortly after rejoining my regiment I obtained a transfer to the Army Outward Bound School in North Wales as an instructor. At least I was getting back to my climbing roots. It was while I was at the school that I was invited on my first Himalayan expedition, the British Indian Nepalese Services expedition to the unclimbed Annapurna II (7937m/26,040ft). It was a fascinating trip. Two of us travelled out by ship with all the expedition gear, a delightfully leisured way of going climbing, reminiscent of the pre-war Everest expeditions. A train journey with much of the expedition baggage packed into our compartment took us to Patna, from where we flew in a DC3 to Kathmandu.

Our leader was Colonel Jimmy Roberts, who was military attaché in Kathmandu. As a result we had a busy round of receptions and parties before setting out for our mountain. Kathmandu was a very different place then. There was just one hotel, run by a flamboyant White Russian called Boris, very few tourists and no trekkers. We started our walk to the mountain from the British Embassy compound and didn't see a single foreigner on our 16-day approach march to the northern flanks of Annapurna II. The climb itself was a traditional snow plod with a sting in the tail on the final summit ridge, which was steep and airy. As the youngest member of the British team I was lucky to go to the summit with Dick Grant, a captain in the Royal Marines.

The following year I resigned my commission, in part to join a civilian expedition to Nuptse, the third peak of Everest. This was a very different kind of enterprise to Annapurna II. It comprised eight talented climbers but they hardly knew each other. Once again I travelled out by sea to look after the expedition gear, while the bulk of the team drove out, in those days an adventure in itself. I don't think any of us fully appreciated the scale of the challenge. This was my first visit to Sola Khumbu. As in the previous

*Our camp site at Tengpoche looking towards the South Faces of Nuptse and Lhotse, with the summit of Everest behind them. Our Nuptse tents were similar to those used in the '53 Everest expedition.*

year, we started our walk from Kathmandu and met only three other foreigners in the three months we were on expedition. One of them was Peter Aufschnaiter, who had been with Harrer in their seven years in Tibet.

Our first view of Nuptse was a shock. Most mountains, Everest included, suggest an obvious line for a first ascent. Nuptse didn't. The only feasible route seemed up its huge South Face by a series of ice arêtes and rock buttresses leading up to a snow gully that reached the summit ridge. Considering how basic our gear was, it is surprising we ever reached the top. Yet by sheer individual perseverance and downright bloody-mindedness we worked our way up this huge face, fixing ropes, some of which we had bought in the Sherpa villages, until at last Dennis Davis and the Sherpa Tachei made a first ascent, followed next day by Les Brown, Jim Swallow and myself.

Despite our success on Nuptse, at this stage my focus was still more on the Alps than the Himalaya. We travelled back overland in a pair of beat-up Hillman Husky estate cars, and I was dropped off in Chamonix to meet up with Don Whillans with whom I hoped to tackle the North Wall of the Eiger. I was ready for it, but the weather wasn't. We did, however, achieve the first ascent of the Central Pillar of Frêney, a superb buttress on the south side of Mont Blanc. That year I was away from England for nine months, returning in September to join Unilever as a management trainee.

I was going to become a weekend climber, putting expeditions behind me. It didn't last long. Whillans invited me to join an expedition to Patagonia and my boss in Unilever advised me that I needed to decide where my priorities lay. I left the business world without any clear idea of what I was going to do when I returned from Patagonia. In addition, I had met Wendy in January and fallen in love. By May we were married – a sign for many to settle down to a steady career, but that was last thing Wendy wanted. We decided we might as well have a summer in the Alps and it was at the end of the season that I made the

*Don Whillans, left, and
Mick Burke with one of the
revolutionary box tents Whillans
designed for the Annapurna
expedition. Our route up the South
Face, in the background, followed
the left-hand buttress.*

first British ascent of the North Wall of the Eiger with Ian Clough. It was a test-
piece climb that I really wanted to complete. It also enabled me to see a way
of making a living around climbing as a writer, photographer and lecturer.

It was in the late sixties that I started exploring the possibility of once again
climbing in the greater ranges. The Himalaya had been closed to climbers
from 1965 through to 1969 because of conflict in the area but was now opening up once again and it was around this time that I came across a photograph
of the South Face of Annapurna. It immediately caught my imagination —
even bigger and certainly steeper than the South Face of Nuptse.

I plunged into the project almost on impulse and only then began to realize all its implications. For a start, we would need a larger team than we had
had on Nuptse. We ended up with a team of ten supported by six Sherpas. We
were sponsored by the Mount Everest Foundation — the first expedition they had underwritten since the
ascent of Kangchenjunga in 1955.

This was the first expedition I had ever led. I had never considered myself to be the organizing type,
though I think I learned a great deal as commander of a troop of tanks in my army days. That was a
little bit like leading an expedition — a crew of four in each of the three tanks, and National Servicemen
which meant one's troopers were probably less amenable than the regulars of today. I quickly discovered
that leadership was not so much a matter of giving orders, as capturing the loyalty and enthusiasm of a
team through consultation and inspiration. It was to be much the same on the mountain, but without
the authority of military discipline and with a team of particularly rugged individualists.

In many ways the South Face of Annapurna was my most challenging climb. Although I had the
experience of the South Face of Nuptse behind me, Annapurna was both higher and more complex.
There was the challenge of planning the logistics, managing my climbers and struggling with the effects
of altitude. We had crises from the very beginning. The ship carrying all the expedition gear broke down
in the Indian Ocean and was over a month late reaching Bombay. This meant borrowing gear and mountain food from a British army expedition on the north side of the mountain to enable us at least to make

*High on the rocky ridge leading to Nuptse's South Face, Les Brown, wearing typical alpine gear of the early sixties, is silhouetted against Ama Dablam's shapely pyramid.*

a start until Ian Clough, my trusty companion of the North Wall of the Eiger, personally escorted our equipment all the way overland from Bombay.

We had almost been overtaken by the monsoon. It was snowing every day and Don Whillans and Dougal Haston were ensconced in the top camp waiting for a break in the weather. Most of the team were climbed out and there was little more than a trickle of supplies reaching the front. Ian Clough and I were at the penultimate camp and had almost given up hope, the weather was so bad. Then the front pair snatched a break in the weather, when the lower part of the mountain was still swathed in cloud, and made a bold push to the summit.

At the very moment of victory, tragedy struck. Ian Clough was the last man down from the mountain. He had been working with the Sherpas to clear our camps. There was one particularly dangerous spot near the bottom where the route went below a serac wall. We had all gone beneath it a dozen times or more. You were in the danger area for only about five minutes and, as Ian passed through, the wall collapsed. We were able to recover his body and buried him below the face where he had contributed so much to our success through selfless work in support of the lead climbers. We returned to Kathmandu with mixed feelings, a deep sadness at the loss of a good friend and yet satisfaction at having achieved success. It was to be a pattern that was to happen all too often in the future.

Back in Kathmandu I also found I was being asked to refocus and turn my mind to an expedition to another mountain – Everest no less. News had come through that the Japanese had failed on the South West Face and I had already been invited to be climbing leader of an international expedition due to make the next attempt in 1971. Up to now all my attention had been devoted to the South Face of Annapurna, with the Japanese still to make their Everest attempt. But now the International Expedition was front of the queue and Jimmy Roberts and Norman Dyhrenfurth, the joint leaders, wanted to consult me about next year's climb. But I was drained from everything that had happened on Annapurna. It had been hard enough leading a group of friends of my own choosing – what would it be like with a group of top

*Ian Clough in the Whillans Box*
*at Camp 5. We made the first*
*ascent of the Central Pillar of*
*Frêney and the first British ascent*
*of the North Wall of the Eiger*
*together. Tragically, he was killed*
*in an avalanche in the final stages*
*of the Annapurna expedition.*

climbers from different countries, none of whom I knew? I decided therefore to pull out of the International expedition, but my near involvement had kindled a preoccupation with Everest that was to verge on the obsessional. I had learned so much on the South Face of Annapurna. I felt not only that I now knew how to put together an expedition to climb Everest South West Face but also that I desperately wanted to meet that challenge entirely on my own terms. The problem was that the mountain was fully booked for the next five years, with several expeditions already eyeing the particular challenge of the South West Face.

In the first instance, I knew I wanted to be the one who masterminded the first ascent of the South West Face of Everest. It was only after I had actually climbed Everest myself a decade later that I realized just how important it was to me to stand on the world's highest point.

This book is a condensation of my accounts of four expeditions to Everest. Each expedition is therefore described immediately after the event. No doubt I'd perceive aspects of all four expeditions from a different perspective today, with the help of hindsight and our ability to filter out events with which we feel uncomfortable. I haven't attempted to do this since I believe that a first impression is both fresher and more accurate. In reading over the original books I found there were incidents that I had forgotten or which over the course of time my memory had subtly altered.

Everest was to have a huge influence over my life for a 15-year period after our ascent of the South Face of Annapurna. It was to put great pressures on my family, was to give me moments of intense elation and absolute despair and was to teach me a great deal about myself, about the challenges of leadership and organization and about working with my fellow climbers. In its course some friendships were strengthened, others damaged or even destroyed. There was a strong element of theatre engendered from the size of some of the expeditions and the level of media interest. I had to become an expert in dealing with sponsors, selling ideas, making deals, planning complex logistics and of writing under pressure. All this was taking me far from the fundamentals of climbing and yet had its own fascination,

*Mick Burke leading a pitch on Annapurna's Rock Band at a height of around 7500m (24,600ft). This proved the crux of the climb and was probably the hardest technical climbing done at that altitude at that time.*

appealing to different aspects of my psyche and, for that matter, ego. But I was determined not to loose sight of the foundations of my love of climbing, the moments of being out in front, on rock or snow, picking out a route, or of sitting on a belay gazing at the mountains stretched below and around.

My driving force was not so much to stand on the highest point on earth, but the fascination of finding new ways to that point, of confronting the seemingly impossible and using my skill, intellectual and physical, to overcome the problem. Indeed, a friend of mine once commented, in a slightly accusatory tone, that I spoke little of the romance of climbing and more about the challenge of solving problems, and I think to a degree he was right. Be it a rock climb in the Lake District or a new way up Everest, it's the problem that I find all-absorbing — of how to use a few wrinkly little holds and tenuous cracks in front of my nose on a rock climb, or how to surmount a huge mountain face. In the case of the South West Face of Everest in 1975, I perceived a need for a large team, fixed ropes, oxygen and all the impedimenta that necessitated complex logistics and planning. In every instance it was the process that I found fascinating, but this did not blind me to the beauty of the mountains around me. If anything, the intensity of the experience enhanced my wonder at that very beauty and at the same time in moments of stress, particularly in the course of a big expedition, the grandeur of the surroundings had a soothing, therapeutic quality.

Why Everest and not some other mountain? The glib answer is that it's the biggest and the cynical might comment that therefore it's the mountain that will gain climbers the greatest fame or attract the most sponsors, and to a degree they are right. But I think it goes further and deeper than that. There is a magnificence, a compulsive attraction, in the superlative — one that has lured so many climbers over the years and, through their efforts and stories, has built a tradition around Everest that is almost tangible as you walk past the Rongbuk Monastery towards the northern Base Camp or climb Kalapatar and gaze into the Western Cwm.

All these factors kept drawing me back to Everest.

The challenge of Everest, showing the ridges and faces by which the mountain has been attempted from the 1920s to the present day. Mallory tackled the North Ridge from Tibet. Hillary and Tenzing's 1953 first ascent was made from Nepal by the South Col. The Americans mastered the West Ridge by the Hornbein Couloir on the North Face in 1963. By the 1970s the challenge had shifted to the South West Face.

1

'One of the joys of mountaineering in this fast-shrinking world is that mountaineers for many generations to come will still be able to discover untrodden corners in the greater mountain ranges of the earth. We, however, shall always feel fortunate and privileged to have been able to unravel the complex problems that were presented by the world's highest and steepest mountain face.'

# Everest: South West Face 1972–1975
## A Campaign Accomplished

# Beginnings

T HE GULLY STRETCHED endlessly in front of me; six steps, a rest, breathless in the snow – then another six steps. Aware of Ang Pema just behind me, determined not to let him overtake, not to weaken, I looked up and the top seemed to get no closer; I concentrated on the snow in front of my nose. Ten steps this time; I succeeded in making eight, and then lay panting against the snow; time and distance slipped by slowly. The top was just above – just ten slow steps – and suddenly, after two months' effort with the same magnificent view, a new world opened out before me. It was 1961 and I was on Nuptse, the third peak of Everest. We had been climbing its South Face, and this day was our fulfilment – we were going for the summit.

My first impression was one of boundless space, of a sea of brown rolling hills, flecked by the occasional snowcap, reaching to a distant horizon. In a way this view is even more striking than that of Everest, just the other side of the deep gorge described by the Western Cwm. Its summit is a mere 900m (2950ft) above where we were standing that day – less than the height of Snowdon – a squat, black pyramid, veined with snow and ice, towering above the void of the Western Cwm.

From the summit of Nuptse we had a unique view of the South West Face of Everest, but that day I'm afraid I cannot claim to have formed an immediate ambition to tackle it. We had been too close to our limits on this 7855m (25,770ft) mountain to entertain thoughts of technical climbing at even greater heights. In 1961 we weren't ready for it.

The first time I heard the South West Face of Everest mentioned as a possible objective was in the summer of 1965. I was climbing with John Harlin, the flamboyant and controversial American who swept through the European climbing scene in the early sixties. We were planning to tackle the Eiger Direct that summer, and did a number of training climbs together. John was always full of far-fetched schemes, some of which remained castles in the air, but others surprisingly came off. He was

*My first view of the South West Face of Everest – from the summit of Nuptse in 1961. It would be nice to claim I immediately dreamt of climbing it, but I was so knackered, I couldn't imagine getting any higher than I was at that moment.*

'I weighed the claims of a small team on a known route against the lure of that unclimbed 600m (2000ft) above the high points of the two previous expeditions on the South West Face. The entire concept of a South West Face expedition, with all its challenges, was still extremely attractive to me – perhaps because the challenge was so very great.'

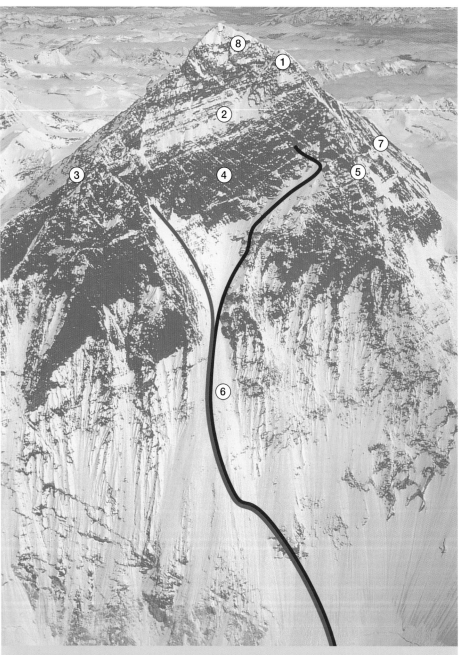

*The South West Face of Everest showing the routes taken by earlier expeditions in their attempts.*

KEY

━━━ Japanese routes: Spring 1969, Spring 1970

━━━ International Expedition route in Spring 1971. International Expedition in Spring 1972 and the Japanese of Autumn 1973, which followed the same line but tried to traverse right on to the South East Face

1  South Summit
2  Summit Snow Field
3  West Ridge
4  Rock Band
5  South Pillar
6  Great Central Gully
7  South East Ridge
8  Hillary Step

dreaming of an international expedition to the South West Face, which never got further than dreams.

I backed out of the Eiger Direct project that autumn but not before I came to know Dougal Haston; we'd met in passing in Chamonix and Leysin, but on the Eiger Direct we spent a certain amount of time together, sharing snow holes and doing some climbing on the face. Dougal was single-minded and even then knew exactly what he wanted to do in life – to climb to the limit – and knowing this, he was very easy to work and climb with. There was no manoeuvring for position on a climb to get the best pitch, or to avoid some of the harder or more dangerous work. He just took everything as it came.

Tragically, John Harlin was killed in the final stages of the climb; we lost a good friend and mountaineering lost one of its most colourful and imaginative inno-vators. Had he lived, the South West Face of Everest might well have been another of his achievements. Instead, he planted the germ of an idea in the minds of Dougal and myself. We had been bitten by the Everest bug. But there was an immediate

*Dougal Haston was a pivotal member of my Everest teams and had already been to the foot of the Rock Band with the International Expedition. A brilliant climber, focused and enigmatic, Dougal became a cult figure.*

problem. The Nepalese government had just banned moun-taineering in Nepal and by the time their frontiers were reopened in 1969 there was already a queue of contenders for the South West Face of Everest, led by the Japanese.

The crux of the South West Face is the notorious Rock Band, a wall of sheer rock stretching across the face that starts at around 8300m (27,230ft). Expeditions had to find a way round it. At its left-hand end is a deep-cut gully and, follow-ing a thorough reconnaissance in 1969, the Japanese were set to tackle this approach the following spring. They reached 8000m (26,250ft), just below the Rock Band, but were thwarted by lack of snow in the gully and danger of stone fall. The fact that their large expedition was divided in objective between the South West Face and the familiar South East Ridge probably did not help matters.

The International Everest Expedition was next in what had become a very long queue for Everest. Norman Dyhrenfurth assembled a well-equipped team for spring 1971, but again one with a dual objective. Some would go for a new line on the West Ridge. Among those dedicated to the South West Face were the UK representatives, Dougal Haston and Don Whillans. Dissension manifested itself before they reached the Rock Band, with Austrian complaints that the Brits were hogging the lead. A ten-day storm and the death of a team member undermined the prospects of the West Ridge team, who voted to switch to the South Col until that route was abandoned too, and the expedition almost fell apart under acrimony, illness and withdrawals. This left Whillans and Haston, supported by the Japanese climbers Uemura and Ito, to tackle the Rock Band.

Knowing that part of the Japanese difficulties in 1970 had been their failure to find a suitable camp site at the foot of the left-hand gully from which to launch their assault, Whillans decided to explore the right-hand flank of the Rock Band instead.

He and Haston succeeded in establishing a Camp 6 (8300m/27,230ft) at the foot of a narrow gully, filled with snow. Rounding a corner, Whillans could see the possiblity of an easier line across to the South Ridge but he rejected this compromise route as avoiding the challenge of the Rock Band. Meanwhile Austrian muttering against the British continued and supplies for Camp 6 thinned to a trickle. Don and Dougal succeeded in climbing about 27m (90ft) up the gully but then ran out of rope. It was painfully obvious that they were not going to get sufficient supplies to make a sustained effort on the Rock Band, let alone a summit bid once that was climbed. Don had reached the high point and came sliding back down the rope to Dougal. 'I think we've had it', he said.

Don and Dougal were invited back to the South West Face the following year by Dr Karl Herrligkoffer, a Munich doctor with a long and highly controversial record of expedition organizing behind him. Dougal backed off this European expedition, as did I when approached, but Don agreed to go. Like the rest of us, he had many doubts about Herrligkoffer, but nevertheless had a deep and burning desire to reach the summit of Everest. Perhaps in some respects his motives were material, as mine had been. Such an achievement would undoubtedly have crowned his career as a mountaineer and established him in a strong position. I suspect he was very aware of both this and the actual financial rewards that would have accompanied his success. But his desire to go to the top of Everest was much more deep-rooted. Throughout his climbing career, he has always favoured bold, obvious lines; he has never really bothered with a contrived route that works its way subtly up a rock face or, for that matter, up a

*Don Whillans went to the summit of Annapurna South Face with Dougal Haston in 1970 and had twice tackled the South West Face of Everest, but I made the controversial decision to leave him behind in 1972.*

mountain. Climbing with him over a period of time, I found that whereas I simply enjoyed the process of climbing and worried little about the nature of the climb, Don would only set out on a climb that he felt was worthwhile. Everest, to him, was much more than the means of making a good living. It represented the ultimate superlative – the ultimate strong and simple objective. To attain it he was prepared to cope with an expedition that was anything but ideal in composition.

Once Dougal and I had withdrawn from the British contingent, Don enlisted Doug Scott and Hamish MacInnes. Doug was an powerful climber who combined a preference for pioneering routes in remote places with an interest in American aid climbing. His expeditions have taken him from Baffin Island to the Hindu Kush, and in 1971 he was the first Briton to climb the Salathé Wall in Yosemite.

Hamish MacInnes was an old friend of mine, as well as Don's. We had shared an epic attempt on the South West Pillar of the Dru when Don probably saved Hamish's life, hauling him semiconscious up most of the climb after Hamish had been hit on the head by a falling stone. Hamish had set his sights on Everest earlier than any of us, taking off for the mountain (from Scotland via New Zealand) in 1953 with fellow Scot, John Cunningham. They had heard that the Swiss, who attempted

Everest in the spring and autumn of 1952, had left dumps of food and oxygen all the way up the mountain. The two Scots were hoping to use these supplies for a super-lightweight attempt. By the time they got in position, John Hunt and his Sassenachs had already beaten them to it, so they exchanged their objective to Pumo Ri, a very attractive unclimbed, 7000-m (23,000-ft) peak, immediately opposite the Everest Icefall. The expedition had been on a shoestring. They had jumped the Nepalese frontier, had employed a Sherpa to help carry their gear for a short time, but dismissed him when he complained of carrying a load of over 30kg (66lb). They were already carrying 40kg (88lb) each. They parted with the Sherpa without ill-feeling, and the latter even presented them with a fork, since they were being forced to use pitons as eating utensils. Back in Britain, Hamish had established himself in Glencoe and become a world authority on mountain rescue. His good BBC and media contacts made him especially attractive to Herrligkoffer who was always in need of funds, earning him the sardonic nickname 'Sterlingscoffer' from Don Whillans.

Most things that could do so went wrong with Herrligkoffer's expedition, some of

*One of my oldest friends, Hamish MacInnes had taken me on the first winter ascent of Raven's Gully and we climbed the South West Pillar of the Dru together. He was to be deputy leader of the 1975 expedition.*

them down to his ignoring basic acclimatization procedure, and communication was not helped by the fact that he conducted proceedings entirely from Base Camp, when he wasn't rushing back to Germany to procure the quality of down clothing the Sherpas had threatened to go on strike for. The old animosity between the Austrian contingent and the British lingered on from the previous year. Whillans and Scott established Camp 5, the Austrians pushed on to Camp 6, both using ropes left by the International Expedition. When the weather broke and this second attempt at the right-hand gully was abandoned, it is academic whether Kuen and Huber had got any higher than Whillans and Haston the year before. So the South West Face of Everest remained tantalizingly unclimbed.

I had been trying to get permission to make an attempt ever since I heard of the failure of the International Expedition, but Everest was now booked as far ahead as 1976. It seemed a long time to wait. Then in January 1972 I heard that an Italian team, which was down for a reconnaissance that autumn and a full-scale expedition for spring 1973, might be pulling out. I hoped for the latter slot, since tackling Everest in the autumn presented a large number of problems.

The two periods during which you can climb in Nepal have very different characteristics. The pre-monsoon season is squeezed between the clearing of the winter snows, around the beginning of March, and the arrival of the monsoon at the end of May; the post-monsoon season starts at the end of the monsoon – any time between mid-September to early October – and then trails off into the gathering winter cold. During the pre-monsoon season, the weather tends to be more unsettled. However, there are two advantages in climbing in the spring. First, the temperature is getting progressively warmer during the course of the expedition so that when the team is

'Another challenge on Everest is to try to climb the mountain without oxygen.

in a position to make a summit bid – hopefully, before the arrival of the monsoon rains – the weather is also at its warmest. In addition, the winds in the spring do not seem to be anything like as serious as they are in the autumn. In the autumn you have the converse effect; when the team starts off, it is relatively warm in the immediate lee of the monsoon and then, as they climb higher up the mountain, it becomes progressively colder. Much more serious during the autumn are the high-altitude jet-stream winds which seem to blow continuously from about 7500m (24,600ft). It is for this reason that the record of expeditions attempting mountains of over 8000m (26,250ft) in the post-monsoon season has been very poor.

Another reason why I did not like the idea of trying the South West Face of Everest in the autumn of 1972 was that we would have no time at all to organize the expedition, since we could not really get under way until we had learned the fate of Dr Herrligkoffer's expedition. From initial reports in March and early April, they seemed to be making good progress and there was the probability that they could well climb the mountain. I very much doubted if they would try the true South West Face, but even if they managed to get round the escape route which Don had spied in 1971 and reach the summit of Everest, we would probably have had considerable difficulties in raising funds for an attempt on the true South West Face route.

When in mid-April we learned that we would almost certainly be able to get the post-monsoon slot in 1972, I felt that we had to commit ourselves. But I was still extremely worried about trying to organize a South West Face Expedition at such short notice, in such a doubtful period of the year, and with the likelihood that we would not have the best Sherpas at the height of the trekking season.

Then I had another idea. Why not attempt Everest by the known South Col route, but with a lightweight expedition? This would mean that there would be nothing like the same financial involvement, and yet the challenge would be there, and probably with a small expedition it would be very much more fun. I attacked the new concept with enthusiasm. Just how small can you pare down an Everest expedition? The ultimate, of course, would be one man, on his own. This had been tried back in 1934 when Maurice Wilson attempted to climb Everest from the north. No experienced alpinist, he was a dreamer and mystic, who slipped into Tibet in native dress with three Sherpas and a single pony carrying all his equipment. His body was found in 1935 quite close to Camp 3 on the north side of Everest. There was another solo attempt in 1947, by a Canadian adventurer named Earl Denman. He claimed to have reached 7000m (23,000ft) – a height higher than the North Col, but there was no evidence to back up his claim. He was only away from Darjeeling for five weeks.

'This is the only way that a truly lightweight Everest expedition could succeed'

*Doug Scott was a strong climber with a string of exploratory expeditions behind him, as well as some American big wall-climbing experience. He had had one close look at the South West Face on Herrligkoffer's contentious expedition and was keen to return.*

The scale of Everest is so vast that it is difficult to conceive of a successful solo attempt. All the expeditions to Everest had been on the heavy side, with strong back up of Sherpas. The only exception was another unofficial expedition of four climbers, three Americans and one Swiss, led by Woodrow Wilson Sayre, a grandson of the former US President. Their declared objective was Gyachung Kang, a magnificent peak of 7952m (26,089ft), which in itself was probably beyond their capabilities. The party was comparatively inexperienced, badly equipped and had no porters. Reaching the Gyachung Kang region, they slipped over the Tibetan frontier on to the Rongbuk Glacier, and succeeded in climbing well above the North Col of Everest to a height of 7600m (25,000ft). This was a remarkable achievement, but the attempt was fairly heavily castigated in conventional climbing circles of the early 1960s. Yet I wonder. There are quite a few mountaineers today who are beginning to feel that this type of venture is true mountaineering, while the massive expeditions are getting quite a long way from it.

Another challenge on Everest, of course, is to try to climb the mountain without oxygen. This is the only way that a truly lightweight expedition could succeed, since the weight of the oxygen bottles needed on the upper slopes of the mountain means that you need a fair number of load-carriers; consequently the size of the expedition must inevitably escalate. There is a definite appeal in the thought of man, unaided, reaching the summit of Everest. It would undoubtedly be a really huge challenge, since from all the evidence gained so far, particularly from the prewar expeditions, the height of 8500m (28,000ft) seems to be a critical one without the use of oxygen. The climber who tries to reach the summit of Everest without oxygen is certainly taking huge risks, not only with his life but perhaps also with his future health.

I wasn't ready to abandon oxygen, but began putting together plans for a South Col attempt with a climbing team of four, with two in support and six Sherpas. Dougal Haston was already a member of the scheme; the question was, who else to invite? I decided upon Nick Estcourt and Mick Burke. Both of them had been with me on the South Face of Annapurna in 1970 and we had climbed together for years. Nick was a computer programmer and essentially an amateur climber. He had to ask his employers for leave of absence again, knowing full well that it probably wouldn't do his career any good and would be unpaid. But the lure of an Everest expedition was irresistible. Nick had performed extremely well on the South Face of

Annapurna. He had drive, was tremendously competitive by nature, and always extremely methodical.

Mick Burke had made several outstanding routes, particularly on larger mountains. It was he who instigated the first British Cerro Torre expedition in 1967, when Dougal Haston, Peter Crewe, Martin Boysen and he made a very strong attempt on what might well be the world's most difficult mountain. He followed this with the first British ascent of the Nose of El Capitan in Yosemite, leading all the way. Although he had practically no experience, he decided to make his career in filming and managed to get a place at the London Film School. He took an active part in making the film on the South Face of Annapurna. He and I always had a slightly odd relationship. He was argumentative and fiercely aware of what he considered his rights and his position in the climbing rat race. Both of us had the capacity to lose our tempers and then very quickly simmer down and see the other's point of view. Our friendship remained intact over a number of years.

I needed two more climbers in a support role, who would act as long-stops and run the basic administration of the expedition while we were making our summit bid. Mike Thompson, one of my oldest friends, was an obvious choice. He had been with us on Annapurna in a similar role. In his mid-thirties, an anthropologist by career, he was a reasonable, without being an outstanding, mountaineer, and wonderfully good at getting on with other people. Mike and I had been to Sandhurst together and both of us had tired of the Army at roughly the same time. The Army released me without argument, but had felt that Mike was of greater value to them. So Mike stood for Parliament. Every citizen in the British Isles (at that time anyway) had a constitutional right to stand for Parliament, yet no soldier was allowed to go in for politics, so the Army had no choice but to release him. It cost Mike about £250 by the time he had lost his deposit and paid his solicitor's fees. The final member of the team was our expedition doctor, Peter Steele, who had been the doctor on the International Expedition, had worked in Nepal and could speak Nepali.

So there we were in May 1972 with permission to climb Everest reasonably assured, an exciting prospect of a small expedition, and an enthusiastic team. And yet the presence of the South West Face still nagged at me. As May dragged out, it became increasingly evident that Herrligkoffer's expedition were getting into severe difficulties, and then, at the end of May, came the news. The Britons had pulled out and, a few days later, the entire team had withdrawn from Everest. The South West Face was still unclimbed.

My mind was in a turmoil for a period of about ten days as I weighed the claims of a small team on a known route against the lure of that unclimbed 600m (2000ft) above the high points of the two previous expeditions on the South West Face. The entire concept of a South West Face expedition, with all its challenges, was still extremely attractive to me – perhaps because the challenge was so very great. And so, in mid-June, I came to my decision. We changed to an all-out assault on the South West Face of Everest.

Previous page: *The Everest massif from the air looking eastward. Lhotse, fourth highest mountain in the world, is on the far right, Makalu, fifth highest, is in the right-hand middle ground and Kangchenjunga, third highest, 130km (80 miles) away, dominates the sky line left of centre.*

From the day I made that decision, we were to have eight weeks to increase the size of the team, raise all the extra money required – approximately £60,000 – and get together the mass of equipment that such a large expedition would involve. The scale of the thing we were about to undertake was tremendously exciting, even though the odds seemed to be stacked against us. The first thing was to adapt my basic planning to the larger objective. We were obviously going to have to increase the size of the team, but I was anxious to keep it as compact as possible. I wanted to add four more members to the six we already had. At this stage I envisaged two of them being lead climbers so that I should have, in effect, six potential leaders and four who would adopt support roles. Although there are a huge number of very talented climbers in this country today, there are comparatively few who have real high-altitude experience. From this point of view, both Doug Scott and Hamish MacInnes were obvious choices, since they had both performed well on Everest, reaching heights of nearly 8000m (26,250ft). I therefore invited them to join me for the autumn attempt and they both promptly accepted.

But I left out Don Whillans, the one person both the media and the climbing world expected me to take. We had done some of our best alpine climbing together and he had reached the summit of Annapurna with Dougal Haston in 1970. He had then been my deputy leader and had contributed a great deal to our success. His forthright, abrasive style had complemented my own approach, but it had also created stress. One of the problems had been that when we had climbed together in the Alps, Don had indisputably held the initiative. He had been that bit more experienced and was also stronger than I. It would be very difficult for him to accept a reversal of those roles. He was a strong leader in his own right, had now been to Everest twice, and knew the mountain much better than I. It would not have been easy to run the expedition in the way that I wanted with Don taking part and so I decided to leave him behind.

To make up the rest of the team I was especially pleased to have lured my old friend Jimmy Roberts away from Mountain Travel, his Kathmandu trekking business, in the height of the season to be my deputy leader; his vast Himalayan experience and enormous rapport with the Sherpas would be invaluable at Base Camp. Another good man there would be former Gurkha captain Kelvin Kent who had run Base Camp admirably for me on Annapurna and would do the same on Everest. The immediate burden of work fell on the more than capable shoulders of Edinburgh climbing shop proprietor Graham Tiso, who not only got the right gear together in record time but also fulfilled a vital role on the mountain itself and was a useful climber in his own right. When Mike Thompson dropped out of the new-look venture, his place was taken by Dave Bathgate, an Edinburgh climber with an impressive winter-climbing reputation and a couple of Peruvian expeditions under his belt, who came recommended by Dougal; Dr Barney Rosedale replaced Dr Peter Steele. And so we had a complete team. We also had about eight weeks to put together the entire expedition and we did it.

*25 August–14 September 1972*

# The Approach March

NORMALLY EXPEDITIONS FLY from Kathmandu to Luglha which is easier and cheaper, since air freight costs less than employing porters. However, since we were planning to make our approach through the monsoon, we could not be guaranteed sufficient good weather for the plane to fly. Jimmy Roberts had therefore recommended that we make the 270-km (170-mile) approach march all the way from Kathmandu, which would certainly give us ample opportunity to acclimatize. With us would travel 400 porters, recruited from the surrounding villages, as well as cook-boys and mail-runners, and 40 Sherpas, 14 of whom were designated high-altitude Sherpas who would expect to carry loads on the South West Face itself. The remaining Icefall porters would not carry higher than Camp 2 in the Western Cwm, but I was planning to promote ten of them to the rank of high-altitude Sherpas once we saw how they performed.

We had two sirdars, Pembatharke being the chief sirdar, who would primarily be

in charge of directing the Sherpas on the mountain itself, while Sona Hishy, a younger man, was to be our administrative sirdar. He would look after our supplies from Base Camp and help to make the approach march run smoothly. This pair highlighted the changing role and development of their community. Pembatharke was very much a Sherpa of the old style. He could neither read nor write, had a rugged simplicity in his attitude to life and yet, at the same time, was highly intelligent and shrewd. He certainly had a magnificent climbing record on Everest, and in 1970 with me on the South Face of Annapurna; while on

the International Expedition he had been loyal to Don and Dougal in organizing and keeping the Sherpas going on the tenuous line of communications behind them.

His opposite number and in theory his assistant, Sona Hishy, was very different. Aged 26, he had been educated at one of the Edmund Hillary schools, spoke and wrote good English, and had even visited the United States. He had done more trekking with tourists than climbing on expeditions. While Pembatharke had a magnificent physique and looked the very prototype of a leader of men, Sona Hishy was tall, slender and a much more complex character. He was extremely efficient, but was also to prove to be the Sherpa shop-steward.

The routine of the approach march quickly fell into a well-defined pattern. We had set out in a bright spell in the monsoon, and the sun blazed down, hot and

*Left: The forests we walked through in were lush and leech-laden in the monsoon rains. Right: Sona Hishy, our deputy sirdar, was something of a shop steward, always keen to pick on issues. Our sirdar Pembatharke, (below right with his wife), was more easy going, very much the traditional Sherpa. He had been with us on Annapurna.*

heavy, through gaps in the piled clouds, which still clung to the higher hills. Everything was green — a green much richer than anything one saw in the drier pre-monsoon season. There were wild flowers everywhere, little jewels of red and pink, blue and purple. Spiders' webs, gleaming with diamond drops of water, festooned the shrubs. The hillside, however steep, was carved into terraces, each one with a low mud wall imprisoning the waters of the monsoon rains. A thick green carpet of rice shoots grew in these terraced pools. There was a constant trickle of running water from the many streams coursing down the hills, and the houses clustered in little groups. Each had brown earthen walls with a veranda across the ground floor, small wooden-slatted windows and a roof made from weathered wooden slats or thatch.

Although the Everest route had now become a tourist trail, particularly in the post-monsoon period, with the constant march of trekkers, there seemed hardly any change at all from when I had walked the same path back in 1961. The Nepalese were as gentle and courteous as ever — the girls with their golden nose studs and earrings had a shy, gentle beauty. The first day there was a soft, kind balm in the air after our weeks of wheeler-dealing, frantic worry and activity. We were already slipping into an easy, methodical routine, resting beneath our umbrellas and stopping about three o'clock in the afternoon for the evening's halt. It took us 14 days to walk to Namche Bazar at the pace of our porters. Today hundreds of trekkers follow this trail. Making it during the monsoon gave it a special character and we all became thoroughly neurotic about leeches, which in some areas seemed to cling to almost every blade of grass and would get on to the walls of the tents at night, then drop with unerring precision upon the heads of their unsuspecting victims. We were now in the Sherpa heartland of Sola Khumbu. Before climbers started going to Everest in the 1920s, the Sherpas' economy was based on a combination of subsistence farming in the sparse, gravelly fields of the mountains, and trading between Tibet and India. With the Communist invasion of Tibet, part of their economy was seriously disrupted. This loss in trade was, however, already being replaced by their role as high-altitude porters as an increasing number of expeditions came to Nepal to climb in the Himalaya.

Then, from the mid-sixties onwards, another development further increased their relative wealth. Trekking became more and more popular. One of the early founders was Jimmy Roberts. In the last few years trekking has boomed, and an increasing number of Sherpas have found trekking more remunerative and less arduous than mountaineering expeditions. Nevertheless, there are still a few Sherpas, Pembatharke is undoubtedly one, who prefer the rugged adventure of climbing on a Himalayan expedition to the more sophisticated and inevitably sub-servient work of looking after rich tourists on treks through Nepal. Others of our Sherpas, however, very sensibly looked upon prestigious expeditions, such as one to Everest, as useful stepping-stones in their careers as trekking Sherpas.

The Sherpas, like most other mountain people, have never been able to afford the luxury of being romantic about their mountains. They tend to take them for granted

and their position is similar to that of the Swiss peasants in the 1850s, whose interest in their mountains started only when outsiders came and offered to pay money for their help. The difference between the Sherpas and the Swiss, however, was that when the early Victorian alpinists started venturing into the Alps they knew even less about the problems of mountaineering than the Swiss peasants they took with them. The Swiss peasant, therefore, initially assumed the role of guide and expert in the mountains, a role he was to keep until the end of the nineteenth century. The Sherpas were employed as carriers rather than guides. The mountaineers who came to the Himalaya already had a background of climbing in the Alps; consequently, they were experts and had to look after the Sherpas in the mountains, rather than vice versa. There have been, of course, some notable exceptions to this. Tenzing, who accompanied Hillary to the summit of Everest, was able to climb with the European members of the team on a level footing, especially, of course, as he had already been most of the way up Everest with the Swiss before the British team ever got there.

With recent developments in mountaineering in the Himalaya, disparity between climbers and Sherpas has become greater. Now that mountaineers are tackling high-standard technical problems at altitude, there are comparatively few, if any, Sherpas who have the advanced technical knowledge even to think of taking part in the lead

*One recompense for the rains of the monsoon was the profusion of wild flowers, like these gentians.*

*Dave Bathgate on the path leading into Namche Bazar. Although the village had grown since my first visit in 1961, it was still quite small, with few Sherpa lodges and no hotels. Today, it is very changed, with electricity, satellite dishes and all the paraphernalia of tourism.*

climbing, and they might even have difficulty in coping with the fixed ropes on particularly steep sections of the expedition.

The attitude of the Sherpas to mountaineering is practical and materialistic. For a start, they regard every European expedition as vastly rich, since who else could possibly afford the luxury of doing anything quite as pointless as climbing a mountain? The very resources we display, the mounds of gear we bring in, the standard of life we adopt on the mountain, all contribute to this impression. To us, equipment is purely functional, enabling us to climb the mountain. To the Sherpa, it is part of his wages, which he can exchange for goods or cash. So its quality is crucial. It was failure to understand this that caused some of Dr Herrligkoffer's early problems.

We reached Namche Bazar on 6 September. In 1961 we didn't see one European for the entire period of our Nuptse expedition after leaving Kathmandu, but today Namche has become a tourist centre, with little restaurants serving omelettes and tea at inflated prices. There are also a couple of shops selling carpets and other goods for tourists. It was at Namche Bazar we paid off our 400 porters recruited from around Kathmandu to take on local Sherpas. This was a question of trades-union job delineation – once in Sherpa country you employ Sherpas. Most of our newly employed porters were women, who carried the same loads as the men. Some of them were ancient crones who looked in their sixties, others were young girls. Rather like postwar Kentish hop-pickers, they all seemed to regard their projected journey, first to Tengpoche and then to Base Camp, as a glorious, well-paid holiday.

I had not been able to relax entirely on the approach march, for I had spent much of
the time, as I wandered in the rain through the Nepali countryside, thinking of how
we were going to climb the South West Face. I talked to the others of my plans, based
largely on the experience of Dougal on the International Expedition. A basic question was how many camps we should use. Dougal had recommended having a
seventh above the Rock Band and this seemed to make good sense at first, though
stocking it would stretch our resources. But mulling things over with him and
Hamish during the approach, we settled on the plan of fixed-roping the Rock Band
from Camp 6, then making the summit bid from this lower camp instead. Oxygen

*Porters swathed in plastic against the rain. Keeping them contented with their lot was vital to the progress of the expedition. The majority saw the walk in as a wonderful paid holiday.*

was another problem. Each cylinder weighed 8kg (17lb) and contained just over 1000 litres of oxygen, enough for about four hours. We planned on letting the climbers use oxygen from 7000m (23,000ft) upwards, to try to keep them going for the final summit push, while the Sherpas would start using it from Camp 5 at just under 8000m (26,250ft). The problem is that once a climber or Sherpa is using oxygen, his effective payload is reduced to about 7kg (15lb), since his oxygen cylinder for climbing takes up half the acceptable load of around 16kg (35lb). To achieve a fast build-up from Camp 5 upwards, one would need a large number of carriers at each camp to maintain the flow. A further complication was presented by the fact that the camp sites have a limited capacity. This was especially the case at Camp 4 at 7500m (24,600ft), which had room for only three platforms.

Another fundamental decision, which to me had never seemed in doubt, was our choice of route up the Rock Band. The Japanese had headed for the left-hand side, where there are two clearly defined breaks, one a ramp leading out on to the West Ridge, and the other a deep chimney-like gully cutting up through the Rock Band. Doug Scott had named it Gardyloo during the Herrligkoffer expedition, and had suggested, even before we set out, that this might offer a possible line of ascent. Dougal, on the other hand, had been to the very foot of another gully which pierced the defences of the Rock Band on its right-hand side. He described this as being filled with snow and looking comparatively straightforward. It is interesting to speculate just why Whillans and Haston abandoned the Japanese line up to the left, to make their long traverse below the Rock Band over to the right. One of the key problems was that of camp sites, and in the spring of 1970, the Japanese had failed to find a suitable site for their Camp 5 at the foot of the Rock Band. There was insufficient snow on the face to cut out a platform, and they did not have enough alloy platforms to construct artificial standings for their tents. Don had detected possible sites for Camp 5 on the right-hand side of the Great Central Gully, which runs up towards the Rock Band, and Camp 5 was duly established there. From their site of Camp 5 it would have been extremely difficult to get back across to the possible left-hand line. The route to the right, across the foot of the Rock Band, seemed fairly straightforward, however, so they had adopted this approach.

Since there was a line of fixed ropes, which we might well be able to use, and since the gully through the Rock Band did not seem too difficult, there appeared to be no doubt that this was the route we should take.

I had made my initial plans on the basis of climbers and Sherpas, without worrying about who would do what job, and how each person would fit into the role allotted to him. Now I was going to have to give people their roles on the expedition and realized all too well how critical this could be.

My team was selected on the basis that I had six lead climbers, any one of whom would be capable of reaching the summit of Everest. Each would also expect, and need, to have a share of the lead climbing if his morale and interest in the climb were going to be sustained. These were Dave Bathgate, Mick Burke, Nick Estcourt, Dougal

Haston, Hamish MacInnes and Doug Scott. Then there were five of us who would have to be in support. Initially, I had given myself a role as lead climber, but then had increasingly felt that it would be better for me to stay in support, as far as possible in the camp just below that of the lead climbers. On the South Face of Annapurna, I had found it difficult to conduct the expedition from the front.

My other support climbers, Graham Tiso, Kelvin Kent, Barney Rosedale and Colonel Jimmy Roberts (deputy leader and base camp manager) were going to be extremely important, for each camp needed someone to supervise the Sherpas, allot loads, maintain morale and take radio calls. As it turned out, I could have used more climbers performing this role. The lead climbers were not suited by temperament to such a job, and anyway I needed to keep them as fresh as possible for the final push.

The pairing of my lead climbers resolved itself by compatibility into Dougal and Hamish, Doug and Mick, Nick and Dave. The far more difficult question was sorting out their batting order for tackling the various objectives up the route, particularly above Camp 5. Pair one would have the least satisfying task, since they would merely be establishing the lower part of the face, and then making the route from Camp 5 to 6. I was hoping that, having made the route, they would also be able to stay up in support for the summit bid. In a way, acceptance of this role required the greatest level of unselfishness and the highest degree of reliability. I decided to cast Nick and Dave for this somewhat unenviable task, for I knew I could rely totally on their loyal support in what, at first glance, seemed a lesser role. Dougal and Hamish were by far the most experienced pair, and Dougal particularly was recognized by the entire team as having the greatest drive on the mountain. He was acknowledged by all to be at the top of the pecking order. As for Hamish, he was also a very competent cameraman, which Dougal certainly wasn't, and we had a film to make. There was little to choose as a pair between Doug and Mick, and Dave and Nick. Doug did have the advantage that he had been to almost 8000m (26,250ft) and Mick was chief cameraman of the expedition, so needed the maximum chance to get the best film possible.

Bearing all these considerations in mind, I decided to designate Mick and Doug as pair two, with the responsibility of making the route from Camps 3 to 4 and then from Camp 6 up the Rock Band and the first summit attempt, holding Dougal and Hamish back for the final summit attempt. This made sense and because of the latter pair's complete self-confidence, they would be able to cope with a reserve role, knowing full well that on them would rest our main chance of reaching the summit of Everest. I had a feeling that the chances of Doug and Mick could be no more than outside, after the enormous effort they would have to make in forcing the Rock Band.

I announced the plan at Tengpoche, a day's march beyond Namche Bazar, where we were going to have a couple of days' acclimatization rest. Naturally Nick and Dave were disappointed but, such was their loyalty to the expedition, they accepted their role without argument and fulfilled it with enthusiasm.

The main monastery of the Khumbu region is at Tengpoche and, like expeditions before us, we made our official visit to the Lama to present some money to the monastery and enable our Sherpas and ourselves to receive his blessing for the climb. We went through a low door to a little yard with marigolds and flowers in window boxes around it and into the Lama's sparsely furnished room. I was ushered in and made my *namaste* (greeting) to him, bobbing my head; Kelvin and Hamish came in afterwards and did the same. Then all our Sherpas trooped in, in what seemed to be an order of seniority – Pembatharke first, followed by Sona Hishy and then Phurkipa, the eldest of our Sherpas, and finally all the others. The older ones bowed down to have their heads touched, the younger ones went right down on their hands and knees, touching the floor with their heads, and then back into the standing position – three times before coming forward for the blessing. Each had a white ceremonial gauze scarf in which was wrapped his offering. We sat there, eating biscuits and drinking tea, for about an hour. During that time some of the tranquillity and the settled peace of the monastic existence rolled over us.

We left Tengpoche on 11 September and pressed on through the monsoon clouds to Pheriche and Lobuche, no more than a couple of yak herders' huts at the side of the glacier. At Lobuche it snowed hard in the night, so it seemed a good moment to issue all their equipment to the Icefall Sherpas who had now joined us. The camp took on the appearance of a bazaar, as Graham Tiso broke open the boxes and lined them up like a series of market stalls. Our temporary porters, who were going to carry the gear up to Base Camp, watched the hand-out in a spirit which was both light-hearted and critical. This was the moment that had caused the crisis on the Herrligkoffer expedition. I was just praying that they would be happy with what we presented to them. You could tell at a glance the difference between our high-altitude porters who had been employed all the way from Kathmandu and the Icefall Sherpas whom we had only just hired. The latter were less well dressed, their clothes the relics of previous expeditions; few spoke English and they looked altogether rougher and older. Jimmy Roberts' Mountain Travel Sherpas looked like mountain guides – they barely condescended to use the clothing we had issued, preferring for the approach march gear they considered more elegant. Some of them, Pertemba particularly, reminded me of the French guides, with smart peaked cap and well-cut breeches. However, they all seemed satisfied at this stage with what they had been issued.

By now we had an addition to the team in the form of Tony Tighe, an Australian friend of Dougal's who had planned to be in the area under his own steam at the same time as us and had asked if he might help out at Base Camp. A good mixer, he was to become a definite asset.

The following day dawned fine, our timing seemed perfect; to all intents and purposes 14 September marked the end of the monsoon. Now the sun blazed from a cloudless sky and yet there was a bite in the air that removed all traces of haze. And it was on the 14th that Dougal and Hamish, feeling almost no effect at all from the altitude, made the long walk from Lobuche to the site of Base Camp.

*1 September – 30 October 1972*

# The First Attempt

BASE CAMP ON EVEREST is a bleak place; it is situated on the glacier itself, among rocky debris carved by the glacier in the previous millennia. It resembles a vast, derelict granite quarry whose unworked stones have been left in haphazard piles; the rocks are comparatively young and unweathered, edges unrounded by erosion of wind and weather. There was rock dust everywhere, as if from a recent blasting. At close quarters it is a stark, almost ugly place, contrasting with the austere beauty of the surrounding mountains; a wilderness of rock and snow and ice, whose only reminder of man was the worst possible – man's pollution of almost anything he touches. The rubbish of previous expeditions was everywhere – rusty tins, plastic bags, decaying packing cases. Yet that first night, the very austerity of the setting must have seemed precious to Dougal and Hamish in their small orange tent, at the head of the Khumbu Glacier. A few days later this was to become a village of tents with a population of more than 50.

The thing that commanded their immediate attention was the Khumbu Icefall, the gateway to Everest, a vast frozen cataract, tumbling nearly 900m (2950ft) between a subsidiary spur of Nuptse and one from Everest. Had it been water it would have been a gigantic waterfall, but as ice it was even more impressive. The huge but slow pressure of the glacier above in the Western Cwm inexorably thrusts the ice before it, over the drop of the Icefall, breaking up the smooth-flowing river of ice that forms the bed of the Cwm into a convoluted chaos of ice walls, towers and pinnacles, all of which must eventually topple. Dougal and Hamish were the experienced hands set to find a route through this maze. Entering the Icefall undoubtedly has an element of Russian roulette. There is no possibility of making a safe route. All you can do is to try and pick out a route that is as safe as possible, but there will always be sections that are threatened by ice towers, which – sooner or later – must collapse. You just hope that no one happens to be beneath them when they do. If climbers and Sherpas only had to go through the danger area once

*Base Camp after the first storm in early October. The snow never cleared and by the end of the expedition night-time temperatures were down to -40ºC (-40ºF).*

'Entering the Icefall undoubtedly has an element of Russian roulette…all you can do is to try and pick out a route that is as safe as possible, but there will always be sections that are threatened by ice towers, which – sooner or later – must collapse. You just hope that no one happens to be beneath them when they do.'

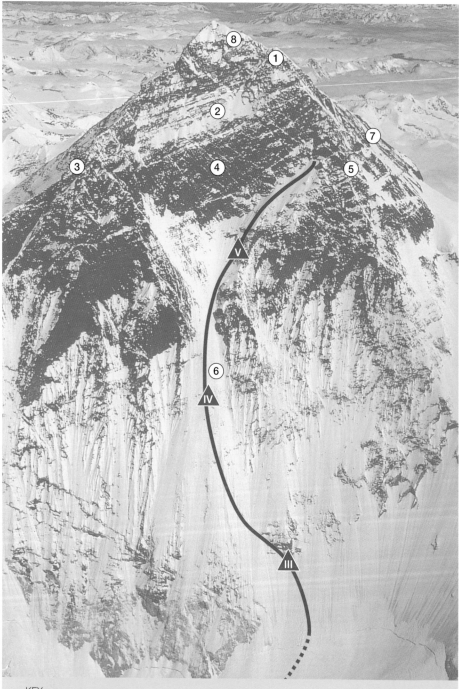

*The South West Face of Everest showing the route and camps on our 1972 attempt.*

KEY

| | |
|---|---|
| ——— | Climbing with fixed rope |
| ▪▪▪▪▪▪ | Climbing without fixed rope |
| ▲ V | Camp |

1 South Summit
2 Summit Snow Field
3 West Ridge
4 Rock Band

5 South Pillar
6 Great Central Gully
7 South East Ridge
8 Hillary Step

during an expedition the risks would be comparatively slight. The problem with the Everest Icefall is that some climbers must go through these danger areas every day and it is the Sherpas who are exposed to the greatest risk, particularly the Icefall porters whose job it is to keep Camp 2 in the Western Cwm stocked with food and gear.

On the 16th, we first set foot on Everest in earnest. Dougal, Hamish and five Sherpas with 1.5–m (5–ft) sections of alloy ladders, rope, snow stakes and deadmen (not corpses, but plates which are buried in the snow to provide a compact yet very reliable anchor), set out before dawn. They had picked out a line the day before and now zigzagged steadily up. The harsh angularity of the ice was hidden by the covering of monsoon snows and they were able to make rapid progress, bridging the occasional open crevasse with one of their ladders. Hamish was in his element; being, perhaps, a frustrated structural engineer, he revels in making complex pulley systems, bridges and anything mechanical. By midday, when the heat of the sun becomes intolerable and the snow unstable, they had reached almost halfway, and the following morning they returned to push the route up to the foot of the final steep wall before the top of the Icefall. It was now my turn, with Dave Bathgate, to force the last section. They had warned us it was going to be difficult. This was not a style of climbing I had undertaken before. Pushing up a 9-m (30–ft) ladder from a comparatively narrow snow ledge is no joke. It was just as well we had six Sherpas with us. We also had Phurkipa, our 'road-mender', coming along behind with Nick Estcourt to improve the route. Phurkipa was the oldest of our Sherpas. Then 55, he had been on innumerable expeditions, including the spring Everest trip with Doug, who had recommended him.

Another small wall barred our way. This was to be the only real climbing I was to have on the entire expedition – a mere 6-m (20-ft) vertical ice wall. I cut a step, kicked in my crampons, forgot the altitude for a few minutes in my concentration and apprehension. Beyond, the view was not encouraging, a trough surrounded by instability. Dave and I made a couple of tentative forays before deciding to return. I have always been intensely competitive in my climbing and could not help feeling disappointed that I had not made better progress. In fact it took two more days and some further heroic bridge engineering from Hamish before we established our route through the Icefall, and then it had to be made safe for the porters to ferry the 5 tonnes of oxygen cylinders, climbing equipment, tentage and food through to Camp 1 and on to Camp 2, our Advanced Base at the foot of the face.

While all this was going on, we selected the eight best Icefall porters to promote to high-altitude work and then found ourselves facing the Great Sleeping Bag

Strike. The Sherpas were demanding two sleeping bags. We pointed out that we all had one sleeping bag and they could always get into their down suits if it was very cold. They said down suits were outer clothing, so didn't count. Sleeping bags have a high market value in Sherpa country, but our Sherpas insisted their resale potential was not the point; they were cold at night, which was probably true, as our bags were a bit big for them. The argument, translated between my English, Kelvin Kent's Nepali and Sona Hishy's Sherpa, raged back and forth. I offered to have some more sleeping bags flown out from England. The Sherpas wouldn't wait. They said they wouldn't go up the mountain next day without an extra bag. There was only one solution. I collected ten lightweight bags from the rest of a grudging team. That night I confessed to my tape diary: 'Climbing Everest is a logistic problem – it's a man-management problem, a complex labour problem, and there's just a little bit of climbing in it too.' Kelvin, a former Gurkha officer who sat up until two o'clock with the Sherpas, said they had needed to get this off their chests and it was as much as anything about their fear of the Icefall. This is undoubtedly true from the way they pray incessantly as they plod up it. But next day they went up.

The weather now began to deteriorate, damaging parts of the line through the Icefall, crushing tents and delaying route-making to Camp 2. Was this the last kick of the monsoon? I worried about the inexperienced Nick and Dave trying to push out the route in these conditions and decided to send up Hamish and Dougal to give them a hand. But I could tell Doug and Mick feared this might become a habit and threaten their turn for the top. A week had gone by since we had succeeded in climbing the Icefall, but a day's heavy snowfall, combined with a few more days of bad visibility, had set us back about four days – days which did not seem to matter too much at the start of an expedition, but were to prove all-important later on.

It is only when you start walking up it that you begin to gain a true idea of the gigantic scale of the Western Cwm. At first, the South West Face is hidden coyly behind a subsidiary spur from the West Ridge then, as you work your way up and across to the left-hand side of the cwm, it comes slowly into full sight, foreshortened, massive, the Great Central Gully leading upwards like an arrow to the guts of

Previous page: *Camp 1 at the head of the Icefall with the West Ridge of Nuptse to the left, the West Shoulder of Everest, right, and Pumo Ri rising above the valley below.*

the face – the Rock Band, which stretches across like a wall. It looks deceptively short and even more deceptively close to the summit.

The Sherpas dictated the site of Camp 2 by dumping their loads and heading back down. We were about half a mile from the foot of the face, where the International Expedition had had their Camp 2. After having to slog up the cwm in snowshoes, the snow on the face proved firm and perfect for crampons, so Nick and Dave made short work next day of running the rope out to Camp 3 next day on a little rock buttress. I, meanwhile, installed myself at Camp 2, where I could keep an eye on the flow of supplies from below and be in touch with Doug and Mick who were establishing Camp 3 with a view to pushing on to the site of Camp 4. This was when the second storm intervened. It lasted only two days, but it set us back another four in our race against the winter winds, as Doug and Mick had retreated to Camp 2. They found Camp 3 in a shambles on their return and left their Sherpas to re-establish it as they set out for Camp 4.

I had decided that climbers should use oxygen from Camp 3 onwards. Once you get badly run down at altitude, there is very little opportunity for recovery, since even Base Camp, at 5425m (17,800ft), is situated at too high an altitude for real rest and recuperation. Mick had already been feeling the strain, but during the spring expedition Doug had not found it necessary to use oxygen until above Camp 4, and even from there up to Camp 5 the benefit he gained from the set was dubious, since it was faulty for most of the time. So he was sceptical now as to how much good it would do, taking into consideration the weight of the cylinders against the benefit gained. He agreed to give it a try, but soon abandoned his cylinder as they kicked laboriously up the hard snow slope, their two Sherpas following with spare reels of rope. It was typical of Mick that despite his altitude problems he was determined not only to do his share of pushing the route out but also to get it recorded on film.

The climbing now became more awkward, over a series of ice and rock steps. There was insufficient snow to use the deadman anchors, and even ice pitons were difficult to place. They were on the front points of their crampons, the wind tearing at their clothing, trying to push them back down the slope. Their last 90-m (300–ft)

rope came to an end still 20m (65ft) below the site of the camp. They could see the gleaming corner of one of the platforms sticking tantalizingly out of the snow just above them. The slope was littered with the flotsam of previous expeditions, tattered fabric, warped alloy poles from the tents and boxes sticking out of the ice. But there was also rope. They managed to pull some, left from the spring attempt, out of the snow and use it for those last 20 metres to the site of Camp 4. They found the camp devastated by rockfall since Doug had last been there just five months before; the Japanese platforms, rather like bedsteads dumped on a scrap heap, were hanging from their anchor points at an angle. But Herrligkoffer's platforms looked as if they would be usable once they had been dug out. In just one and a half day's hard work, Doug and Mick had forced the route to an altitude of 7500m (24,600ft).

At Camp 4 there were no level spaces, and even the ledges cut in the shallow covering of snow quickly filled in with spindrift which became instantly iron hard. You had to use constant vigilance, both to avoid slipping yourself or dropping anything. It was Dougal and Hamish who dug out the platforms left by the German expedition and erected two of our boxes. Hardly a breath of wind brushed the upper part of the face on 13 and 14 October as Hamish and Dougal pushed up the great snow couloir leading up towards the Rock Band. On their second day they ran out of oxygen. 'We were almost glad, afterwards, that we had run out,' commented Dougal. 'It showed us that we, also, could climb without oxygen, like the Sherpas who were carrying our ropes.'

Two days' work and they had run out the rope to a point just short of the site of Camp 5. Although both were climbing strongly, they had used up all their stock of fixed rope, and so turned back. It was still only halfway through October, and yet we had now reached a height of almost 8000m (26,250ft). We were in a very strong position. The morale of the Sherpas was excellent. In my original planning I had allowed for the Sherpas to do just two carries from Camp 3 to 4, before they returned to Camp 2 for a rest. But Pembatharke, on his way back down to Camp 2 after helping Hamish and Dougal make the route up the Great Central Gully, volunteered, out of the blue, that the Sherpas would be prepared to make three carries in succession. This made a considerable difference to my logistic planning, for we still had a lot of loads to get up to our high camps. I myself moved up to Camp 4 with four Sherpas to help ferry loads to Camp 5 before Nick and Dave moved in for their turn at the front. But at this point the winds returned with a deafening roar, cascading down the Great Central Gully, hammering our tents with a river of spindrift, ice and rocks, pinning us down for five frustrating and terrifying days. I was on the verge of evacuating the mountain when on the morning of the 20th I realized everything had become silent once more. There was no wind and outside the tent was a brilliant clear day. This was a day to go up, not down.

It was a struggle. My oxygen supply didn't seem to be working properly. Ang Phu and Jangbo surged ahead as I plodded up the endless snow couloir in absolute misery. But when I reached Camp 5 all the effort and struggle was made infinitely

Previous page: *Porters carrying gear up the Western Cwm. The South West Face is on the left, Lhotse in the background and the North Face of Nuptse on the right. The route crosses the huge crevasse in the foreground by a convenient snow bridge.*

*Dave Bathgate getting back to Camp 4 after a carry to Camp 5 in ferociously high winds. The box tents were pitched on frames left by the European expedition.*

worthwhile by the incredible view. We were now level with the summit of Nuptse on the other side of the Western Cwm, a spot where I had stood 11 years before. At that time I could not have foretold that I should ever be at nearly 8000m (26,250ft) on Everest, or the course of my life that had led me to this point. I was content. We carried two loads up to Camp 5 and that single day of fine weather brought all my optimism back to life. Perhaps we had a chance of reaching the summit after all. Back at Camp 4, I was determined to maintain our toehold on the face. But we were to be given only one day's grace. The wind returned – mind destroying, physically destroying, soul destroying. Nick and Dave who had replaced me at Camp 4 had it demolished around them. I called a retreat.

This time the storm raged for five days but it is amazing how quickly pessimism can turn to optimism with a change in the weather. At the height of the storm, although I don't think any of us contemplated giving up, everything had seemed as black as possible. Camp 4 would be a write-off, it was going to take several days to resume communications through the collapsed sections of the Icefall, and at least a week to redeploy; and yet, when the storm ended and the sun blazed down into the Western Cwm, all seemed different and we were full of hope once more.

My immediate problem was that I had got two of my teams of lead climbers out of sequence for their pre-allocated jobs. Before the storm I had sent Nick and Dave down to Camp 1 to help bring up more loads. According to the original plan, Nick and Dave were down to do the route from Camp 5 to 6, leaving Doug and Mick to tackle the Rock Band. Logistics suggested switching these roles, as Doug and Mick were already moving back up to Camps 4 and 5. But my instincts told me to stick with the original plan. This meant I needed to get Nick and Dave back up and out in front without holding up our advance. My decision caused an inevitable row with Nick who saw a chance to tackle the Rock Band being denied him yet again. But the tensions of our storm-bound days were forgotten as we made progress up the face.

# Return to the Face

ACROSS THE FACE, the wind gusted at more than 100km/hour (60mph), blowing up clouds of spindrift, blinding the climbers and making any form of work on the wrecked camp site impossible. Mick and Doug had taken four hours to plod up the line of fixed ropes to Camp 4 – ropes that had to be cleared of snow every foot of the way; but with the two Sherpas Ang Phurba and Anu, who were staying up with them, they had a long task ahead.

From below, the boxes looked in reasonable shape – still erect, brightly coloured huts clinging to the slope. But on reaching them Mick and Doug discovered they were filled with spindrift, like snow cubes parcelled in canvas. The frames of two of them had collapsed, and the snow inside had set as hard as concrete, hiding all the stoves and cooking pans left behind when the camp had been abandoned. There was no sign of any of the stores which had been carried up to Camp 4 before the storm; these, too, were concealed under the compacted spindrift. In some ways it was worse than establishing a camp from scratch; poles were bent, sockets jammed with ice, vital pieces missing – and the line of shadow creeping up the face was a tide of darkness that would bring an instant drop in temperature. Fingers and toes were already nipped, but you couldn't hurry; everything had to be systematic; anything dropped was lost forever. It was dark before they had patched up two boxes for the night.

Even though tired from the effort of the previous day, next morning Doug made a carry up to Camp 5 with two Sherpas, while Mick did his best to dig out all the gear left at Camp 4 before the storm. I was particularly anxious to learn exactly what we had at Camp 4, for my planning of the build-up to Camp 5. With Doug's carry, we had just enough gear at 5 for him to move up with Mick on the following day, and this is what they did.

They had another camp to establish, this time from scratch. A platform had to be dug, tents erected, all in the chilling cold. But at least Camp 5 was a more relaxing place than 4; it was situated in the shelter of an overhanging rock wall, on a broad

*Ang Phurba proved an outstanding performer, here carrying a load below the Rock Band on his way from Camp 5 to the high point. He accompanied me in pushing the route on to what was to be the high point of the expedition.*

rock ledge covered in snow. While Mick dug out a platform, Doug ranged around the area taking photographs.

Attempting to get more in the frame of the camera, he stepped back, but still not getting quite enough, stepped back again, over the edge! Unroped, without his axe, it was fortunate that he had removed his gloves to take the pictures as he shot down the 50-degree slope of hard snow, towards a vertical drop of about 600m (2000ft). With bare hands clawing at the snow, he kicked in with his cramponed boots and somehow, on the very brink of the drop, brought himself to a stop. He was still sufficiently cool to take a unique photograph looking straight down at Camp 4, 4500m (14,750ft) below, before kicking back up to the ledge!

Mick, digging away at the snow, had been blissfully unaware of this near-fatal accident. That night, they were both badly shaken by the experience, exhausted by the effort of making the camp and chilled by the bitter cold of Camp 5. Up to this point Doug had fought shy of sleeping tablets, never trusting them, but now, perhaps in a state of shock and because of the savage cold, even inside the tent, he took three, which knocked him out for the night.

Next morning, 5 November, dawned fine, without a breath of wind on the mountain. My build-up seemed to be working out. Nick and Dave had spent the night at Camp 4 and were moving up to 5 to join Mick and Doug. I was still at Camp 2 and anxious to supervise the build-up from the orchestra stalls, though I was planning to move up to Camp 5 when the route had been established to 6. Things never go completely to plan, however.

Doug and Mick had shot their bolt excavating Camp 4 in the intense cold and they were in no state to help make the route to Camp 6. They wanted to come down. My decision in the circumstances to push the fresh Hamish and Dougal up to tackle the Rock Band was not appreciated by the other pair, particularly Doug. We had a blazing row in which he accused me of being no better than Herrligkoffer in the way I manipulated people and I told him that if he felt like that he should start heading for Kathmandu. But as we reached the climax of our argument, we temporized, each realizing we could not afford to wreck the expedition and also unwilling to break up the friendship we had built up over the previous weeks. Whether I had been right or wrong in my decision is immaterial. The important factor was that Doug and Mick, though believing me wrong, accepted my decision and gave Hamish and Dougal their loyal support.

Meanwhile Dave and Nick were pushing towards Camp 6. Nick's oxygen ran out as he traversed the snowfield below the Rock Band. His diary records the sheer desperation of cold and altitude:

I was obsessed with the need to reach Camp 6, and didn't notice the time. Eventually, 12m (40ft) short of 6, the rope went tight, so assuming I had run out all 140m (460ft), stopped to put in a deadman. I took my rucksack off, to take out the dozen pegs that were in it to leave at the high point. I fumbled and

*Ang Phurba repairing the box tent at Camp 5. The gully in shadow just in from the top left of the picture is the line we would take through the Rock Band the following year.*

dropped the rucksack, which held my oxygen unit and spare gear, and watched it cartwheeling down the slope out of sight. I very nearly cried. I was so disgusted with my mistake; I'd never dropped anything like that before in all the time I'd been climbing. Then I pulled in the rope so that I could tie it as tautly as possible to the dead man, and fully 12m (40ft) came in – it must have been sticking somewhere when I had pulled it before and I could have got all the way to Camp 6 after all. In retrospect, though, it's just as well I didn't, since that last 12 metres could easily have taken half an hour, and later on that length of time could have made all the difference between being dead and staying alive.

It was only then that I realized how late it was getting. The sun was dropping below the mountains on the far horizon. I actually said to myself, 'That is an absolutely fantastic view – but you shouldn't be seeing it – not from here anyway.' It's incredible how much colder it gets the moment the sun goes down. And it chose that very moment to start blowing. At first it wasn't too bad, but by the time I had got back to Pertemba, the wind was unbearable. We were having to go back straight into it, and it wasn't in gusts; it was a continuous blast of spindrift; you couldn't open your eyes, couldn't face into it.

Pertemba seemed in a befuddled state from the long wait and the lack of oxygen. I said, 'We'll get down fast now, Pertemba,' and led the way down. The descent was a nightmare.

Dave was very relieved to see me. He had spent the last hour holding the box up. A whipcrack of wind had lifted up the floor with him lying on it, and had

smashed the frame. After this he had had to hold it up braced across the box. Even so, he had a brew ready for me. I had a long chat with Pertemba. He made a very relevant remark when he said: 'We nearly died.' And we bloody well did. If I had been able to pull that extra 12 metres of rope through first time off and had actually reached the site of Camp 6 – and I should have done, I was in that kind of mood – we should probably have started down two hours later, and I think under those circumstances we should have been lucky to survive.

There was no question of their staying up at Camp 5 to help build up supplies. Nick and Dave had taken themselves beyond normal limits in an effort to make it possible for others to have their summit bid.

I felt good as I climbed back up to Camp 5 and the following morning I set off with Ang Phurba to complete Nick's heroic route to Camp 6. There were a number of ledges on a spur dropping down from the foot of the Rock Band, on one of which I should have to find a camp site. At this point I was able to look straight up into the gully that Dougal had described as the way through the Rock Band. He had said that in 1971 it was a straightforward snow gully, but now, looking up, I could see very little snow. Indeed, it barely seemed a gully at all, more a fissure in the rock wall, narrow, steep, in places overhanging. It looked hard; but then I shut the problem from my mind. I had programmed myself to establish Camp 6, and just completing this simple task was taking all my own resources. The gully was Dougal's problem.

At last I was going to get a little lead climbing, as I tied on to the end of the rope left dangling by Nick and started to pick my way across towards the rocky spur, kicked steps up a steep little snow slope and then pulled over a rock step. A length of rope, left from the spring expedition, protruded from the snows and was attached to a big boulder on a ledge reaching out to the crest of the spur. It was exposed to the wind, but got plenty of sun and what a situation! Just round the corner we could gaze down on the South Col, over 300m (1000ft) below; immediately across from us was the great mass of Lhotse, its summit only a little higher than the site of Camp 6.

I took off my pack and set off down the ropes to Camp 5. Ang Phurba had already got down and, as I arrived, thrust a steaming mug of lemon tea into my hand. When we had first met Ang Phurba we had no idea of how outstanding a performance he was to produce on the mountain. Slightly built, a bit of a dandy, always elegantly dressed in gear issued by other expeditions, it had been difficult to imagine him having the endurance to keep going at altitude and yet he was proving to be one our most outstanding Sherpas.

I had planned to do another carry myself to Camp 6 but the urgent need to sort out our oxygen situation intervened. Meanwhile Hamish and Dougal had arrived at Camp 5 before we had consolidated Camp 6 for them. I volunteered myself to make one last carry to Camp 6 and then, with both Hamish and Dougal and Doug and Mick ensconced in Camp 5, I retreated to Camp 4, only too aware we had very few days left, our lead climbers were barely supplied and there was the most technically difficult climbing to come. The weather forecast had reported winds of 200km/hour (125mph) over the summit.

For Dougal, who had been here before, the wind was the chief enemy as he led off. 'I had experienced many bad storms, many high winds, but this was a new dimension of wind speed, and it was basically fine weather. I reached the position where the equipment was dumped and at just about that point the wind stopped gusting and moved into continuous movement. Thinking was difficult. I had to turn away and crouch. Two things were blatantly self-evident. There was no way we could attempt to climb on the Rock Band and no way a tent could be pitched.' As for the so-called escape route, which Don Whillans had observed on to the South East Ridge, Dougal realized it would have been suicidal in the gusts. 'There was nothing to do but turn round. I jerked my head downwards. Doug nodded.'

Dougal's news on the evening radio call wasn't really a surprise, and once we had mastered our disappointment, I wanted to clear the mountain as quickly as possible. Camp 1 was rather sad, stripped of all its tents – just the scattered debris of an expedition. Hamish and Dougal were in front. I went down the Icefall with Doug Scott, finding the upper part changed from when I had last seen it six weeks before. Crevasses had opened out, séracs had fallen and the route wound its way through the debris. Strangely, we had little sense of danger now, perhaps becoming immune to the feeling after our weeks on the mountain. I spent an hour photographing a particularly spectacular section of the Icefall, which, only two hours later, was to collapse – with disastrous results.

We were over halfway down when we met Tony Tighe on his way up to meet us. He was tremendously excited at the prospect of getting a glimpse into the Western Cwm. He had spent the last eight weeks at Base Camp fulfilling unexciting but invaluable duties, taking all the radio calls, helping Jimmy Roberts with general

*Ang Phurba cooking at Camp 5. It was so cold we had to toast the wireless batteries over the stove to make them work.*

administration and the assembly of loads for the mountain. At times he had even taken on the role of diplomat. It is all too easy while on the mountain to resent people having the easy life at Base Camp, to wonder why supplies were not coming up to the front line more quickly, and grumbles were often passed back to Base Camp over the radio. Tony would soften them

down and, in passing them on to Jimmy, would take the sting out of them. In every way he had fulfilled an important role on the expedition through his mature good sense, his kindness and his efficiency. The last day I felt I had to give him some kind of reward for everything he had done for us, knew how much he longed to see into the Western Cwm, to get an inkling of the excitement and struggle we had known and enjoyed all these days. And so I had invited him to come up and meet us.

He was brimming over with happiness when we met him. He had come up with 20 Sherpas who were going to Camp 1 to meet those bringing the loads down from Camp 2. Having dropped behind them, being less fit than they, he was now on his own – nothing unusual since the track through the Icefall was clearly marked and all the crevasses bridged, all difficult sections fixed roped.

We passed him, got back down to Base Camp, to the first wash in six weeks. There was a feeling of the start of the holidays, talk of the meals we were going to have in Kathmandu, dreams of getting home. The afternoon wore on; then suddenly there was a rising babble of voices among the Sherpas. They were obviously worried – they seem to have an almost extrasensory perception of trouble. Kelvin called me over.

'There's some kind of trouble in the Icefall,' he said.

'What is it?' I asked.

'I'm not sure,' Kelvin replied. 'They're not at all certain, but they seem to think there's been a big collapse.'

There was nothing we could do but wait. A large party straggled into sight, followed by another, each with their stories of the collapse they had had to circumnavigate. It appeared that the Sherpas had had a miraculous escape, but there was a terrible growing certainty that Tony had been engulfed in the collapse. Our search parties found nothing. Tony had vanished completely under the tons of ice. We had tried and failed. We knew when we snatched that vacancy in the queue for Everest that we would be fighting against long odds, that chances were thin. Then surely this is part of the challenge of climbing? But for us the face had proved impossible. We had been beaten by a combination of high winds and extreme cold. I am confident that no other party could have done much better that autumn.

Can the South West Face be climbed? I am confident that in the pre-monsoon season it can; the escape route round the side would give an almost certain way to success but in taking this the real challenge of the South West Face would be evaded. Tackling the South West Face will require a combination of high-standard technical climbing at an altitude higher than almost any other mountain in the world, together with the logistic build-up necessary to support at least two climbers – ideally four – at Camp 6 with oxygen, food and equipment.

It is interesting to note that the pattern of failure is very similar to that experienced by prewar expeditions attempting the first ascent of Everest. Nearly all these reached a height of around 8300m

*Tony Tighe, the Australian who helped us at Base Camp throughout the expedition. He was killed by a sérac collapse in the Icefall on the last day of the expedition.*

*Dougal Haston returning from our high point after the decision to abandon the expedition. There was insufficient snow in the groove that led up through the Rock Band and consequently it would have been too difficult in the extreme cold and high winds.*

(27,230ft) to be defeated by the technical difficulties of the Yellow Band and the altitude. Today we can cope with a very much higher standard of difficulty at altitude, thanks to improvements in equipment, but I cannot help wondering whether those improvements are yet sufficient to enable climbers to tackle what, in effect, is a high-standard alpine problem at an altitude of over 8300 metres. The critical factor is oxygen, both the reliability of the supply and, even more important, the weight of the cylinder. If this weight could be reduced by half, the logistic problem also would be reduced by very nearly the same proportion, making it that much easier to sustain climbers in a siege at altitude.

Another important factor is the choice of the route itself. Whillans and Haston had adopted the right-hand route up the Rock Band primarily because they had found a convenient site for Camp 5 on the right-hand side of the Great Central Gully. From here it would have been difficult to get back across to the break on the left-hand side of the Rock Band, the line that the Japanese had favoured in 1969 and 1970. This latter line seems to have some distinct advantages. Throughout its length it appears to be a snow and ice gully in photographs taken over a period of years. The gully on the right, on the other hand, seems less reliable. The left-hand gully also has the advantage that it is shorter, being approximately 150m (500ft) in length, while the right-hand one is probably about 245m (800ft). Camp 5 could be situated near the foot of the Rock Band where there seems to be a snow-covered ledge on a small promontory, although even if this were to prove unusable, platforms such as those at Camp 4 could always be constructed. The great advantage of this step would be that Camp 6 would then be above the Rock Band, somewhere on the broad snowfield that stretches back to the right-hand side of the upper part of the face, where an easy-angled snow gully leads to the col between the South Summit and the main summit. The route would be more pleasing aesthetically, for there is not the easy option of an obvious escape off the face and, at the same time, it might prove more practicable.

And so the siege goes on. Is it worth it – worth the expense – worth organizing large expeditions (for you would never climb it with a small one) – the discomfort – the possible loss of life – and all the ballyhoo which must inevitably accompany an Everest expedition? I think it is.

Before leaving Kathmandu for home I filed an application for another attempt on the South West Face in the next available spring slot.

# A Second Chance

THE SOUTH WEST FACE of Everest remained filed under unfinished business while we all got on with other enjoyable climbing projects. I could not believe that it would not have been climbed by the time the Nepalese government got around to granting me another slot, so I was mentally discounting it, even when another strong Japanese expedition failed to crack the Rock Band in autumn 1973. Then one morning in December 1973 a cable arrived from Kathmandu. It was from Mike Cheney at Mountain Travel, Jimmy Roberts' trekking agency. It read: 'Canadians cancelled for autumn 1975 stop Do you want to apply Reply urgent Cheney.'

Suddenly all my nicely laid plans were upset; I had another chance of going for the South West Face at the wrong time of year. It took me several days to decide. If I were to attempt the South West Face again I felt strongly that it should be in the spring rather than in the autumn. Every consideration of reason and common sense said, 'Don't go!' But the fact that Everest is the highest mountain in the world, the variety of mountaineering challenges it presents, the richness of its history, combine to make it difficult for any mountaineer to resist. And for me it had a special magnetism. I had been there before and failed, and in the end I knew that I could not let pass the opportunity to go to Everest again, even if an attempt on the South West Face seemed impractical. I applied, and four months later heard we had permission for Everest in the autumn of 1975.

Maybe I could revive my earlier plans for a lightweight South Col expedition? The Japanese who had recently failed on the South West Face had managed to put two men on the summit by the South Col as late as 26 October. They had had a team of 36 climbers. Our challenge would be to do it with 12. Doug Scott and Dougal Haston were not convinced. Doug asked me how we'd all feel if we arrived in the Western Cwm and conditions seemed suitable for an attempt on the South West Face, and yet by the very nature and size of the expedition we were forced to pursue our plan for making a lightweight push by the South Col. We should always be aware of the

*Walking up to Namche Bazar in the morning sunshine. Learning from 1972, we set out earlier in 1975 and we were more fortunate with the weather.*

'We round a corner and there is the British Raj in all its glory, neatly lined up erected tents, crowds kept at a distance and we sit down at tables in the mess tent and are brought steaming kettles full of tea. For a mountaineer surely a Bonington Everest expedition is one of the last great imperial experiences that life can offer.' Peter Boardman

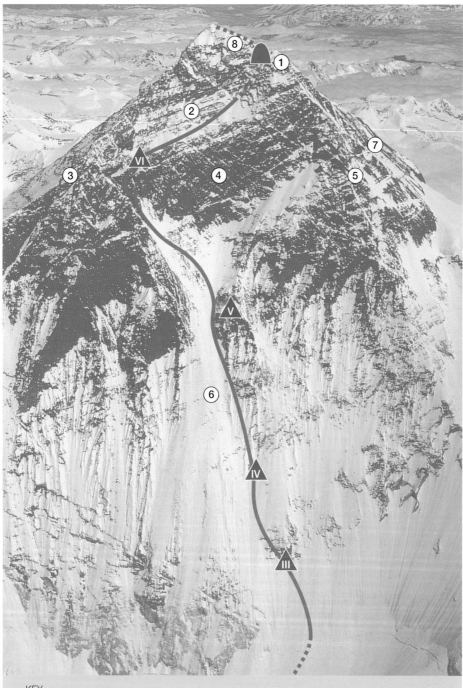

*The South West Face of Everest showing the route and camps on the successful 1975 climb.*

KEY

| | |
|---|---|
| —— | Climbing with fixed rope |
| ▪▪▪▪▪ | Climbing without fixed rope |
| 🔺 | Doug and Dougal's bivvy on way down |
| ▲ | Camp |

1 South Summit
2 Summit Snow Field
3 West Ridge
4 Rock Band
5 South Pillar

6 Great Central Gully
7 South East Ridge
8 Hillary Step

South West Face towering above us with its intriguing unknowns of the Rock Band and the upper stretches of the mountain. This was the real challenge and until it had been met and overcome any other route or style in climbing could only be a second best. I shared their feelings, but knew all too well that it was I who would have to spend the next year putting together the strong expedition that we should need to give us the slightest chance of success.

The key problems were the cold and the high winds of the post-monsoon period. Somehow we had to get into position to make a summit bid before the arrival of the winds which seem to come at any time from early to mid-October. An obvious way would be to start earlier, but here one is limited by the monsoon, which continues until towards the end of September. The Japanese had reported fine mornings followed by snow most afternoons when they had established their Base Camp on 25 August. This, therefore – three weeks earlier than we had started in 1972 – seemed a reasonable target to aim for.

The next essential would be greater speed in climbing the mountain. Inevitably this meant a larger team would be required to give greater carrying power. In 1972, with 11 climbers and 40 Sherpas, there had been several occasions when we had had to delay our advance on the mountain in order to build up supplies at one of the camps. I had to find a balance between having a large enough team to ensure that we could maintain our speed up the mountain and yet, at the same time, avoid becoming unwieldy. We needed better tentage that could stand up to the high winds, the heavy snowfall and the stones that raked the face. By the end of the previous expedition, hardly a tent remained undamaged.

Finally, and perhaps most important of all, we needed to find a better route through the Rock Band. It is surprising that the Japanese in 1973 followed the same line as ourselves and previous expeditions, particularly since the first Japanese expedition had been confident that there was a route through the Rock Band over on the left. They had decided, however, that the Rock Band was too difficult for a first ascent and favoured the tactics of Herrligkoffer's expedition, proposing to take the so-called escape route on to the South East Ridge. In fact, they were unable to establish their sixth camp. Examination of our own performance in 1972, and that of all the other expeditions to the face, seemed to show that the right-hand route was a blind alley. Both Doug Scott and I were very attracted to the deep-cut gully which appeared to penetrate the left-hand side of the Rock Band. You could not see all the way into the back of it, but a tongue of snow led into it and there seemed a good chance that this could continue a good way up. The problem might be to find an escape from the gully out on to the Upper Snowfield, but it was thought likely that the difficult climbing would be for a comparatively short section.

Another advantage of attempting the Rock Band from the left was that we should be able to tackle it from Camp 5, ensuring that our lines of communication would be that much shorter, with the climbers sleeping lower and, therefore, going more strongly. If successful, we should be able to have our Camp 6 above the Rock

Band – admittedly, with a long traverse across the Upper Snowfield to the foot of the South Summit gully – but this seemed acceptable since the main difficulties would then be over.

We had our permission, we had a new plan, now all we needed was to raise £100,000, an outrageous sum by 1970s expeditioning standards. It is here that I am eternally grateful for the expertise of my literary agent, George Greenfield, and his introduction to Alan Tritton of Barclays Bank International, who took us on – and with us a not inconsiderable amount of media and Barclays customer flak.

After our 1972 failure I had been shaken, even hurt, by the criticism of a number of mountaineers whose opinion I respect, both of the value of the route and the size of the expedition we had used to tackle it. The fundamental question was whether the South West Face could be considered a worthwhile objective. I think it was. There is a natural evolution from attempting a mountain by its easiest route, on Everest, the South East Ridge, then tackling other, perhaps harder, facets such as the North Ridge or the West Ridge and then, finally, the steep walls embraced by the ridges. This same evolution has taken place in the mountains of the Alps, like the Matterhorn and the Eiger, and the steps forward on to harder ground were often accompanied by controversy over new techniques used or risks taken. The South West Face of Everest was not 'The Ultimate Challenge' of mountaineering (the title used for the American edition of our 1972 book) – there is no such thing, for no sooner is one 'last great problem' solved than another is found. But it was an intriguing problem which would continue to nag mountaineers until it was solved.

There was no doubt in my mind about the worth of the route; inevitably I did wonder about the means we were going to use to climb it. My own philosophy is that one should use the minimum force or number of climbers necessary to give some chance of success. In the Himalaya there has been a growing trend towards very lightweight expeditions tackling increasingly difficult problems, often using an alpine-style approach, abandoning the concept of set camps, high-altitude porters and fixed ropes, for a continuous movement up the mountain, carrying everything on the backs of the party and bivouacking each night. This is an exciting and very satisfying concept – one which Haston, Scott, Boysen and I followed on Changabang in 1974. Another pleasing feature of this approach is that the entire team can go to the summit together, thus all share in the climax of the expedition.

On the South West Face of Everest, however, there could be no question of such an approach. I found the sheer immensity of the problem fascinating. It needed a whole set of new concepts in planning, equipment and timing to give any chance of success at all. Perhaps I am a frustrated field marshal, my passion for war games and my early military career providing a clue in this direction, but I both enjoyed, and at times was frightened by, the scale of the responsibility I had undertaken – to form a sound plan and then to make it work in practice.

It could be argued that we should have waited, or even allowed some future generation with improved equipment, or longer necks, to make a lightweight push

*Breakfast on the approach. Walking into the mountain gave us all some time to acclimatize and me a chance to think ahead and weigh up climbing permutations. Maybe I am a frustrated field marshal.*

straight up the face. I have a feeling, however, that if each generation just sat back, abandoning the challenge of the moment to the people of the future, we would never make any progress at all. None of the team gave more than a 50-50 chance of success and some of them – especially at the beginning – gave us no chance at all, yet could not resist the invitation to join. Their attitude mirrored that of the majority of mountaineers.

Certainly none of my 1972 lead climbers could resist the chance of completing the job, with the exception of Dave Bathgate, but in his place I could call on one of my oldest climbing friends, Martin Boysen, a competitive and outstanding rock-climber who had not been available in 1972. Hamish MacInnes signed up as deputy leader, organized our oxygen system and designed some new super-strong box tents; Nick Estcourt shouldered the job of expedition treasurer and paymaster; and Mick Burke would once more double as high-altitude cameraman. I needed two more lead climbers to bring the number up to eight. Paul 'Tut' Braithwaite, with experience in the Pamirs and Baffin Island, came on Doug Scott's recommendation and it was Tut who suggested the youngest recruit to the team, the 23-year-old Peter Boardman who already had an impressive record of climbs in the Hindu Kush.

In supporting roles, Dave Clarke took on the chore of organizing equipment; my old Army friend Mike Thompson was persuaded to be i/c food; Ronnie Richards shouldered transport and communications; Mike Cheney, our invaluable contact in Kathmandu, agreed to manage Base Camp and recommended ex-Gurkha captain Adrian Gordon with his fluent Nepali for Advanced Base manager. Our doctor was Charlie Clarke, a keen expedition climber in his own right, whose suave Islington exterior belied a steady strength of character on the mountain. When it was pointed out that there might be enough work for two we invited Jim Duff, a young doctor already working in Nepal as a medical officer. We needed one more climber and took

'Climbing Everest using siege tactics is like a ponderous game of leapfrog, each group

Allen Fyffe, a climbing instructor from Glenmore Lodge in the Cairngorms with a strong winter climbing record, though in signing him up I created a problem for myself, for Allen was definitely a lead climber and this gave an uneven number. There was also a representative from Barclays, one from the *Sunday Times* and a four-man BBC team. I sometimes wondered how I was going to control them all.

We chose to send our 20 tonnes of food and equipment well ahead of time overland to Kathmandu. It took Bob Stoodley's team of four a heroic 24 days in two 16-tonne trucks, and from the dump in Mike Cheney's garden the loads were ferried by plane to Lughla and by porter to Khumde to await our arrival. Jimmy Roberts had suggested Pertemba as expedition sirdar. He had been one of our outstanding high-altitude porters in 1972 and I had been impressed by both his performance and personality. Though at 26 he was young for the responsibility, I was happy to agree with the suggestion. His deputy, Ang Phu, had also put up a good showing in 1972. With the gear taken care of early, I explored what help my logistics might receive from computer programming, courtesy of my old friend Ian McNaught-Davis. I quickly discovered it was impossible to get the computer to do it all for you; rather, it represented a quick check on one's own planning. We made a climbing game in which I gave the order for movement and load-carrying, and the computer would swiftly calculate the finish at the end of each day. We played this through three times but always reached a logistic bottleneck around Camp 4. As a result of this, I developed a formula for planning the most effective distribution of manpower in the early and mid-stages of the expedition, which seemed to solve the problem. Not only did this work so well that we followed it almost exactly in practice, but also – when we changed the siting of our camps in the later stages of the expedition – I found I was able to adapt mentally to the changing situation quickly, even at 7700m (25,250ft). I prepared a programme for the climb which would, in theory, enable us to make a summit bid towards the end of September.

At the end of July 1975, however, when we flew out to Kathmandu, I did not dare believe that we could possibly achieve these targets. There were so many unknown factors – the weather, performance of the Sherpas, the state of the snow, our ability to acclimatize in a very fast ascent. On the eve of our departure even our best friends gave us no more than an even chance of success – these were the odds quoted by John Hunt, chairman of our committee of management, at our press conference. Some members of the team felt even this to be optimistic.

Thanks to Mike Cheney's master-minding and Pertemba's hands-on management, the approach march made life easy for the climbers in the Nepalese foothills.

out in front, usually a foursome, making the route from one camp to the next'

*Overleaf: The barn in the Sherpa village of Khumde, journey's end for our two truckloads of gear that had been ferried up from Luglha airstrip ahead of the monsoon. We camped around it below Kangtaiga, left, and Tamserku, towering in the background.*

To Peter Boardman everything about the walk in was a fresh experience, as he recorded in his diary:

We round a corner and there is the British Raj in all its glory, neatly lined up erected tents, crowds kept at a distance and we sit down at tables in the mess tent and are brought steaming kettles full of tea. For a mountaineer surely a Bonington Everest expedition is one of the last great imperial experiences that life can offer.

Once again I spent much of the time balancing pairs of climbers in my mind. In 1972 I had gone through the same thought process and resolved on giving everyone a clear role in advance all the way to the summit bid. Climbing Everest using siege tactics is like a ponderous game of leapfrog, each group out in front, usually a foursome, making the route from one camp to the next and then retiring for a rest, thus enabling the lead climbers to remain sufficiently fresh to contend with the challenge of the final 600m (2000ft) of the mountain and at the same time to maintain the momentum of the ascent. The advantage of this approach was that, in theory, once everyone had accepted their role, they automatically made the best of it. In practice, however, it did not work out so well, since it presupposed that everything would go to plan, a most unlikely eventuality on a mountain the size of Everest. Having given team members a role expectancy, they inevitably became very possessive about it. I remembered the row with Doug.

This time, therefore, I resolved to avoid committing myself to giving individuals a specific role within a climbing team any earlier than absolutely necessary. But because of the leapfrog principle, the initial grouping of team members could determine their position on the mountain in the final vital stages, affecting the logical choice of the summit pair. I consequently spent many hours, as I walked up and down the winding paths of the foothills, fitting together the different combination of lead climbers and also trying to formulate my own response to the challenge of leading this tremendously talented and strong-willed group of mountaineers.

My thinking changed and developed with the days, but I managed to keep most of my thoughts to myself. In the past I have often made life difficult both for myself and my team by thinking out aloud, plunging into speech when thoughts have only been part formed. This has inevitably led to what has seemed like changes of mind, upsetting everyone concerned. Instead I began talking to my lead climbers about their potential roles on the climb, starting with Dougal Haston, Nick Estcourt and

Mick Burke on the way to Khumde. After our arrival I recorded their reactions in my tape-diary:

> Their various attitudes are quite interesting. Dougal's approach is undoubtedly that of a prima donna; he reckons that he wants to get to the top, that he deserves the top and he's certainly the best person to go there. I'm inclined to agree with him. At the same time, though, one must be very aware that forcing the Rock Band, pushing the route out above it, might be just as exacting and every bit as vital. I don't think Dougal, if I ever put him in a position where he was forcing above the Rock Band, would agree to drop back and let someone else go for the top.

Anyway, we talked round his role and the one that I had seen for him was one that he's happy to fit in with, establishing Camp 4 and pushing the route out towards Camp 5, as a member of my third lead climbing party, with Hamish MacInnes and two of the others whom I have still not decided upon.

We swapped round some names. Dougal did raise the point – wouldn't it be ideal if he and Doug Scott were paired up. I countered this though with the fact that I couldn't possibly put the strongest pair together right at the beginning, both from a morale point of view and also because I wanted to even out the abilities of each of my lead-climbing teams. At this stage I think it unlikely that Doug and Dougal will end up climbing together; I think I'd rather use them in successive summit bids, to ensure that a second attempt is as strong as the first.

I also talked to Nick Estcourt. He's a bit uncertain of himself in many ways, can be obsessive over small things, but in the big important ones is very unselfish. Nick just said, 'I leave it entirely to you, Chris; you know I'll do anything you ask me to do.' It's great having this kind of support but I can't help worrying that perhaps I end up taking advantage of him, using him for a key role on the way up the climb that I know requires a highly developed sense of social responsibility.

I talked to Mick Burke as well. Last expedition he was much more tense because he hadn't got his own role in life clear. This time he's more relaxed, largely I suspect because he has a secure career with the BBC, and even more important, his role in the expedition is secure in that whatever happens he's the star of the BBC team; he's got everything to gain and very little to lose. Mick said, 'Just play it along as you see best; I'll fit in with whatever you want.' He then grinned at me and said, 'You've got one hell of a job; I don't envy you one little bit.'

Our expedition doctor Charlie Clarke was, like Pete Boardman, experiencing the road to Everest for the first time:

Kharikhola – 11 August 1975: I wonder what the life-cycle of a leech is? I still worry about the dangers of the Icefall. Enormous avalanches sweeping down off Nuptse; tottering ice towers just waiting for me personally; or the horror of being off-route in mist and hearing the groaning of avalanches and séracs. I have other fantasies about going to the top, but these will shortly be dashed when I find how unpleasant it is.

The bridge below Namche – 13 August 1975: The majestic scale is impossible to capture on film and it is only by having to walk up the Dudh Kosi that one realizes how enormous it all is. Here in camp I watched, I made certain I saw, the slaughter of our dinner – a large, black goat. I've never seen an execution before and one is certainly enough. The squealing creature was dragged over a tree trunk and then, with a single blow of a kukri, the head was severed and leapt forward on the rope around the neck, followed by two jets of blood. I was very nearly sick and thought how tenuously the whole of our individual lives is held together. I think about death a lot – not my own particularly – but the practical aspects of what we'll have to do. It's rather like being at war, this expedition, with the Sherpas as our mercenaries. I think many of us are scared, but no one will bring himself to discuss it – Chris just turned off it a few days ago. It's so odd how Tony Tighe is talked about as though he's still around, and morbidly fascinating to hear Nick discussing Dougal's floppy hat as the one Tony used to wear. I like Dougal very much, in a quiet sort of way. I wonder what he thinks about all the time.

So, to Khumde tomorrow and the action really starts. I do wonder how enjoyable this expedition will be and, unlike others, I don't think I must look for too much individual pleasure. It will be a collective thing – probably, as Mick said, irrelevant of the outcome, 'It doesn't seem to alter your joy at the end of an expedition whether or not you've climbed the mountain.'

We reached Khumde on 14 August, just 12 days after leaving Kathmandu. Dave Clarke and Ronnie Richards had pressed on a day ahead to start unpacking the gear and by the time we reached the village the tents were already up and piles of boxes neatly covered by tarpaulins were scattered over the small field in which we were to camp. The gentle limbo of the approach march was over.

Although it rained each afternoon, the mornings were clear and still — ideal weather for getting started on the Everest Icefall. I resolved, therefore, to send Nick Estcourt and Dougal Haston ahead on 17 August to find a site for Base Camp and make a first reconnaissance. I also had the chance of talking to Hamish and Doug Scott about their roles on the expedition. In my diary I described the conversation:

I laid out my ideas and plans, and discussed the composition of the lead teams on the face. I definitely want Hamish to set up the boxes at Camp 4. I think that is one of the most important moves on the expedition, for unless this camp is secure, we won't be able to keep up the flow of supplies on the face. With a bit of luck he will also be able to site Camp 5 and make sure that's all right. It's really good having his advice and support — he's so wonderfully relaxed about it all and yet, at the same time, very canny.

I also talked to Doug. Doug was very reasonable. I think he likes the idea of having a crack at the Rock Band and would even take on one of the genuinely sacrificial roles — for instance, forcing the route across the Upper Icefields, as close to the South Summit as possible, thus putting it on a plate for the next pair through. He just commented: 'There's no point getting uptight about it. You never know — the weather might close in and anything could happen to change the role you think you're going to get.' I think he really means it and that means that he will be relaxed. I must say, he is one of the biggest, most unselfish people I have got amongst the lead climbers.

I still couldn't help worrying about the size of the team. Being big meant we had the reserves we might need, but there were going to be a lot of people sitting around at times, and there's nothing like idleness for making people discontented. This was something I realized I was going to have to watch.

It was a relief to set out for the final stage of our walk to Base Camp, pausing for chang at the tea houses, calling at Tengpoche monastery for the Head Lama's blessing and arriving at Base Camp on 22 August. Base Camp was as bleak as ever, the rubbish of a Japanese Ladies' expedition strewing the rocks just below the site that Nick and Dougal had chosen. That day they were already up in the Icefall, making the first reconnaissance. We were starting on the right note in our race against the autumnal winds and cold. There was much to do, and barely enough people to do it all. Each day a group went up into the Icefall to push the route out towards its top. Back at Base Camp we resigned ourselves to administrative chores.

On the 24th I settled down in one of the big box tents with Dougal, Hamish and Ronnie Richards to alter the Sherpas' crampons. The size we had ordered was too big for most of them and to get them to fit on their boots we had to shorten the arm

*Mingma Nuru, the young deaf-mute who was tragically drowned in a glacier stream while carrying a load up to Base Camp.*

linking the heel-piece to the main set of spikes. Hamish was the expert at this rough engineering, while the rest of us riveted on the straps and altered the screw-on sections. It was about 10.30 when Pertemba came into the tent and told me that I was wanted for a ceremony to consecrate the Base Camp altar. This was the first time any of us had heard about it. Slightly mystified, I followed him out to find all the Sherpas assembled round a pile of stones which had been built up into a simple altar. Purna, our cook, was the self-appointed master of ceremonies and thrust into my hand a tray on which was balanced a bottle of local rum and around which was heaped rice and tsampa smeared with margarine. A ceremonial scarf was placed around my neck and another around the bottle of rum. Phurkipa was chanting a prayer from a tattered book of Tibetan script, while the rest of the Sherpas were shouting and laughing. The entire ceremony was typical of the Sherpa temperament, light-hearted yet very serious, all at the same time. The Sherpas were throwing handfuls of rice and tsampa over Pertemba, myself and each other; laughter and muttered prayers mingled, while I clutched my top-heavy tray, fearful that the bottle of rum might topple over. I imagined that this would have been a terrible omen. A flagpole, decked with prayer flags, the expedition flag and that of the BBC television show 'Blue Peter' was heaved into position on the altar; Pertemba then placed his offering on the altar and I followed suit, making a *namaste* at Pertemba's bidding. Every morning before setting out into the Icefall, the juniper fire was lit and each Sherpa made an offering of a little tsampa or rice on the altar.

The ceremony over, we had to come to terms with an increasingly worrying problem. The previous evening it had been reported that one of the porters who had set out that day from Gorak Shep had failed to return. He was a young deaf and dumb lad called Mingma, whom Doug Scott had befriended. At that stage none of the Sherpas was worried, thinking that perhaps he'd missed the path on his way back and had spent the night out. The following morning, however, he still hadn't turned up and it was obvious that something could perhaps be wrong; being deaf and dumb, if he had only strayed a little distance from the path and had sprained an ankle, he would have had no means of calling attention to himself. We were going to have to mount a search. Gazing over the rocky wilderness of the Khumbu Glacier, I was appalled by the extent of the area we should have to cover. It was Adrian Gordon who found his body in a stream. Doug, because he was the last person to employ the boy, had an unwarranted sense of guilt. But the ever-pragmatic Mick Burke pointed out that the Sherpas were not unduly troubled because they could shrug it off with a thought that his time had come and he had gone to a better life. Next day we pressed on. Yet I could not help asking myself, once again, whether these climbs were worth the loss of life that so often accompanied them. I have no answer. But a climber can assess the risks, and can accept or reject them. Mingma was not a climber, and can have had no thought of danger. His death was an accident, which might have happened at any time, but he was carrying for us, and we were responsible. We could only pray that there would be no more accidents.

# Getting Back Up

CLIMBING THE ICEFALL is a cross between a medieval assault on a fortress and crossing a dangerous minefield. The first time through, everything seems to be full of lurking threats, of toppling séracs and hidden chasms, but once a trail has been broken, with all the obstacles laddered, one can quickly be lulled into a dangerous illusion of security, for the risk is always there, as we had learned so tragically in 1972, right at the end of the expedition.

Following Nick and Dougal's lead, we took it in relays to press out the route and consolidate it. In the middle was a region we named the Egg Shells because of the complexity of the crevasses and the seeming fragility of the blades of ice, which were holding up a roof of snow. We had to fix an almost continuous track of ladders and fixed ropes to ensure that, if the entire area collapsed, any climbers or Sherpas passing through at the time would have a chance of survival through being clipped into the line of rope. Our minds were constantly on potential avalanche paths at this tail end of the monsoon.

At one point I paired Doug with Dougal. At this stage I had no particular thought of putting them together for a summit bid and their pairing was largely a matter of temporary convenience. Doug described his reaction: 'Every decision Chris made from start to finish was scrutinized minutely. When Chris paired me with Dougal I was conscious that I was with someone special, for everyone knew that Dougal was summit material. Then I wondered what Tut Braithwaite would think of this arrangement, for only recently I had spoken to Tut about Chris's intimation that he wanted me to lead the Rock Band and I had asked Tut if he fancied doing it with me. Now, here I was, out of the blue, paired with the star of our show. All I could do was to go along with the flow and see what turned up next. There was no telling at that stage of the game and no point in thinking it was Dougal and me for the top.'

Back at Base Camp there was plenty of bureaucracy to sort out. Our Sherpas were in excellent spirits and happy with their equipment and bonus scheme. I promised

*Dougal Haston making the route through the Icefall. Only one person at a time can be out in front doing what all mountaineers love doing – actually finding the route and climbing. I tried to give everyone a share of the leading.*

Pertemba that I would try to get at least one Sherpa (which in all probability would be him) to the summit. One night we heard a great commotion in the cooktent where Purna was organizing the funding of the Sherpas' end-of-expedition party. Each Sherpa had to pay a certain amount into the kitty for every Sherpani he had boasted of sleeping with on the approach march!

On 27 August we consolidated the route through the Icefall up to the site of Camp 1 on the lip of the Western Cwm. Charlie Clarke who arrived there next day wrote: 'The Western Cwm was everything I had not expected. It should have been straight, wide, vast. Instead, it was so narrow with the walls of Nuptse and the West Shoulder barely making room for it; certainly the route through this defile is hardly attractive.'

By now the organizational structure was sorting itself out, largely due to the work of Dave Clarke, Adrian Gordon and Mike Cheney. But I still had to finalize the composition of my three lead climbing teams. Group one would be making the route from Camp 2 to 3 – not a particularly interesting or exciting job, but one

*Left: Camp 1 at the head of the Icefall, with Pumo Ri beyond, was situated on a huge bollard of ice which eventually must tumble down the Icefall. Right: Nick Estcourt, Pertemba and other Sherpas preparing loads to carry up the Western Cwm.*

which would put them into the logistical position of going up to Camp 5 eventually. Group three would establish Camp 4 and make the route up to Camp 5. Group two, who would have the long push from Camp 3 to 4, could then be in a position of finishing off the Rock Band later on – or perhaps even pushing the route across above it.

It was on the afternoon of the 28th that I finally made my decision. Doug Scott and Mick Burke were obvious choices for the 2 to 3 run – Doug to force it, Mick to film it. They also got on well together. Nick Estcourt seemed ideal for 3 to 4, a long, interesting stretch which he could get his teeth into, making him available for some of the vital work towards the top. It occurred to me that Nick and Tut Braithwaite would complement each other; Nick, very conscientious but sometimes tense and anxious, Tut, easy-going but, at the same time, very ambitious with a tremendous appetite for hard climbing. I knew Dougal and Hamish were happy about their proposed role in putting up Camp 4 and pushing the route to 5, thus putting Dougal in a good position for the summit, while Hamish could ensure that the platform boxes at Camp 4 were really secure.

For sheer skill in climbing there was no one to touch Martin Boysen and I should have liked him to have had a go at the Rock Band. Not the most methodical of souls, the logical place for him would have been with Doug or Nick, but he had only just caught up with us, from an expedition to the Trango Tower, which had overrun, and seemed in need of a rest. I decided, therefore, to send him up to Camp 4. This left Pete Boardman with the third party, and Ronnie Richards and Allen Fyffe in the first. Finally, I felt it would be sensible to use two Sherpas in the run from Camp 3

to 4. It was one of the longest stretches and the Sherpas would probably be able to carry better loads than the climbers, without oxygen. These were the combinations I announced at lunchtime on the 29th.

There was no question who was going to be needed for the first priority job, however. Hamish recorded in his diary: 'It was Dougal who told me there was the daddy of all crevasses just past Camp 1. He and Nick Estcourt had just come down from there and assured me it was thirty foot across and no way round. "You'll be able to use some of that fiendish gear you've been working on," Dougal said cheerfully.' The structure Hamish created we called the Ballachulish Bridge, in honour of the bridge over Loch Leven that had nearly been completed near Hamish's home in Glencoe. There was one difference between the two bridges, however. Hamish built his in a day, keeping well up to schedule, while the Ballachulish Road Bridge was then a full year over deadline!

It took Doug and Dougal just three days to make their way to the site of Camp 2. The initial stretch was much more complex than it had been in 1972, with a network of wide, deep crevasses. They had hoped to keep to the middle of the glacier all the way up, to avoid the risk of avalanches from the flanks, but about halfway up, the centre was barred by a series of broad crevasses and they were forced into the Nuptse flank. We were running out of ladders, even though we had brought out half as many again as we had used in 1972, and Pertemba had already been sent back to Khumde to purchase more, some of which were ones salvaged by the Sherpas from the Icefall in 1972. We were also rescuing ladders left by other expeditions.

Doug and Dougal reached the site of Camp 2 on 31 August and I followed up two days later. The debris of a huge wet snow avalanche had spilt over the route, covering the marker flags for a stretch of a 100m (330ft). Anyone caught in that would have had little chance of survival. And then the face came into view. I made this an excuse to sit down and rest. I also wanted to examine a new line up the lower part of the face which Doug was keen for us to adopt. It was obvious enough, working its way up a series of snow arêtes on the left-hand side of the face, just opposite the site of Camp 2. It was much more direct, and therefore would probably be much quicker. It was also more open to avalanche risk. After the dog-leg, which crept under the flanks of Nuptse, the track swung into the centre of the cwm and stretched, long and steady, up a shallow depression towards the site of Camp 2. I met Nick Estcourt on his way back down. He didn't like the new line at all, claiming it was in the natural fall line of avalanches from the Great Central Gully, while the right-hand route worked its way up to one side of all the avalanche runnels. Mick and, to a lesser degree, Doug argued for the left-hand line, pointing out how we could easily lose all our fixed ropes on the original route to the right whenever it snowed heavily. But everyone, almost imperceptibly, came back to the original right-hand route and we finally settled on it.

Looking back at the argument I wondered about my own role as leader. Perhaps I should have been more positive, but I wasn't, and I think the way we all changed our points of view and argued round the problem to reach a democratic decision was, in this particular case, the best way we could have done it. We were very closely united by a decision that everyone helped to make. Many months later I was bemused to discover how our consultations had looked to other members of the party. Doug Scott recollects: 'Chris suddenly ended the debate with "We'll go the old way; I've made my decision." It wasn't exactly democratic. He had listened to us rather like a prime minister might consult his civil servants before making his decisions. But here it worked and we were all relieved that a decision had been made.'

Doug is a passionate believer in climbing democracy where all decisions are made through group discussion. What he perhaps isn't fully aware of is how strong his own personality is, and how often it is his decision that is adopted. At the same time, though, he understood my side of the problem and always gave me the fullest support, even when, perhaps, he was unhappy about the way I had gone about it. I had to remember too that an innocent offer on my part to lend a hand, with pushing out the route to Camp 3 for example, could be interpreted by the climbing group allocated the job as a threat to their freedom to be out in front and, for a short time, autonomous within a large expedition. Ruefully I realized my role was similar to that of an admiral in a flagship who had to be careful not to interfere with the tactical day-to-day decisions of the fleet's captains.

At Camp 3 it was like an archaeological

*Camp 2 (Advanced Base) seen in the moonlight below the Lhotse Face. The start of the South West Face is on the left.*

'The morning was so magically beautiful, the cwm swathed in boiling mists,

dig, for we quickly began to unearth the relics left by the 1973 Japanese expedition. There was a complete tent that had obviously been left pitched, filled up with snow and turned to ice. Embedded in it was some food and various belongings – an old anorak, a down boot, an ice axe, an oxygen mask and bits of climbing paraphernalia. It was as if the tent had been left for the day and its occupants had never returned. There were also little plastic bags of seaweed, boiled sweets and tins of fruit, all of which provided a welcome change from our diet and proved perfectly edible. We hacked through the relics of the Japanese expedition, salvaging as much as possible, and then came across the ruins of one of our 1972 box tents. No doubt, had we dug deep enough we should also have found reminders of all the previous expeditions.

Back at Camp 2, discussion focused on the problem of where to put Camp 4. The site used by all the previous expeditions was exposed to avalanche and stone fall from the Rock Band. This was the reason why Hamish had designed such a strong box tent, but it seemed preferable to find some way of avoiding the dangerous camp site altogether, and an idea, which was to change the entire logistic balance of the expedition began to germinate. So far, each expedition had followed its predecessor in siting Camp 4 and had then accepted not only the inherent danger of its situation but also the fact that it was in the wrong place logistically in relation to the other camps. The trouble was that Camp 3 was much too low, too short a day from Camp 2, and Camp 4 was too high. In 1972, the Sherpas had preferred to stay at Camp 2 and then every other day had done a very long day's carry up to Camp 4, a height gain of 900m (2950ft) from 6600m (21,650ft) to 7500m (24,600ft). The climbers had been unable to manage this and had always staged at Camp 3 on the way up. This is what we were planning to do this time. I had always been a little unhappy, however, about the principle of the Sherpas obviously undertaking a very much harder carry than the climbers.

The solution suddenly occurred to me. Bring the site of Camp 4 much lower, to a point just 300m (1000ft) above our existing Camp 3. There was a convenient spur running down from the remaining buttress of the Great Central Gully that looked as if it would give the new camp site some protection from avalanches and at the same time would be a reasonable day's carry for climbers and Sherpas alike from Camp 2. Hamish was immediately enthusiastic, as was Dougal when he returned from a long solitary walk up the Western Cwm to try to spy out the route through the Rock Band. I then put the

Previous page: *Sherpas carrying loads up the Western Cwm below the huge North Face of Nuptse. There was snowfall every afternoon and I had to decide each day whether or not to close the route because of the threat of avalanche.*

Everest in dark blue shadow, Nuptse emerging diamond white, ice crests gleaming'

idea to Pertemba, for his reaction was the most important of all, and he was also in favour. I spent the morning with him making the detailed logistic calculations that the change of site for Camp 4 made necessary. Charlie Clarke described his reaction to my activity in his diary:

Chris is in a state of hyper mania at Camp 2 in the Western Cwm, drawing charts of stores, oxygen, men, being uncontrollably effusive down the radio and Mick has christened him the 'Mad Mahdi'. He is desperate that the master plan unfolds smoothly and above all that the route from Base to Camp 2 is safe, for it is here that the Sherpas go alone and much can go wrong.

He really is a great leader in spite of all the criticism levelled at him. Nobody else has the personality to command us and deep down we respect him. I have a very good relationship with him particularly as I, thank God, am not in the raffle – i.e. the great decision of who goes to the top. This sadly alienates him from most of the lead climbers. Even a little is enough and it's just beginning to show itself. No splits, no factions, no nastiness, but it's all there in their hearts.

I was well aware that one of the problems of having sufficient lead climbers in the expedition to cope with a sustained siege of the Rock Band was maintaining their interest and morale while they waited for their turn out in front. Back at Camp 2, just before taking his turn in the lead, Martin Boysen had been very depressed: 'It really doesn't matter if I'm here or not. I have done sweet Fanny Adams apart from dragging my unwilling body up and down the Icefall.' And yet on the morning of 10 September: 'amazing how one day's depression dissolves into happiness. At Camp 2 I was at my lowest ebb, yet next day walking up the Western Cwm with Pete I felt light-hearted and gloriously happy for the first time. The morning was so magically beautiful, the cwm swathed in boiling mists, Everest in dark blue shadow, Nuptse emerging diamond white, a hundred ice crests gleaming.'

*Left: Camp 3, on the face. It was like an archaeological dig with the remnants of previous expeditions in different layers of snow.*

They spent the night at Camp 3 and the next morning, on 11 September, set out for the site of Camp 4. Pertemba and I, with 12 Sherpas, had already left Camp 2 with loads of box tents, food, fixed rope climbing hardware for the push into the Great Central Gully. The Sherpas pulled ahead of me without any trouble, but I kept plodding – slow but steady up the long line of fixed rope.

Martin had waited for me at Camp 3 and it was good to see him relaxed and happy. We set out together for the new camp, being hit by the sun before we were halfway up the big snow slope that led across to the base of the Great Central Gully.

The heat was immediately oppressive and our upward progress slowed to a crawl. Dougal Haston, Hamish MacInnes and Pete Boardman had already reached the site of the camp and were hacking out their platforms. It didn't look quite as well protected as it had through our binoculars from below. They were digging their way into a shallow snow arête, which hopefully would divide any avalanches from the very considerable broken snow slope above and protect the camp from the worst of their force. The powder-snow avalanches had already carved out channels, down which a torrent of snow was pouring. This was the first time that the complete MacInnes box, with its platforms, special floor of plastic honeycomb sandwiched between plywood and bullet-proofed tarpaulins, was to be tried out. Hamish was in his element, spanner in hand, erecting one of the boxes.

Martin digging a platform just below, observed slightly caustically: 'Pete sits above

acting as Hamish's bolt boy. Dougal squats impassively under the rocks. Pete calls incessantly, "Martin could you secure my rucksack? Martin could you bring my camera up? Martin…" I told him to stop pissing about, expecting me to run around for him, and to come down to help dig out our platform. Am I being unreasonable to be so shirty? I know I am being a bit grumpy, but why should I feel so annoyed? Perhaps it's because Pete is so young, too easily managed by the old stagers. He's such a dreamy bugger and can appear to be so damned helpless. But I like his company and, as for the climbing, he's as tough and determined as anyone.' Eventually the boxes were erected and the foursome settled down to the afternoon routine of brewing tea and cooking the evening meal, our own high-altitude rations being titivated with some Japanese tinned food from Camp 3.

*Left: High-altitude Meccano. Hamish MacInnes at Camp 4, erecting one of the super-strong box tents he had designed for the expedition.* Right: The tarpaulins draped over the box tents were designed to act as chutes so that snow would flow over them rather than build up behind.

The next day 11 Sherpas, accompanied by Mike Thompson, made a carry up to Camp 4, bringing a good stock of rope, deadmen, more boxes and oxygen cylinders, while above the route was being pushed out until the arrival of the afternoon sun drove the lead climbers down to their tents and their diaries. Pete Boardman observed his new team mates cautiously: 'Martin seems to have slotted me light-heartedly as Bramhall middle class. Hamish is friendly and cheerful but Dougal is ever distant.' A feeling of wellbeing induced by roast lamb and fried slices of Christmas pudding was interrupted that evening when a big powder-snow avalanche swept over the camp. Hamish MacInnes describes what it felt like:

I don't know what the time was when we woke up, but we woke with a start! The whole box was vibrating in sympathy with the motion of the snow not so

far away: the face was avalanching. Suddenly there was a thud. The box shook violently. The overhanging rock hadn't been such good protection after all. The thought of hurtling down the South West Face in a box was not a pleasant prospect, even if the structure did rejoice in the name of its designer/ occupant. Next morning the snow appeared to be in a critical condition. But Dougal and I donned our oxygen equipment and struggled resolutely out into a day reminiscent of the damp Scottish Highlands. Martin and Pete were to follow later. The rope rose directly above the camp over a steep step. Dougal went first. I turned on my oxygen cylinder, pulled the face mask in place, and took a deep breath. At least I tried to, but there was no oxygen. As the person responsible for the oxygen equipment, I felt unfairly singled out, as in 1972, in possessing a faulty set. Despite coaxing, it refused to work so finally, in disgust, I threw it into the box and set off without it.

I was making good time; Dougal was only a short way ahead. Looking down on the two boxes, snuggled into the slope like Oxo cubes, I could see Ang Phurba and Tenzing coming up, several rope-lengths behind. Dougal had traversed left towards the rope which led over to the main gully from the upper face. I was ascending in a shallow runnel, but due to ice on the rope, my jumar clamps were not holding too well.

Then I heard a swoosh like a quiet, fast-moving car above me. The avalanche overtook me and I was engulfed in a maelstrom of snow particles. It was like breathing fine white smoke. I could feel it crowding my lungs and sensed the agonizing horror of a drowning man In the last instant before I was hit, I had managed to wrap the rope round my left hand to prevent the jumar sliding down the rope, with the result that my arm was now being stretched

*Porters carrying loads up the fixed rope between Camps 2 and 3.*

unmercifully by the force of the avalanche. I was passing out as the avalanche stopped just as suddenly as it had commenced. I retched distressfully for a good 15 minutes. My bladder had released involuntarily – not that this mattered, since I was stuffed, inside and out, with powder snow. Even my boots, encased in double gaiters, were filled with the stuff. Eventually my breathing reverted to an approximation of that cacophony more usually associated with the bagpipes being tuned, and I made an unsteady descent.

It had been a shattering experience for Hamish which he was lucky to have survived, and when the others set out to place Camp 5, he was forced to retreat to Camp 2, worried about the state of his lungs.

At the previous day's high point Dougal paused to consider the location of the next camp. Camp 5 was the crucial launch point from which to tackle the Rock Band, but since we were this year going to try the left-hand gully, instead of the right, he was anxious to find a more suitable site for it and found the ideal spot on some ledges to the right of the couloir.

Pete Boardman also enjoyed his day out in front, writing: 'Going well on oxygen as long as I keep on plodding and don't try any major bursts of effort that make me gasp too furiously. Soft slides pour down either side of our rib of snow. The channel on our left is continually moving, giving that uncertain feeling one gets in a railway carriage when the train next to one starts moving. It's a strange sensation to plod upwards, the only sound one's own breathing and the thump of the oxygen valve. So much of this expedition is self-preservation, keeping warm and fed, pacing oneself, looking after one's fingers and toes. Today cold toes as usual and Dougal good to follow, despite his self-congratulatory air.'

I decided to go up to Camp 5 myself, get it securely established, start the route out towards the Rock Band and then probably stay there to coordinate the flow of supplies for the assault itself. In this I was breaking one of the rules I had originally set myself, that I should try to be in the camp immediately behind the lead climbers, to keep an eye on their problems without getting involved in tactical decisions. In this instance, however, I felt justified in going out in front. We had changed so much from our original plan, I no longer thought I had the feel of the problem, found it difficult to visualize the site of camps or the distances involved.

Another factor was that Camp 5 was obviously going to be a crucial camp site and I wanted to ensure that it was securely established. Dave Clarke at Camp 2 and Adrian Gordon at Camp 1 had the day-to-day running of the camps and movement of porters well under control, so it seemed that I should be able to run the expedition for a short time from the front, while getting Camp 5 established, and even supervise the final stages of the expedition from this position. Also, I must confess I was itching to have a little session out in front, actually making the route. I decided therefore to move up to Camp 4 with Ronnie Richards and six Sherpas the following day, 15 September.

*15 September – 22 September 1975*

# Through the Rock Band

I PLODDED ON UP the ropes full of forebodings, out of the still shadows into the glare of the sun that was slanting across the lower snowfields of the face from above the South East Ridge. I was out in front, Ronnie Richards a rope-length behind; a puff of snow appeared on the rocks far above, snow crystals glittering in the sun. The puff spread into a boiling cloud, seeming to stretch across the entire wall. There was no sound and, but for memories of Hamish's experience, it wouldn't even have seemed menacing. I took a couple of photographs of the approaching avalanche, noticed Ronnie huddling into the snow, and then quickly, now fearful, turned my own back to the coming onslaught, tried to burrow my chin into the collar of my silk polo neck to stop the snow flooding down my throat. A wind whipped round me, I was in a turbulent blizzard, the snow plucking me from my stance. And then, as suddenly as it had enveloped me, it was gone.

I had been on the very edge of the avalanche. Ronnie had had slightly rougher treatment and was looking like a snowman as he shook himself clear of the snow. I was most worried, however, about our Sherpas, who had set out from Camp 2 after us, and who, when we had last seen them, had just been starting up the line of fixed ropes below Camp 3. Unless they had reached the shelter of the Rock Buttress they could have been in the direct path of the avalanche. Shortly after reaching Camp 4, I was immensely relieved to see them coming up round the corner. They had reached the shelter of the buttress just in time, and the huge avalanche had come pouring over their heads. They were obviously shaken by their experience, but could still raise a smile and were fully prepared to spend the night at Camp 4.

Camp 4 was a mess with tents and gear submerged in snow and we spent the rest of the day digging out the boxes, uncovering the stockpile of gear, excavating new platforms and erecting two further box tents. Next morning Ronnie and I followed the line of fixed rope alongside the raging torrent of powder snow that came pouring down a deep-cut channel in the centre of the gully. I had never seen anything

*Pertemba crossing the snow-covered rocks leading into the left-hand gully through the Rock Band. Tut Braithwaite led this particularly difficult section.*

'At last I came to a deeper patch of snow, put in a deadman and brought him up to me; I set out on another rope-length. The snow got steadily thinner – I got more anxious. "You're meant to be coordinating this bloody expedition, Bonington, not playing silly buggers on dicey snow," I told myself.'

quite like it before. Using oxygen it was possible to take about 30 steps at a time with-out a rest, even though I had about 18kg (40lb) on my back, with all my personal gear, a rope and my oxygen cylinder.

It was about nine o'clock when I reached Dougal's high point; an empty oxygen cylinder was attached to the ice axe he had left in place as an anchor. It was just round a bend in the gully, and the little gully he had noticed was a mere 30m (100ft) away. It was ideal for our purpose. I tied the rope to my harness and set out;

*Sherpas carrying loads up the fixed ropes leading into Camp 5. Camp 2 is visible far below in the Western Cwm. My concern was to ensure that camps were stocked ahead of climbers pushing out the route.*

it was just a question of kicking into deep soft snow, thrusting my ice axe into its full length; no technical difficulty at all, but immensely exciting. I kicked my way into the base of the little gully, probed with an avalanche probe to find a good site, sheltered from the wind, avalanches and the sun; it seemed the safest spot. I buried a deadman, attached the rope to it, and called Ronnie and the Sherpas, who were patiently waiting below, to come and join me. Camp 5 was nearly established. Nearly, but not quite; once the Sherpas had dumped their loads and left us on our

own, in all probability the highest men on earth that 16 September (the same date incidentally that we had reached Base Camp in 1972) we still had to dig out a platform for the box. It took us the rest of the morning, with frequent rests, to erect a box. By about half past one, we were able to lay out the foam mats, get out our sleeping bags and really relax. It was time for a brew; our mouths were parched and furry from breathing in the cold, dry oxygen-air mixture on the way up. The sun had now crept round the buttress above me and had been hammering on our backs as we had finished erecting the box. I searched through one of the kit bags, found the gas stove and some spare cartridges, but there was no sign of the cooking pan, plates or mugs. I was sure I had packed them, searched our rucksacks, but still no sign, and then I realized what had happened. In redistributing loads the previous night I had left them behind at Camp 4.

It might seem a very minor inconvenience to be without cooking and eating utensils, but in fact it was quite serious, for one needs a large pan to melt sufficient snow to make a good brew. At altitude, dehydration is one of the principal debilitating fac-

tors and experts recommend a liquid consumption of at least 4 litres (7 pints) a day. Ronnie rummaged through our high-altitude packs but the only remotely suitable container he could find was a corned-beef tin. We filled the tin with snow, perched it on top of the stove and waited, mouths dry with thirst for the drink, but the tin was the wrong shape and most of the flame was wasted to either side. Ten minutes later there was a dessertspoonful of dirty water in the bottom of the tin; I added more snow, waited another ten minutes; added some more snow still, and after half an hour we had a quarter of a pint of water to share between us. I grabbed the tin, burnt myself and dropped it. The precious water trickled over my sleeping bag. We tried again, and after half an hour had had a small drink each, barely sufficient to moisten our throats. It was now nearly two o'clock, time for the afternoon call.

The radio crackled into life and I called up Camp 4. Mike Thompson was moving up that day to take charge. There was no reply; I then tried all the other camps in turn, still no reply. And then Camp 2 came on the air, called Camp 4 and they started a long discussion on the following day's carry. I waited, frustrated at not being able to get into the wireless conversation, wanting to assume control and make my requirements known. There was a pause and I quickly called Camp 4 again, no reply; then Base Camp came on the air, talking to Camp 2. At last Camp 2 called me. I replied, but they couldn't hear me, and suddenly I realized the awful truth. For some reason, the wireless set was not transmitting. I could hear everything but was unable to communicate with anyone. By this time I'd lost my temper and had begun to bang the damned radio in an effort to make it work. It didn't respond to this treatment, and I continued an impotent listener to the pulsing life of the expedition. Ronnie had been watching me with quiet amusement and at the end of the call,

Left: *Ronnie Richards who went with me to Camp 5.* Right: *Looking back down the Great Central Gully towards Camp 5, tucked safely in a subsidiary gully and the line of Sherpas below it carrying supplies from Camp 4*

when everyone had closed down, methodically settled down to repair the battered set in time for the late afternoon call. On this I asked Doug and Mick to set out for Camp 4 the following morning so that they could join us at Camp 5 on the 18th, by which time I hoped to be near the foot of the Rock Band. That night was the first time we slept on oxygen, a steady flow of one litre per minute, helping us to sleep, stay warm, build up reserves for the next day's climbing. We used, as far as possible, bottles that had already been part emptied to save the full ones for use during the day, though having to change bottles during the night was never a pleasant task.

I woke as usual about three o'clock and started brewing up in our corned-beef tin. I was determined to get in a morning's climbing. The slope, covered in a uniform blanket of snow, seemed to stretch interminably up to the left-hand gully, which we hoped would take us through the Rock Band. We were going to have to run out many rope-lengths just to reach the foot of the Band. Would we need another camp at the foot of the gully for our assault on the Rock Band? Could we sustain such a camp, and then place yet another above? These were just some of the questions I asked myself that morning. I took the lead, kicking into the crisp snow with cramponed boots, crossing diagonally left towards the base of the gully, still some hundreds of metres away. A buttress of black rock thrust out of the snow; should we go to the left or right of it? I decided on the right-hand side, and started kicking straight upwards. The snow was getting softer and I was going through to the rock underneath; the angle steepened, the snow thinned; there was barely enough to take my weight; there certainly wasn't enough snow for a deadman. I swept it away, hoping to find a crack in the rock for a piton, but it was smooth and compact, all sloping downwards in a series of tiny ledges. I teetered on in my blinkered world, encased in oxygen mask and goggles, feeling more and more insecure as I ran out more rope above Ronnie. At last I came to a deeper patch of snow, put in a deadman and brought him up to me; I set out on another rope-length. The snow got steadily thinner – I got more anxious. 'You're meant to be coordinating this bloody expedition, Bonington, not playing silly buggers on dicey snow,' I told myself. Looking upwards, rocks, like treacherous reefs, protruded from the snow. I looked across to the left and realized I'd taken the wrong line; I should have traversed. You don't waste height and effort willingly at getting on for 8000m (26,250ft), but I had no choice. I had to reverse two pitches. On the plus side, Mike Thompson arrived with five Sherpas, bringing more gear and, most important, a cooking pot. Ronnie and I could have our first proper drink for 36 hours. Next day Doug arrived with more rope, followed shortly by Mick Burke, and the four of us concentrated on reaching the Rock Band.

It was a good feeling, looking down the long slope back to Camp 5, past ten tiny figures strung out along the line of fixed rope, a visual demonstration of our momentum up the mountain. Below them was the Western Cwm, patterned with crevasses; Camp 2, little more than a collection of microdots dwarfed by the mountains around it. We were too far above to pick out the porters carrying loads from Camp 1. At the end of the cwm, the summit of Pumo Ri was now 900m (2950ft) below; we were level with the top of Cho Oyu, massive and rounded at 8153m (26,750ft). As we gained height the view had expanded; we could just see over the containing wall of Nuptse, could gaze far to the west at Gaurishankar and Menlungtse, two mountains that were still inviolate. Memories of 1972; I was looking across and down at that bitterly cold, windswept site of Camp 5; the long traverse below the Rock Band to its right-hand end was in full view; we were very nearly at the same level as our high point three years before. But it was all so different; we were so much earlier, had more climbers and Sherpas, the gear was so much better.

A shout from above, the bell-like ring of the first piton being hammered into the Rock Band. A few minutes later I plodded up the rope to join Doug. 'Do you want to go on through and lead the next pitch, youth?' he asked, as I reached him. It had been a good day with over 400m (1310ft) of rope run out. Although we had not been able to see into the gully I was confident that we could force the Rock Band through the sheer momentum of our progress. Nick and Tut had already pitched another box tent when we returned.

I had been giving a lot of thought to the summit push and had changed some of my original ideas. While we had been making our first steps on the face I had

*Nick Estcourt and Tut Braithwaite, who had the crucial role of forcing the Rock Band, the barrier that had stopped five previous expeditions.*

decided that it would be wise to ensure that the first summit bid was as strong as possible; we might not get a second chance. In this respect I felt that Doug Scott and Dougal Haston probably were the strongest pair. They seemed to get on well together, were very experienced and determined, and for each this was the third visit to the South West Face.

Our progress had been so fast, however, that I now had them out of phase. Doug was here at Camp 5 while Dougal was still at Camp 2. It would have been logical for Doug to climb the Rock Band with Nick and Tut, and then for Dougal to move through with one of the other lead climbers to make the summit bid, but I was not happy about such a concept. Hamish was still badly weakened by his experience in the avalanche and had not gone above Camp 2; Allen Fyffe was having difficulty acclimatizing, Pete Boardman, although his performance so far was excellent, was untried and had never climbed with Dougal before the expedition. I was worried that Martin Boysen, a strong contender, might still be run down as a result of his Trango Tower trip. I decided therefore to bring Dougal straight up to Camp 5.

I also had to work out our plans for the ascent of the Rock Band. Tut Braithwaite and Nick Estcourt, supported by Mick Burke and myself, would go into the left-hand gully and try to force our way to the top. I thought that this would probably take two days, by which time Dougal would have reached Camp 5. It was asking a lot of Nick and Tut, for in solving the problem that had defeated all four previous expeditions they would be giving the summit to Doug Scott and Dougal Haston.

Doug offered to come up the following day, the 20th, to give a hand, but I declined. I felt that not only would he need the rest, but also that the Rock Band should be left exclusively to Tut and Nick, as some consolation for not making the first summit bid. I only just managed to make all my plans before the four o'clock call. I was uncomfortably aware that I had not had time to work out any subsequent bids, even though the climbers resting at Camp 2 would undoubtedly be getting anxious about their chances for the summit. Our progress had been so fast that I now had a surfeit of reserve climbers, all justifiably anxious to take their part in the final drama. All I could do was to promise them that I would work out the logistics of subsequent ascents the following afternoon.

Our tracks had filled in during the night but Nick and Tut had rebroken the trail as they plodded back to our high point. It was like the first climb of the day on any crag in Britain; the ritual to decide who should lead the first pitch. Tut had hidden a small piece of rock in a clenched fist and Nick guessed the wrong hand. Tut led. By the time I caught up with them Tut was out of sight round the corner. There was hammering of a piton, scuffling in the snow, but no movement. The climbing was the most difficult we had yet encountered, with insubstantial snow lying over steep smooth rock. There were hardly any piton cracks and insufficient snow for a deadman anchor. It would have been awkward at any altitude, but at around 8225m (27,000m), encased in high-altitude clothing with an oxygen mask clamped over the face, it was desperate.

Cramponed boots slithered on the sloping rock holds, there was nothing for Tut's glove-encased hands. He stuck his axe into the snow, but it just tore through the loosely coagulated powder. He managed to hammer a long ice piton a few centimetres into a crack, clipped into it, and then, taking rope tension from Nick, leant across from one small spur to the next, his balance thrown out by the weight of his rucksack holding oxygen cylinder and spare rope. He reached a haven of balance, panting hard into the set, paused for breath, and then continued the delicate traverse, using three more pitons for protection and aid. This was real climbing; fatigue and altitude, the grinding plods up lines of fixed rope were all forgotten in the riveted concentration of negotiating those few metres. The angle began to ease, the snow deepened, he was in the flared-out funnel leading to the dark gash of the left-hand gully. He buried a snow anchor, fastened the rope and called Nick up to join him. I followed.

Nick led out the next pitch into the mouth of the gully. It was more than 3m (10ft) wide, with sheer, inescapable rock walls towering on either side. The floor of the gully was covered in deep compact snow, sweeping smoothly at an angle of about 50 degrees to a snowclad overhanging bulge, which probably covered a rock jammed between the gully walls. Above this first barrier, it stretched up to a point where the gully curved slightly and seemed to open out, for the upper part was lit by sunlight. A small spindrift avalanche curled down the right-hand retaining wall. It wasn't big enough to be dangerous, but it made me feel vulnerable. We were in a

*Nick Estcourt heading into the mouth of the left-hand gully. His oxygen had run out and he was having a desperate struggle to keep going. Note the spindrift, harbinger of bigger avalanches, pouring down the gully.*

*Tut following Nick, belayed above, up the difficult ramp taking them through the Rock Band. This was almost certainly the hardest bit of climbing ever done at that altitude at the time, and Nick had led the pitch without the help of supplementary oxygen.*

trap; there was no shelter from any big avalanches that might pour down that gully.

In the bottom of the gully we were in deep shade. Nick had run out of oxygen, taken off his mask and abandoned the bottle, but was determined to keep going. It was now Tut's turn to lead and he kicked up the even slope leading to the jammed rock about 15m (50ft) above. He describes what happened next.

On the right there appeared to be a ledge with a possible belay but there were no cracks for pitons and the ledge turned out to be little more than a sloping shelf. I'd run out of rope but managed to pull a spare one out of my sack, tied on and then threw the tangle down to Nick 50 feet below, with the idea that he could sort out the tangle while I negotiated the overhang.

By this time Chris had caught up with us and had started to untangle the rope, muttering abuse about inefficiency and how stupid it had been to just throw the rope down, without first untangling it. He didn't realize that this was an arrangement that Nick and I had already worked out to save time. Chris insisted that I shouldn't move till he'd sorted out the mess. An understanding glance from Nick, but we both kept quiet until he had it sorted out some dozen curses later.

I placed an angle piton on the right and wriggled up the groove behind the rock and the wall behind, my oxygen bottle catching on every protrusion, boots kicking in thin air. At last, panting hard, I was above it. The gully narrowed and steepened; excellent snow conditions made the next section almost enjoyable. Above me were huge overhangs, with powder snow streaming down over them, from either side of the gully. How the hell were we going to get out?

I managed to find a good piton belay, and Nick, moving slowly but with great determination, followed up the rope. I set out again and soon the gully widened. I had to see what there was round the corner, but had now run out of rope. I tied on to my last rope, dropped the slack to Nick and carried on for another 60 feet; then at last I could see out to the right. There seemed to be a gangway leading up to some snow ledges. Too tired even to tell the others, I just kept going until a small rocky step stopped me. It looked easier on the right and I edged my way over, stepped carefully up sloping little rock ledges, nothing much for the hands. I was excited at the prospects offered by the gangway, and totally involved in the climbing. Suddenly my oxygen ran out. I don't think I shall ever forget the feeling of suffocation as I ripped the mask away from my face. I was on the brink of falling, beginning to panic, felt a warm trickle run down my leg. God, what's happening? Scrabbled up the rock arête until at last I reached some firm snow. I collapsed, exhausted. I had no runners out and was over 100 feet above Nick; I'd have had it if I'd fallen. I just dug my axe into the snow and hung on to it till I got my breath back; got a grip of myself. I then got my rucksack off, took the oxygen bottle out, shoved that in the snow and belayed onto it.

Tut had reached a spot where the gully widened out into a small amphitheatre. The main arm of the gully continued up to the left, but a ramp forked out to the right, beneath an impending wall of yellow rock. This seemed to lead out above the Rock Band. Nick, ever courageous, followed up the rope to join Tut. He had almost become accustomed to going without oxygen, and said later that he had felt like a 105-year-old war veteran and had paced himself accordingly.

Tut had stopped about 6m (20ft) below the bottom of the ramp. Nick led on through the beginning of the rocks, brought Tut up to him, but then was determined to have his full share of leading, even though it meant tackling what was obviously going to be a difficult piece of climbing without oxygen. At least he wasn't going to be blinkered by the mask and encumbered by the rucksack containing the bottle. The first few metres were quite straightforward; the ramp sloped off gently and had a reasonable covering of snow; but after 6m (20ft) it tapered into nothing, forcing Nick into the impending wall which, in turn, forced him out of balance. The snow was thin and insubstantial over steep, hideously loose rock. There was nothing for his feet, no holds for his hands. The snow was too soft to use his ice axe. His entire weight was now resting on his left arm which he had jammed behind a boss of snow that had formed between the impending wall above and what was left of the ramp. Somehow he had to get in a piton. He tried to clear the snow away with his other hand, but the rock was either smooth and compact or, on the ramp itself, little more than rubble, cemented together by snow.

I was getting desperate; goggles all misted up, panting helplessly. I was losing strength fast. I think the others thought I was about to fall off, but whatever happened I wasn't going to give up. If I had, and let Tut do it, I'd have kicked myself for years.

Anyway, I found a crack that was about an inch wide, fumbled for a piton that was the right size. It was hanging on my harness behind my back, couldn't see it, didn't have any sense of feel with my gloves. Somehow got an angle peg that was the right size, eased it behind the boss and shoved it into the crack. I then had to get out my hammer, had a desperate struggle to pull it out of my holster. It had jammed somehow, but I couldn't see how. I got it out at last and managed to tap into the piton.

It was obviously useless, but if you pulled it, in just one direction, it was safe. I managed to lean out on it a little bit, walked my feet up, jammed my other arm behind the boss, reached up, dug into the snow and found something, I'm not sure what, and just kept going. It was still hard and there was nothing secure to hold on to or stand on. It was a question of just keeping going. I now came out into the sun, and the snow was even softer, no longer holding the rocks together. I just had to keep going. I couldn't possibly have got back even if I'd wanted to. Another 20 feet, and I found a decent crack, got a good peg in and brought Tut up. Given the conditions it was the hardest pitch I've ever led.

*Dougal Haston peering out of the entrance to the box tent at Camp 5, which had become a small village in preparation for the push up to the top camp above the Rock Band.*

In leading it, Nick had solved the problem of the Rock Band and had led the most difficult pitch on the South West Face of Everest. We had been waiting, cold and anxious, down below. Tut followed Nick up, jumaring up the rope, while Mick Burke and I started back down the fixed ropes. That day the pair in front pushed up another 12m (40ft) on to a snow spur that seemed to lead up onto the Upper Snowfield. We dropped down tired but jubilant. Nick and Tut had cracked the Rock Band.

The return to Camp 5 seemed even farther, even more arduous, than the way up. I stopped for a rest every few metres, slid down the ropes on my backside wherever possible and had to force myself to take each step on the last traverse back to the camp. It was five o'clock, time for the evening call, but I was too tired to think, let alone talk, and asked Doug to take it. With a bit of luck I would come round in an hour's time, and asked him to arrange a later call. It was all I could do to dump my pack frame, pull off my boots and collapse into my sleeping bag. The others were just as tired.

Six o'clock came all too fast however, and I hadn't managed to plan out anything further than our requirements for the following day. Dougal Haston, Mike Thompson, Pertemba and Tenzing were to move up to Camp 5 next morning. Pete Boardman seemed an obvious potential candidate for one of the summit bids after that of Doug and Dougal. So I asked him also to go up to Camp 4, not fully appreciating how the others at Camp 2 would interpret my action. At the end of the call, Martin came up on the radio and asked if I had any plans for him; all I could do was ask him to wait patiently till the next day, the 21st, when I hoped to plan the subsequent ascents in detail.

I spent much of the night trying to balance out different permutations of climbers. I had originally planned on just one subsequent ascent; back in England even this seemed optimistic, but our progress had been so fast that for some days it had seemed we might be able to have a series of ascents as long as the weather lasted. The obvious choices for the second ascent were Tut Braithwaite and Nick Estcourt. They were here at Camp 5, had shown that they were fully capable of making a fast, safe, summit bid and had opened the way for Doug and Dougal. We had discussed the second summit bid and I had told them that they would be making it, but now I began to worry about the wider implications of what I had said. I was all too aware of how frustrated the lead climbers sitting it out at Camp 2 must be. If I allowed Nick and Tut to stay up at Camp 5 for the second summit bid, I should be excluding the rest of the team from all further involvement in the climb as they waited their turns in the queue for the summit. I therefore reluctantly decided I should have to break the news to Nick and Tut that I wanted them to return to Camp 2, to go to the back of the queue, and let some of the others have their turn.

I then began to think of the ascents themselves. I definitely wanted to include at least one Sherpa in the subsequent ascents. Quite apart from having promised Pertemba that I would try to get a Sherpa up, they had done so much to help us, entered so much into the spirit of the expedition that I felt it only fair that they shared in the summit experience. But that meant one less place for the climbers. Then there were the needs of the film. Mick Burke had been moving slightly more slowly than I on the fixed ropes, but he was cheerful and seemed able to pace himself well. I therefore decided to put him into the second summit party. Martin and Pete were two other obvious candidates.

As for myself, I could not resist the lure of the summit and put myself in the third summit team with Nick Estcourt and Tut Braithwaite. The third summit team wouldn't move up to Camp 6 until 27 September. It was now the 21st and I had already been up for a week. But I felt fine, rationalized that this was the best place for me to stay until everyone was ready to come down from the mountain.

I announced the results of my logistic planning at the two o'clock radio call. Martin Boysen recollects the impact at Camp 2: 'We waited tensed with expectation and ambition. Hamish took the call and Chris came over loud and clear in the warm air of the afternoon. "I've decided after a lot of thought…" Wait for it, I listened only for the names not the justifications… "Mick, Martin, Pete and Pertemba…" Thank God for that. "Tut, Nick, Ang Phurba…" I had no further interest in listening; I had been given my chance and now I looked at the others. Poor Allen, his face hardened with disappointment as the names poured out, but not his own. The radio stopped and everyone departed quietly with their own hopes, ambitions and disappointments.'

Back at Camp 5, we were absorbed in our preparations for the morrow, sorting out the loads, ensuring that Doug and Dougal would have everything they needed to push the route out above the Rock Band. The four o'clock call came with more logistic details, last-minute demands for gear to be brought up to the camp the following morning. As the wireless closed down Pertemba told me that Charlie wanted to talk to me privately at seven that night. I waited, intrigued, slightly worried to hear what he had to tell me.

Seven o'clock came. Nobody else would be listening out on any of their radios littered up and down the mountain. Charlie's voice came over the air from Camp 2. He asked me to reconsider my decision to stay on at Camp 5 and take part in the third summit bid, pointed out the length of time that I had been living above 7600m (25,000ft), the fact that my voice was often slurred over the radio, that my calls that day had sometimes been muddled. He also made the point that I was getting out of contact with the situation on the rest of the mountain, my eyes just focused on establishing the top camp and making the summit.

He also told me that he had come to this conclusion without consulting any of the others and was approaching me in his capacity as expedition doctor. It certainly made sense, even brought out some of the doubts that had been lurking in the back of my mind. I agreed to think it over, and then Charlie told me that Hamish would also like to talk to me. There was a pause, and then Hamish's clipped Scots voice crackled through the speaker. 'I've decided to go home, Chris.' I was staggered, but he went on to tell me that he was feeling the after-effects of his experience in the avalanche and was worried about the state of his lungs. I could understand how he felt and accepted his decision. We were all sorry to see Hamish forced to leave when a successful outcome seemed so close. He had done so much to help achieve it.

Once the wireless was switched off, I began to consider my course of action. I had undoubtedly become divorced from the rest of the team down below; I didn't feel, however, that I was suffering from anoxia; but Charlie was right about it being unwise to put myself in that third summit team, for by then, if I stayed at Camp 5, I should have been there for nearly a fortnight, much too long at that altitude under any circumstances, let alone prior to trying to reach the summit of Everest. I

*One of my personal ambitions was to take part in the carry to the top camp. I felt a great sense of contentment. Doug and Dougal had everything they needed, the weather was settled. We had done all we could. Now it was up to them.*

dropped off to sleep concocting further permutations to fill my place.

The following morning, 22 September, eight of us set out for Camp 6. Dougal and Doug left first, for they were going to have to complete the route from the top of the ramp on to the Upper Icefield, where they hoped they would find a suitable camp site. Ang Phurba, probably the strongest and most talented of all the Sherpas, followed close on their heels, dressed in ski pants and sweater, his oxygen set and mask looking incongruous with such attire. Pertemba and Tenzing went at a slightly more leisured rate, while Mike Thompson, Mick Burke and I brought up the rear.

# The Summit

The chapter that follows belongs to Dougal Haston and Doug Scott, and I leave them to tell their story between them in the following entries from their own diaries.

DOUG SCOTT  I caught Dougal up at the bottom of the Rock Band and carried on up into the foot of the gully. I cleared the rope of ice as I jumared up, conscious of the struggle that Tut must have had, firstly traversing into the gully and then clambering over a giant snow-covered chock stone halfway up. I noted the new perspective with interest, for the ropes led through a huge gash – a veritable Devil's Kitchen of a chasm 90m (300ft) deep into the rocks, whereas the rest of Everest had been wide slopes and broad open valleys. At the top of the gully I followed Nick's rope out and up steeply right. I clipped on to the rope, using it as a safety rail, rather than pulling on it directly with my jumars, for he had warned me that the rope was anchored to pegs of dubious quality. It was awkward climbing with a framed rucksack, especially as the straps kept slipping on crucial hard sections. Nick had done a first-class job leading it without oxygen. I was glad to get to his high point and hammer in extra pegs.

Ang Phurba came up the rope next, for Dougal had stopped lower down to adjust his crampons which kept falling off his sponge overboots and also to disentangle the remains of Nick's rope. Ang Phurba belayed me with all the confidence of a regular alpine climber. I think he is the most natural climber I have ever met amongst the Sherpas. After only 9m (30ft) of difficult climbing I tied off the rope and Ang Phurba came up to me. I stood there exhausted from having climbed a vertical 3-m (10-ft) block with too much clothing and too heavy a sack. From there I led out 75m (250ft) of rope to a site for Camp 6. Ang Phurba came up and we both kicked out a small notch in a ridge of snow that could be enlarged to take our summit box tent. Dougal came up with his crampons swinging from his waist.

*Dougal ploughing through unexpectedly deep snow up the famous Hillary Step, Everest's sting in the tail. But both he and Doug now knew they were going to reach the summit.*

DOUGAL HASTON  I hauled on to the proposed site of Camp 6. Straightaway my energy and upward urges came rushing back – there ahead in reality was the way we'd been hypothetically tracing for so long with fingers on photographs, and making us forget everything else was the fact it looked feasible. There was a steepish-looking rock pitch just ahead, but after it seemed like unbroken snow slopes to the couloir. It looked as if progress was inevitable as long as the others were successful in their carry. Ang Phurba kept muttering about a camp site further up under some rocks, but this looked like wasted effort to us, as the traverse line started logically from where we were at the moment. Diplomatically we told him that we were staying there, it being mainly Doug's and my concern, as we were going to have to occupy the camp, and he started off down leaving his valuable load. We began digging in spells, without oxygen, but using some to regain strength during the rests. Mike, Chris and Mick arrived one after the other looking tired, as well they should be. Carrying heavy loads at over 8200m (26,900ft) is no easy occupation.

DOUG SCOTT  Theirs had been a magnificent carry, especially Chris who had now been at Camp 5 and above for eight days, and also Mick who was carrying a dead weight of equipment. He had been at Camp 5 for five days, and Pertemba had worked hard practically every day of the expedition carrying heavy loads and encouraging his Sherpas. While Mike Thompson, who had never been above 7000m (23,000ft) before, had arrived carrying a heavy sack with apparent ease at 8,320m (27,300ft) We sat there talking confidently in the late afternoon sun. There was a strong bond of companionship as there had been all the way up the face. One by one they departed for Camp 5 and they left us with the bare essentials to make this last step to the top of our route and perhaps the summit itself. I yelled our thanks down to Mike as they were sliding back down the rope. He must have known his chances of making a summit bid were slim yet he replied, 'Just you get up, that's all the reward I need.' And that's how it had been from start to finish with all members of the team. It had taken the combined effort of 40 Sherpas and 16 climbers, together with Chris's planning, to get the two of us into this position. We knew how lucky we were being the representatives of such a team and to be given the chance to put the finishing touches to all our efforts. Finally Mick left, having run all the film he had through the cameras. Dougal and I were left alone to dig out a more substantial platform and to erect the two-man summit tent. We were working without oxygen and took frequent rests to recover, but also to look across the Upper Snowfield leading up to the South Summit couloir. After the tent was up Dougal got inside to prepare the evening meal, while I pottered about outside stowing away equipment in a little ice cave and tying empty oxygen bottles around the tent to weigh it down. They hung in festoons on either side of the snow arête. Finally I bundled rope and oxygen bottles into our sacks for the following morning and dived into the tent to join Dougal.

DOUGAL HASTON  Inside, we worked on plans for the next day. We had 500m (1640ft) of rope for fixing along the traverse and hoped to do that, then come back to 6 and make our big push the day after.

I was higher on Everest than I'd ever been before, yet thoughts of the summit were still far away in the thinking and hoping process. It had all seemed so near before in 1971 and 1972: euphoric nights at Camps 5 and 6 when progress had seemed good and one tended to skip the difficult parts with visions of oneself standing at the top of the South West Face, then reality shattering the dreams in progressive phases as realization of certain failure burst the bubble. There had been an inevitability about both previous failures, but still carrying a lot of disappointment. Failure you must accept but that does not make it any easier, especially on a project like the South West Face where so much thinking, willpower and straight physical effort are necessary to get to the higher points. This time it seemed better. We were above the Rock Band and the ground ahead looked climbable, but I kept a rigid limit on my thoughts, contemplating possible progress along the traverse to the exit couloir, nothing more. If that proved possible then I would allow for further up-type thinking.

Our physical situation felt comfortable. Maybe that is a reflection of the degree of progress that we have made in our adaptation to altitude. Many the story we had read or been told about assault camps on the world's highest peak. No one ever seemed to spend a comfortable night at Camp 6 on the South Col route. Their nights seemed to be compounded of sleeplessness, discomfort and thirst. Here there was none of that. The situation was very bearable. We weren't stretched personally, didn't even feel tired or uncomfortable, despite a long day. The stove brewed the hours away — tea, lemon drinks and even a full scale meal with meat and mashed potatoes. Each was deep in his own thoughts with only one slightly urgent communal reaction as a change of oxygen cylinder went wrong and the gas stove roared with white heat. Order was restored before an explosion, with Doug fixing the leak at the same time as I turned off the stove. Emergency over, we laughed, conjuring visions of the reaction at Camp 2 as Camp 6 exploded like a successfully attacked missile target. It would have been a new reason for failure!

Thereafter sleep claimed its way and I moved gently into another world of tangled dreams, eased by a gentle flow of oxygen. The night was only disturbed by a light wind rocking our box and a changing of sleeping cylinders. One would need to be a good or very exhausted sleeper to sleep through a cylinder running out. From a gentle warm comfort one suddenly feels cold, uneasy and very awake. Just after midnight and the changeover, we gave up sleeping and started the long task of preparing for the morning's work.

Shortly after first light I moved out into the blue and white dawn to continue the upward way, leaving Doug wrapped in all the down in the tent mouth, cameras and belays set up for action. There was a rock step lurking ahead that had seemed reasonably close in the setting afternoon sun of the previous day. Now in the clear

first light a truer perspective was established, as I kept on thrusting into the deep powdered 50-degree slope, sliding sideways like a crab out of its element reaching for an object that didn't seem to come any closer. A hundred metres (330ft) of this progress it was, before I could finally fix a piton and eye the rock step. It wasn't long, seven or eight metres (23–26ft), but looked difficult enough. Downward sloping, steep slabs with a layer of powder. Interesting work. Grade 5 at this height. Much concentration and three more pitons saw a delicate rightwards exit and back, temporarily thankful, into deep snow to finish the rope-length and finally give Doug the signal to move.

DOUG SCOTT I traversed across on his rope and up the difficult rocks to his stance. I led out another 120m (400ft) over much easier ground, parallel with the top of the Rock Band. We gradually warmed to the task and began to enjoy our position. After all the months of dreaming, here we were cutting across that Upper Snowfield. Dougal led out the next reel of rope.

DOUGAL HASTON The conditions and climbing difficulty began to change again. Kicking through with crampons there was now no ice beneath. Rock slabs only, which have never been renowned for their adherence to front points. A few tentative movements up, down, sideways proved it existed all around. It seemed the time for a tension traverse. But on what? The rock was shattered loose and worse – no cracks. Scraping away at a large area a small moveable flake appeared. It would have to do. Tapping in the beginnings of an angle, which seemed to be OK to pull on it, not for a fall, I started tensioning across to an inviting-looking snow lump. Thoughts flashed through my mind of a similar traverse nine years before, near the top of the Eiger Direct. There it would have been all over with a slip and suddenly, working it out, things didn't look too good here, if you cared to think in those directions. Not only didn't I care to, I also didn't dare to think of the full consequences and, chasing the dangerous thoughts away, concentrated on tiptoeing progress. Slowly the limit of tension was reached and feet were on some vaguely adhering snow. It would have to do for the present, were my thoughts as I let go the rope and looked around. A couple of probes with the axe brought nothing but a sense of commitment.

'No man is an island,' it is said. I felt very close to a realization of the contrary of this, standing on that semi-secure snow step in the midst of a sea of insecurity. But there was no racing adrenalin only the cold clinical thought of years of experience. About 5m (16ft) away the snow appeared to deepen. It would have to be another tension traverse. Long periods of excavation found no cracks. Tugs on the rope and impatient shouting from Doug. Communication at altitude is bad in awkward situations. One has to take off the oxygen mask to shout. Then when one tries to do this the throat is so dry and painful that nothing comes out. Hoping that Doug would keep his cool, I carried on looking for a piton placement. A reasonable looking crack came to light and two pitons linked up meant the game could go on. This time I felt

*Dougal pushing the route across the summit snowfield on 23 September, the day they laid fixed rope most of the way across to facilitate their ascent and their return the following day. The peak in the background is Lhotse.*

I could put more bearing weight on the anchor. Just as well. Twice the tension limit failed and there was the skidding movement backwards on the scraping slabs. But a third try and a long reach saw me in deep good snow, sucking oxygen violently. The way ahead relented, looking reasonable. My voice gained enough momentum to shout to Doug and soon he was on his way. Following is usually monotone – sliding along on jumars. This one was not so. I could almost see the gleam in Doug's eyes shining through his layers of glasses as he pulled out the first tension piton with his fingers. 'Nasty stuff, youth.' I had to agree as he passed on through.

DOUG SCOTT I continued across further, using up one of our two climbing ropes, before dropping down slightly to belay. We had probably come too high, for there was easier snow below the rocks that led right up towards the South Summit couloir. However, avalanches were still cascading down the mountain, so we climbed up to the rocks in an effort to find good peg anchors for the fixed ropes. We didn't want to return the next day to find them hanging over the Rock Band. Dougal led a short section on easy snow, then all the rope was run out and we turned back for camp.

I sat in the snow to take photographs and watched the sun go down over Gaurishankar. What a place to be! I could look straight down and see Camp 2 1800m (6000ft) down. There were people moving about between tents, obviously preparing to camp for the night. Mounds of equipment were being covered with tarpaulins, one or two wandered out to the crevasse toilet, others stood about in small groups before diving into their tents for the night. A line of shadow crept up the face to Camp 4 by the time I was back to our tent. I again sorted out loads and put in oxygen bottles for the night, while Dougal melted down snow for the evening meal.

We discovered over the radio that only Lhakpa Dorje had made the carry to Camp 6 that day. He had managed to bring up the vital supplies of oxygen but,

*We were able to watch the progress of Doug and Dougal, two tiny spidery dots, as they crossed the summit snowfield in their bid for the summit.*

unfortunately, the food, cine camera and still film we needed had not arrived. Anyway they were not essential, so we could still make our bid for the summit next day. There was also no more rope in camp, but I think we were both secretly relieved about this. Chris had always insisted that whoever made the first summit bid should lay down as much fixed rope as possible so that if that first attempt failed the effort would not be wasted. This made good sense, but it did take a lot of effort up there and we all longed for the time when we could cut loose from the fixed ropes. It was a perfect evening with no wind at all as we sat looking out of the tent doorway supping mugs of tea. Finally the sun was gone from our tent and lit up only the upper snows, golden turning red, before all the mountain was in shadow. We zipped up the tent door and built up quite a fug of warm air heating up water for corned beef hash.

DOUGAL HASTON Five hundred metres (1640ft) of committing ground was a good day's work on any point of the mountain. The fact that it was all above 8200m (26,900ft) made our performance-level high and, more to the point, we hadn't exhausted ourselves in doing it. This was crucial because deterioration is rapid at such altitudes. Over tea we discussed what to take next day. I still reckoned deep down on the possibility of a bivouac. Doug seemed reluctant to admit to the straight fact, but didn't disagree when I mentioned packing a tent sac and stove. The packs weren't going to be light. Two oxygen cylinders each would be needed for the undoubtedly long day, plus three 50-metre ropes, also various pitons and karabiners. Even if a bivouac was contemplated we couldn't pack a sleeping bag. This would have been pushing weight too much. The bivouac idea was only for an emergency and we would have hastened that emergency by slowing ourselves down through too much weight – so we tried to avoid the possibility by going as lightly as possible. The only extra I allowed myself was a pair of down socks, reckoning they could be invaluable for warming very cold or even frostbitten feet and hands. There was no sense of drama that evening. Not even any unusual conversation. We radioed down and told those at Camp 2 what we were doing, ate the rest of our food and fell asleep.

DOUG SCOTT  About one in the morning we awoke to a rising wind. It was buffeting the tent, shaking it about and pelting it with spindrift, snow and ice chips. I lay there wondering what the morning would bring, for if the wind increased in violence we should surely not be able to move. At about two thirty we began slowly to wind ourselves up for the climb. We put a brew on and heated up the remains of the corned beef hash for breakfast. The wind speed was decreasing slightly as we put on our frozen boots and zipped up our suits. Dougal chose his duvet suit, whilst I took only my windproofs, hoping to move faster and easier without the restriction of tightly packed feathers around my legs. I had never got round to sorting out a duvet suit that fitted me properly .

Because of the intense cold it was essential to put on crampons, harnesses, even the rucksack and oxygen system in the warmth of the tent. Just after three thirty we emerged to get straight on to the ropes and away to the end. It was a blustery morning, difficult in the dark and miserable in the cold. It was one of those mornings when you keep going because he does and he, no doubt, because you do. By the time we had passed the end of the fixed ropes the sun popped up from behind the South Summit and we awoke to the new day. It was exhilarating to part company with our safety line, for that is after all what fixed ropes are. They facilitate troop movements, but at the same time they do detract from the adventure of the climb. Now at last we were committed and it felt good to be out on our own.

DOUGAL HASTON  There's something surrealistic about being alone high on Everest at this hour. No end to the strange beauty of the experience. Alone, enclosed in a mask with the harsh rattle of your breathing echoing in your ears. Already far in the west behind Cho Oyu a few pale strands of the day and ahead and all around a deep midnight blue with the South Summit sharply, whitely, defined in my line of vision and the always predawn wind picking up stray runnels of spindrift and swirling them gently, but not malignantly, around me. Movement was relaxed and easy. Passing by yesterday's tension points only a brief flash of them came into memory. They were stored for future remembrances, but the today mind was geared for more to come. Not geared with any sense of nervousness or foreboding just happily relaxed, waiting – anticipating. Signs of life on the rope behind indicated that Doug was following apace and I waited at yesterday's abandoned oxygen cylinders as he came up with the sun, almost haloed in silhouette, uncountable peaks as his background. But no saint this. 'All right, youth?' in a flat Nottingham accent. 'Yeah, yourself?'

A nod and the appearance of a camera for sunrise pictures answered this question, so I tied on the rope and started breaking new ground. The entrance to the couloir wasn't particularly good, but there again it was not outstandingly bad by Himalayan

'The snow stayed the same, but not only was it steeper, we were on open wind-blown

standards, merely knee-deep powder snow with the occasional make-you-think hard patch where there was no snow base on the rock. On the last part before entering the couloir proper there was a longish section of this where we just climbed together relying on each other's ability, rope trailing in between, there being no belays to speak of.

The rope-length before the rock step changed into beautiful, hard front pointing snow-ice but the pleasure suddenly seemed to diminish. Leading, my progress started to get slower. By now the signs were well known. I knew it wasn't me. One just doesn't degenerate so quickly. Oxygen again. It seemed early for a cylinder to run out. Forcing it, I reached a stance beneath the rock step. Rucksack off. Check cylinder gauge first. Still plenty left. That's got to be bad. It must be the system. Doug comes up. We both start investigating. Over an hour we played with it. No avail. Strangely enough I felt quite calm and resigned about everything. I say strangely, because if the system had proved irreparable then our summit chance would have been ruined. There was only a quiet cloud of disappointment creeping over our heads. Doug decided to try extreme unction. 'Let's take it apart piece by piece, kid. There's nothing to lose.' I merely nodded as he started prising apart the jubilee clip that held the tube onto the mouthpiece. At last something positive – a lump of ice was securely blocked in the junction. Carving it out with a knife, we tentatively stuck the two points together again, then shut off the flow so that we could register oxygen being used. A couple of hard sucks on the mask – that was it. I could breathe freely again.

Doug started out on the rock step, leaving me contemplating the escape we'd just had. I was still thinking very calmly about it, but could just about start to imagine what my feelings of disgust would have been like down below if we'd been turned back by mechanical failure. Self-failure you have to accept, bitter though it can be. Defeat by bad weather also, but to be turned back by failure of a humanly con-structed system would have left a mental scar. But now it was upward thinking again. Idly, but carefully, I watched Doug. He was climbing well. Slowly, relaxed, putting in the odd piton for protection. Only his strange masked and hump-backed appearance gave any indication that he was climbing hard rock at 8500m (28,000ft).

DOUG SCOTT At first I worked my way across from Dougal's stance easily in deep soft snow, but then it steepened and thinned out until it was all a veneer covering the yellow amorphous rock underneath. I went up quite steeply for 9m (30ft) hop-ing the front points of my crampons were dug well into the sandy rock underneath

slopes and there was a hard breakable crust. Classic wind-slab avalanche conditions'

the snow. I managed to get in three pegs in a cluster, hoping that one of them might hold, should I fall off. However, the 9m (30ft) were less steep and the snow lay thicker, which was fortunate seeing as I had run out of oxygen. I reached a stance of about 30m (100ft) above Dougal and with heaving lungs I started to anchor off the rope. I pounded in the last of our rock pegs and yelled to Dougal to come up. While he was prussiking up the rope I took photographs and changed over to my remaining full bottle of oxygen. I left the empty bottle tied on the pegs.

We were now into the South Summit couloir and a way seemed clear to the top of the South West Face. We led another rope-length each and stopped for a chat about the route. Dougal's sporting instincts came to the fore – he fancied a direct gully straight up to the Hillary Step. I wasn't keen on account of the soft snow, so he shrugged his shoulders and continued off towards the South Summit. I didn't know whether the direct way would have been any less strenuous, but from now on the route to the South Summit became increasingly difficult.

DOUGAL HASTON  The South West Face wasn't going to relax its opposition one little bit. That became very evident as I ploughed into the first rope-length above the rock step. I had met many bad types of snow conditions in 18 years of climbing. Chris and I had once been shoulder deep retreating from a winter attempt on a new line on the North Face of the Grandes Jorasses. The snow in the couloir wasn't that deep, but it seemed much worse to handle. In the Alps we had been retreating, now we were trying to make progress. Progress? The word seemed almost laughable as I moved more and more slowly. A first step and in up to the waist. Attempts to move upwards only resulted in a deeper sinking motion. Time for new techniques: steps up, sink in, then start clearing away the slope in front like some breast-stroking snow plough and eventually you pack enough together to be able to move a little further and sink in only to your knees. Two work-loaded rope-lengths like this brought us to the choice of going leftwards on the more direct line I had suggested to Doug in an earlier moment of somewhat undisciplined thinking. By now my head was in control again and I scarcely gave it a glance, thinking that at the current rate of progress we'd be lucky to make even the South Summit.

It seemed that conditions would have to improve but they didn't. The slope steepened to 60 degrees and I swung rightwards, heading for a rock step in an attempt to get out of this treadmill of nature. No relief for us. The snow stayed the same, but not only was it steeper, we were now on open wind-blown slopes and there was a hard breakable crust. Classic wind-slab avalanche conditions. In some kind of maniacal cold anger I ploughed on. There was no point in stopping for belays. There weren't any possibilities. I had a rhythm, so kept the evil stroking upwards with Doug tight on my heels. Two feet in a hole, I'd bang the slope to shatter the crust, push away the debris, move up, sink in. Thigh. Sweep away. Knees. Gain a metre. Then repeat the process. It was useful having Doug right behind, as sometimes, when it was particularly difficult to make progress, he was able to stick two hands in my back to stop me sliding backwards. Hours were flashing like minutes, but it was still upward gain.

DOUG SCOTT  I took over the awful work just as it was beginning to ease off. I clambered over some rocks poking out of the snow and noticed that there was a cave between the rocks and the névé ice – a good bivvy for later perhaps. Just before the South Summit I rested while Dougal came up. I continued round the South Summit rock while Dougal got his breath. I was crawling on all fours with the wind blowing up spindrift snow all around. I collapsed into a belay position just below the frontier ridge and took in the rope as Dougal came up my tracks. After a few minutes' rest we both stood up and climbed on to the ridge and there before us was Tibet.

After all those months spent in the Western Cwm over this and two other expeditions now at last we could look out of the cwm to the world beyond – the rolling brown lands of Tibet in the north and northeast to Kangchenjunga and just below us Makalu and Chomo Lonzo. Neither of us said much. We just stood there absorbed in the scene.

DOUGAL HASTON  The wind was going round the South Summit like a mad maypole. The face was finished, successfully climbed, but there was no calm to give much thought to rejoicing. It should have been a moment for elation but wasn't. Certainly we'd climbed the face but neither of us wanted to stop there. The summit was beckoning.

Often in the Alps it seems fine to complete one's route and not go to the summit, but in the Himalayas it's somewhat different. An expedition is not regarded as being totally successful unless the top is reached. Everything was known to us about the way ahead. This was the South East Ridge, the original Hillary/Tenzing route of 1953. It was reckoned to be mainly snow, without too much technical difficulty. But snow on the ridge similar to the snow in the couloir would provide a greater obstacle to progress than any technical difficulties. There were dilemmas hanging around and question marks on all plans.

My head was considering sitting in the tent sac until sunset or later, then climbing the ridge when it would be, theoretically, frozen hard. Doug saw the logic of this thinking but obviously wasn't too happy about it. No other suggestions were forthcoming from his direction however, so I got into the tent sac, got the stove going to give our thinking power a boost with some hot water. Doug began scooping a shallow snow cave in the side of the cornice, showing that he hadn't totally rejected the

*Looking back on the initial
section of the South East
Ridge. The South Summit
is in the centre rear, with
Lhotse on the left and the
South Col bottom left.*

idea. The hot water passing over our raw, damaged throat linings brought our slide
into lethargic pessimism to a sharp halt.

Swinging his pack onto his back Doug croaked, 'Look after the rope, I'm going to
at least try a rope-length to sample conditions. If it's too bad we'll bivouac. If not we
carry on as far as possible.'

I couldn't find any fault with this reasoning, so grabbed the rope as he disappeared
back into Nepal. The way it was going quickly through my hands augured well.
Reaching the end Doug gave a 'come on' signal. Following quickly I realized that
there were now summit possibilities in the wind. Conditions were by no means
excellent, but relative to those in the couloir they merited the title reasonable. There
was no need to say anything as I reached Doug. He just stepped aside, changed the
rope around and I continued. Savage, wonderful country. On the left the South West
Face dropped away steeply, to the right wild curving cornices pointed the way to
Tibet. Much care was needed but there was a certain elation in our movements. The
Hillary Step appeared, unlike any photograph we had seen. No rock step this year,
just a break in the continuity of the snow ridge. Seventy degrees of steepness and
24m (80ft) of length. It was my turn to explore again. Conditions reverted to bad, but
by now I'd become so inured to the technique that even the extra ten degrees didn't
present too much problem.

DOUG SCOTT  As I belayed Dougal up the Hillary Step it gradually dawned upon
me that we were going to reach the summit of Big E. I took another photograph of
Dougal and wound on the film to find that it was finished. I didn't think I had any
more film in my rucksack, for I had left film and spare gloves with the bivvy sheet
and stove at the South Summit. I took off my oxygen mask and rucksack and put
them on the ridge in front of me. I was sat astride it, one leg in Nepal the other in

Tibet. I hoped Dougal's steps would hold, for I could think of no other place to put his rope than between my teeth as I rummaged around in my sack. I found a cassette of colour film that had somehow got left behind several days before. The cold was intense and the brittle film kept breaking off. The wind was strong and blew the snow Dougal was sending down the Nepalese side right back into the air and over into Tibet. I fitted the film into the camera and followed him up. This was the place where Ed Hillary had chimneyed his way up the crevasse between the rock and the ice. Now with all the monsoon snow on the mountain it was well banked up, but with snow the consistency of sugar it looked decidedly difficult.

A wide whaleback ridge ran up the last 275m (900ft). It was just a matter of trail-breaking. Sometimes the crust would hold for a few steps and then suddenly we would be stumbling around as it broke through to our knees. All the way along we were fully aware of the enormous monsoon cornices, overhanging the 3000-m (10,000-ft) East Face of Everest. We therefore kept well to the left.

It was while trail-breaking on this last section that I noticed my mind seemed to be operating in two parts, one external to my head. In my head I referred to the external part somewhere over my left should. I rationalized the situation with it, making reference to it about not going too far right in the area of the cornice, and it would urge me to keep well to the left. Whenever I stumbled through the crust it suggested that I slowed down and picked my way through more carefully. In general it seemed to give me confidence and seemed such a natural phenomenon that I hardly gave it a second thought at that time. Dougal took over the trail-breaking and headed up the final slope to the top – and a red flag flying there. The snow improved and he slackened his pace to let me come alongside. We then walked up side by side the last few paces to the top, arriving there together.

All the world lay before us. The summit was everything and more that a summit should be. My usually reticent partner became expansive, his face broke out into a broad smile and we stood there hugging each other and thumping each other's backs. The implications of reaching the highest mountain in the world surely had some bearings on our feelings, I'm sure they did on mine, but I can't say that it was that strong. I can't say either that I felt any relief that the struggle was over. In fact, in some ways it seemed a shame that it was, for we had been fully programmed and now we had to switch off and go back into reverse. But not yet, for the view was so staggering, the disappearing sun so full of colour that the setting held us in awe. I was absorbed by the brown hills of Tibet. They only looked like hills from our lofty summit. They were really high mountains, some of them 7300m (24,000ft) high, but with hardly any snow to indicate their importance. I could see silver threads of rivers meandering down between them, flowing north and west to bigger rivers, which might have included the Tsangpo. Towards the east Kangchenjunga caught the setting sun, although around to the south clouds boiled down in the Nepalese valleys and far down behind a vast front of black cloud was advancing towards us from the plains of India. It flickered lightning ominously. There was no rush though for it

Overleaf: *Dougal just below the summit of Everest in the gathering dusk. The summit of Nuptse is on the left in the middle ground and Menlungtse, in Tibet, is to the immediate left of his head on the skyline.*

would be a long time coming over Everest – time to pick out the north side route – the Rongbuk Glacier, the East Rongbuk Glacier and Changtse in between. There was the North Col, and the place Odell was standing when he last saw Mallory and Irvine climb up towards him. Wonder if they made it? Their route was hidden by the convex slope – no sign of them, edge out a bit further – no nothing. Not with all the monsoon snow, my external mind pointed out.

The only sign of anyone was the flag. It was some time before I got round to looking at it. It was an unwelcome intrusion and there had been more to do than look at manmade objects. Still, you couldn't help but look at it, seeing as how it was a tripod and pole nearly 5 feet (1.5m) high with a rosary of red ribbons attached to the top. Take a photograph. Ah, yes! Dougal ought to get some of me. He hadn't taken a single photograph on the whole trip. 'Here you are, youth. Take a snap for my mother.' I passed him my camera. 'Better take another one, your glove's in front of the lens. Now a black and white one.' He's never been keen on photography, but he obliged.

DOUGAL HASTON We were sampling a unique moment in our lives. Down and over into the brown plains of Tibet a purple shadow of Everest was projected for what must have been something like 300km (200 miles). On these north and east sides there was a sense of wildness and remoteness, almost untouchability. Miraculous events seemed to be taking place in the region of the sun. One moment it seemed to dip behind a cloud layer lying a little above the horizon. End Game – thought we. But then the cloud dropped faster than the sun and out it came again. Three times in all. I began to feel like Saul on the road to Damascus. More materially, right in front of me was an aluminium survey pole with a strip of red canvas attached. The Japanese Ladies in the spring hadn't mentioned leaving or seeing anything. Puzzlement for a moment. Then the only answer. There had been a Chinese ascent of the North Ridge claimed just after the Japanese ascent. Some doubt, however, had been cast on the validity of this, due to the summit pictures lacking the detail associated with previous summit shots. It was good to have the ultimate proof in front of us. Having to play the doubt game in climbing is never a pleasant experience.

Slowly creeping into the euphoria came one very insistent thought as the sun finally won its race with the clouds and slid over the edge. The thought? Well, we were after all on the top of the world but it was still a long way back to Camp 6 and it was going to be very dark soon and then what would we do? We knew we could get back to the South Summit in the half light. On the previous nights there had been a very bright moon and it seemed reasonable to assume we could retrace our steps down the face if this came out. If it didn't, as a last resort we could bivouac. That after all was the reason for bringing the tent sac. I'd always reckoned a bivouac possible at such altitude, but that doesn't mean to say I looked upon the project with a great degree of enthusiasm. We finally turned our backs to the summit and set off down.

Our tracks were already freezing up, making the going reasonable. An abseil got rid of the Hillary Step with the rope left in place. Moving together we were soon

back at our little cave. Much cloud activity didn't bode well for the appearance of a moon. The oxygen cylinders dribbled out their last drops of usefulness and became mere burdens. Standing vaguely waiting for some light to happen, it was good to take off the tanks and mask. Lighter feeling but not lighter headed. Slowly, as it clouded over, the choices were gradually cut down. We decided to have a look at the possibility of a descent in the dark, knowing the up-trail to be deep and maybe now frozen, but a tentative 15-m (50-ft) grope on the South West Face side of the ridge into the strong night wind with finger and toes going solid finally slammed all the alternative choices to a bivouac out of mind. Dropping back to the sheltered side I told Doug the news. There was nothing really to say. He started enlarging the hole.

DOUG SCOTT  Dougal melted snow on the stove once again while I continued digging into the hillside. After we had had a few sips of warm water, Dougal joined me and we quickly enlarged the snow cave, digging away with our ice axes, pushing the loose snow out through the entrance. By nine o'clock it was big enough to lie down in, we pushed out more snow against the entrance and reduced it to a narrow slit. We were now out of the wind, which was fortunate, as already our oxygen bottles were empty, or our sets had refused to function. The little stove, too, was soon used up. So there we lay on top of our rucksacks and the bivvy sheet, wishing perhaps we had given more thought to the possibility of bivouacking, for we had no food and no sleeping bags. I was wearing only the clothes that I had climbed up in, a silk vest, a wool jumper, a nylon pile suit and my wind suit. I don't think we were ever worried about surviving for we had read of other climbers who had spent the night out on Everest without much gear, although lower down. However they had all subsequently had some fingers and toes cut off. What worried us was the quality of survival and we brought all the strength of our dulled listless minds to bear upon that. I shivered uncontrollably and took off my gloves, boots and socks to rub life back into my extremities for hours at a time. We were so wrapped up in our own personal miseries that we hardly noticed each other, though at one point Dougal unzipped the front of his duvet suit and kindly allowed me to put my bare left foot under his right armpit and my other at his crutch which seemed to help. Without oxygen there didn't seem to be any internal heat being created, so I mostly sat and rubbed and rubbed my fingers and toes. This was no time for sleep. It needed the utmost vigilance to concentrate on survival, keeping my boots upright out of the snow, keeping the snow off my bare hands and feet, warming my socks against my stomach, keeping my head from brushing snow off the roof of the cave. The temperature was probably -30°C (-22°F). It was so cold that at first when I left a sock on my rucksack the foot of the sock went as stiff as a board. Most of the night I dug away at the cave just to keep warm, hacking away at the back with the ice axe into the hard snow and pushing it out through the doorway. By the dawn it was to be big enough to sleep five people lying down!

Our minds started to wander with the stress and the lack of sleep and oxygen.

Dougal quite clearly spoke out to Dave Clarke. He had quite a long and involved conversation with him. I found myself talking to my feet. I personalized them to such an extent that they were two separate beings needing help. The left one was very slow to warm up and, after conversations with the right one, we decided I had better concentrate on rubbing it hard. And all the time my external mind was putting its spoke in as well.

DOUGAL HASTON I was locked in suffering silence except for the occasional quiet conversation with Dave Clarke. Hallucination or dream? It seemed comforting and occasionally directed my mind away from the cold. That stopped and then it was a retreat so far into silence that I seemed to be going to sleep. Shaking awake I decided to stay this way. We'd heard too many tales of people in survival situations falling asleep and not waking up. It seemed as if we'd both come to this conclusion and Doug's incoherent speech served to keep both awake. There was no escaping the cold. Every position was tried. Holding together, feet in each other's armpits, rubbing, moving around the hole constantly, exercising arms. Just no way to catch a vestige of warmth. But during all this the hours were passing. I don't think anything we did or said that night was very rational or planned. Suffering from lack of oxygen, cold, tiredness, but with a terrible will to get through the night, all our survival instincts came right up front. These and our wills saw the night to a successful end.

First light came and we were able to start the process of preparing for downward movement. Checks showed an ability to stand up and move. Extremities had sight numbness, but no frostbite. Kidney pains were locking us in an almost bent-in-two position. Boots were difficult to get on. I gave up my frozen inner boots and used duvet boots as a replacement. The sun came up, but with no hope of getting any warmth to our bodies. Movement was the only way and soon we were across the cornice, saying adieu to Tibet and starting off back down the face. The warmth of movement was almost orgasmic in its intensity as the blood started recirculating. Aware of the possibilities of lack of oxygen hallucinations and their potentially dire effects, we kept a wary eye on each other as we belayed down the first few pitches.

DOUG SCOTT We had not slept or eaten for nearly 30 hours, we had actually spent the night out in China, and we had done it at 8750m (28,700ft) without oxygen. Eventually we made the fixed rope and at 9 am fell into our sleeping bags at Camp 6. I put the stove on and looked around for something to eat and came across the radio. We had been so absorbed in surviving the night and the descent that at times it had all seemed so much like a dream, just the two of us and no one else in the world to share the cold swirling snow. The radio brought us back to reality, it crackled into life. Answering voice – Chris concerned, relieved – happy with the success. Put on a good voice I thought, don't want to sound slurred, although I felt it. 'No, I don't think we are frostbitten,' I said, for by then our fingers and toes were tingling.

The quality of survival had been good.

# Success and Tragedy

Back at camp 2, we had followed the progress of Doug and Dougal through our binoculars and the 600mm lens of the camera. They were tiny black dots, whose spidery arms and legs were just visible in the eyepiece. On the 24th we first picked them out near the end of their traverse across the line of rope they had fixed the previous day. They were making good progress, for it was only nine o'clock in the morning and they were already at the foot of the gully leading up to the South Summit. They vanished into it and the hours through the day began to drag out, with someone every few minutes taking a look through the binoculars at the head of the gully. Surely we must have somehow missed them as they came out of the gully. Perhaps they had gone onto the other side of the ridge.

It was four o'clock. Nick Estcourt was gazing through the 600mm lens. He let out a shout. He had seen someone at the top of the gully; we crowded around, impatiently waiting our turn to look. Surely they're on their way down. They must be. And then the realization came that they were on their way up, they should make the summit, but at that time of day a night bivouac was going to be inevitable. I don't think any of us slept well that night or really relaxed until the following morning we saw the two tiny figures crawl back across the long traverse to Camp 6. Then there was the joyous call that they were home, that they'd made the summit, and had no more than frost nip as their payment for the highest bivouac that has ever been undertaken and one of the boldest bids that has ever been made on the summit of Everest. There was a feeling throughout the expedition of undiluted joy; I couldn't help crying as I ended my wireless conversation with Doug. Dougal could hardly talk; his throat was so parched and sore.

They were on their way down, but the second party was already on its way up. Martin Boysen, Pete Boardman, Mick Burke and Pertemba had set out from Camp 5 that morning, prepared either for a summit bid or a semi-rescue operation if Dougal and Doug were in a bad way. The momentary euphoria soon wore off; I was going to

*Pertemba emerging from the South Summit gully onto the col just beyond the South Summit. Doug and Dougal had taken most of the day to plough up the soft snow, but on the second ascent Pete Boardman and Pertemba had the benefit of their steps and made it in just over an hour.*

'It was four o'clock. Nick Estcourt was gazing through the 600mm lens.
He let out a shout. He had seen someone at the top of the gully; we crowded
around, impatiently waiting our turn to look. Surely they're on their way
down. They must be.'

have to sit through two more summit bids, powerless to do anything but wait and hope that nothing went wrong. I knew that the next few days, until all eight climbers returned safely, were going to be hell. I sat at Camp 2, tensed and anxious, waiting for the two o'clock call, when I should learn that my second summit party were ensconced at Camp 6. They had with them two Sherpas, Lhakpa Dorje and Mingma, who were going to carry up the vital bottles of oxygen for their bid.

It was Martin who came on the air. He told me that Mick had not yet arrived and that Lhakpa Dorje had also failed to make it. Only Mingma had reached them. As a result they had only enough oxygen for Pete, Pertemba and Martin for their summit bid the following day. They were therefore going to have to tell Mick that he would have to stand down, particularly as he seemed the slowest of the four; they had been at the site of Camp 6 for over two hours and there was still no sign of him. I think I had been quietly worrying about Mick, in the very back of my mind. When I had decided to drop out of the third summit bid and return to Camp 2 I put it to Mick that he also had been up at Camp 5 for some time. (He had arrived with Doug on the 18th and so by the morning of the 23rd, when I dropped back, he had been there for six nights compared to my eight. By the 25th, however, on his way up to Camp 6 he had been up there for eight nights as well.) He had replied that he felt he was still going well and that he would be able to get a good rest in the next few days. I knew how determined he was, how savagely disappointed he would be if, having told him he could take part in the second summit bid, I changed the decision, and so I had let him stay.

But now my anxiety, triggered by Martin's, burst out with all the violence of suppressed tension. I told him very strongly that under no circumstances did I want Mick to go for the summit next day. I wanted him to come back down. Martin was shaken by the violence of my reaction and after he went off the air I realized I was perhaps ordering the impossible. Once climbers have got to the top camp on Everest they are very much on their own. Up to that point, they are members of a team, dependent on each other and the overall control of a leader, but the summit bid was different. This was a climbing situation that you might get on a smaller expedition or in the Alps. It was their lives, in their own hands, and only they could decide upon their course of action. We kept the radio open and I had told Martin that Mick was to call me as soon as he reached camp. When Mick arrived a short time later he had plausible excuses for his delay. He had been sorting out the fixed rope and swapping faulty oxygen sets with the Sherpas to enable them to keep load-carrying. There was no point in having a confrontation by radio. All I could do was to exhort them all to stick together and that if anyone did retreat, that they should all return. Even this exhortation was fairly meaningless in the reality of the situation. A line of fixed rope, followed by tracks, stretched towards the summit of Everest just 450m (1475ft) above. I was asking too much. They talked it over that night and agreed that if anyone was going so slowly that he might jeopardize their chances of reaching the summit, he should turn back, before reaching the end of the fixed rope.

They were ready to start at four-thirty the following morning. It was an ominous dawn. Although there was no wind, a thin high haze covered the western horizon and a tide of cloud was fast lapping up the valley bottoms, filling the Western Cwm below them and creeping up the face itself. The weather seemed on the point of change and they all realized that they were going to have to move fast to avoid making a bivouac.

Martin Boysen, ever impatient, was away first, Pete Boardman was next, closely followed by Pertemba, and Mick Burke brought up the rear. Martin suffered an early and bitter setback when his oxygen set packed up and he lost a crampon, this misfortune effectively putting him out of the summit bid; the others overtook him and despairingly he retreated to the tent. 'I crawled inside and howled with anguish, frustration and self-pity. Later the sun crept round, but a strong breeze sprang up. I poked my head out and scanned the gully. Two tiny specks were visible, one just below the summit ridge. I wondered where Mick was and eventually spied him at the bottom of the gully as the two figures above reached the crest. It was only eleven o'clock – they were doing well. I closed the door. I could hardly bear to watch.'

Pete Boardman and Pertemba had made good progress, climbing unroped beyond the end of the fixed ropes along the track leading to the foot of the South Summit Gully and then on up to its top. Although some of the tracks had been filled in by wind-driven spindrift, the snow was much better consolidated than it had been two

*Pertemba on the narrow ridge just beyond the South Summit. The cloud had crept up the face, engulfing them in a thin mist. The wind was steadily rising but visibility was still quite reasonable.*

days before. Pete had glanced back once or twice, had seen a distant figure on the traverse across the Upper Snowfield but had assumed that this was Martin or Mick sitting watching them and that they both would return to camp.

On reaching the South Summit, Pertemba had trouble with his oxygen when his set jammed. The problem was similar to the one that had beset Dougal and they spent an hour fiddling with it before they managed to clear the 5cm (2in) of ice blocking the airflow. Even so, they were still making excellent time. They changed their oxygen bottles and forged on towards the summit, roped up, but climbing together.

The cloud had now crept up the face, engulfing them in a thin mist. The wind was rising steadily, but visibility was still quite reasonable. They could see the line of tracks snaking up the South East Ridge in front of them and felt comfortably in control of the situation.

They reached the top at about ten past one, a very fast time indeed, even allowing for the tracks left by the first summit pair. They were not rewarded by the magnificent view that Doug and Dougal had enjoyed, for they were still enclosed in fine

wind-driven mist, the Chinese maypole the only sign that they were standing on the highest point on earth. Pete was wearing a specially decorated T-shirt presented to him by the Mynydd Mountaineering Club in honour of the occasion. It was like a medieval knight's surcoat worn over his down suit of armour. Pertemba took out a Nepalese flag, which they attached to the Chinese emblem. They took photographs of each other and Pete addressed the world on miniature tape recorder: 'Hello, here is the first bit of recorded sound from the summit of Mount Everest. Would you like to say a word to the viewers, Pertemba?' A muffled sound followed, due to Pertemba still being encased in his oxygen mask, but when asked if he was tired, there came a very firm 'No'. Pete then went on to outline the details of their ascent and the weather conditions and signed off with the cheerful comment, 'Well, I can't see a Barclays Bank branch anywhere.' In this totally relaxed mood they ate some chocolate and mint cake, and then set off down. They still had plenty of time; it was barely one-forty.

They had not gone more than a few hundred metres when to their utter amazement a figure began to take shape through the mist. Pete Boardman tells what happened next:

Mick was sitting on the snow only a few hundred metres down an easy angled snow slope from the summit. He congratulated us and said he wanted to film us on a bump on the ridge and pretend it was the summit, but I told him about the Chinese maypole. Then he asked us to go back to the summit with him. I agreed reluctantly and he, sensing my reluctance, changed his mind and said he'd go up and film it and then come straight down after us. He borrowed

*Mick Burke caught up with Pete and Pertemba as they started back down from the summit. This is the last sighting of Mick, who continued on towards the summit alone.*

Pertemba's camera to take some stills on the top and we walked back 15m (50ft) and then walked past him, while he filmed us I took a couple of pictures of him. He had the Blue Peter flag and an auto-load camera with him. He asked us to wait for him by the big rock on the South Summit where Pertemba and I had dumped our first oxygen cylinders and some rope and film on the way up. I told him that Pertemba was wanting to move roped with me – so he should catch us up fairly quickly. I said, 'See you soon,' and we moved back down the ridge to the South Summit.

After they parted company the weather began to deteriorate fast. Pete and Pertemba continued down to wait with increasing apprehension:

All the winds of Asia seemed to be trying to blow us from the ridge. A decision was needed. It was four in the afternoon and the skies were already darkening around the South Summit of Everest. I threw my iced and useless snow goggles away into the whiteness and tried, clumsily mitted, to clear the ice from my eyelashes. I bowed my head into the spin-drift and tried to peer along the ridge. Mick should have met us at least three-quarters of an hour before. We had been waiting for nearly one and a half hours. There was no sign of Doug and Dougal's bivouac site. The sky and cornices and whirling snow merged together, visibility was reduced to 3m (10ft) and all tracks were obliterated. Pertemba and I huddled

next to the rock of the South Summit where Mick had asked us to wait for him. Pertemba said he could not feel his toes or fingers and mine, too, were nailed with cold. I thought of Mick wearing his glasses and blinded by spindrift, nego-tiating the short length of fixed rope on the Hillary Step, the fragile one foot windslab on the Nepal side and the cornices on the Tibetan side of the ridge. I thought of our own predicament, with the 245m (800ft) of the South Summit Gully – guarded by a 18-m (60-ft) rock step halfway – to descend, and then half of the 600-m (2000-ft) great traverse above the Rock Band to cross before reach-ing the end of the fixed ropes that extended across from Camp 6. It had taken Doug and Dougal three hours in the dawn sunshine after their bivouac to reach Camp 6 – but now we had only an hour of light left. At 8750m (28,700ft) the boundary between a controlled and an uncontrolled situation is narrow and we had crossed that boundary within minutes – a strong wind and sun shining through clouds had turned into a violent blizzard of driving snow.

A decision was needed. I pointed at my watch and said, 'We'll wait ten more minutes.' Pertemba agreed. That helped us – it shifted some responsibility to

*Pete on the summit of Everest at just after one o'clock. He was wearing a T-shirt given to him by his local mountaineering club and recorded a few words on his tape recorder. The Chinese expedition's maypole flies the Nepalese flag, placed there by Pertemba.*

the watch. I fumbled in my sack and pulled out our stove to leave behind. The time was up. At first we went the wrong way, too far towards the South Col. About 45m (150ft) down we traversed back until we found what we thought was the South Summit gully. There was a momentary lessening in the blizzard, and I looked up to see the rock of the South Summit. There was still no sign of Mick and it was now about half past four. The decision had been made and now we had to fight for our own lives and think downwards. The early afternoon had drifted into approaching night and our success was turning into tragedy.

Pertemba is not a technical climber, not used to moving away from fixed ropes or in bad conditions. At first he was slow. For three pitches I kicked down furiously, placed a deadman and virtually pulled him down in the sliding, blowing powder snow. But Pertemba is strong and adaptable. He began to move faster and soon we were able to move together. Were we in the gully? I felt panic surge inside. Then I saw twin rocks in the snow that I recognized from the morning. We descended diagonally from there and in the dusk saw Doug's oxygen cyl-inder that marked the top of the fixed rope over the rock step. We abseiled down to the end of the rope and tied a spare rope we had to the end and descended the other 45m (150ft). From there we descended down and across for 300m (1000ft) towards the end of the fixed ropes. As soon as we started the traverse we were covered by a powder-snow avalanche from the summit slopes. Fortunately our oxygen cylinders were still functioning and we could breathe. We threaded our way blindly across the thin runnels of ice and snow that covered the sloping rocks. I felt a brush of snow on my head and looked up to see another big avalanche coming, channelled straight at me. I looked across. Pertemba was crouched to hold my fall, and was whipping in the rope between us tight to my waist. I smashed my axe into the ice and hung on. The surging snow buffeted over and around me for minutes. Then it stopped. Pertemba had held; the axe had stayed in the ice. We moved on. It was a miracle that we found the end of the fixed ropes in the dark marked by two oxygen cylinders sticking out of the snow. On the fixed rope Pertemba slowed down and I pulled him mercilessly until he shouted that one of his crampons had fallen off. The rope between us snagged and, in flicking it free, I tumbled over a 4.5-m (15-ft) rock step to be held on the fixed rope. At one point a section of the rope had been swept away. At half past seven we stumbled into the summit boxes at Camp 6. Martin was there and I burst into tears.

Back at Camp 2 we had waited, helpless, through the day. In the early morning we had glimpsed two figures, probably Pete and Pertemba, near the foot of the South Summit gully and were filled with hope for a fast safe ascent, but then the cloud had rolled over us and all we could see through the occasional break were banners of spindrift being blown from the top of the Rock Band and the South East Ridge.

After two o'clock we kept the radio permanently open, could detect the growing anxiety in Martin's voice whenever he called us, as the wind hammering his little tent rose through the afternoon. It became dark, and there was still no sign of them. We were all sitting, tensed and silent round the piled boxes of the mess tent at Camp 2; the only sounds, the wind howling across the face above us and the crackle and buzz of the radio. A severe storm had broken and a bivouac would be an even more serious business than it had been for Doug and Dougal.

And then at seven o'clock Martin's voice came through. There was a momentary glimmer of relief; they were back. But our hopes were quickly dashed by the agony in his voice as he told us that only Pete and Pertemba had returned and that Pete would tell me what had happened.

None of us could believe that Mick was dead; he'd stagger back along the ropes in an hour or so's time; he'd bivouac, and return to Camp 6 the following morning; the same irrepressible cocky Mick whom we'd known for so many years on so many climbs. But as the night dragged out, the fury of the storm increased; it raged throughout the following day and as the hours crept by our hopes began to vanish, to be replaced with anxiety not only for Mick but for the safety of the three now pinned down, tired and exhausted, at the end of the Upper Snowfield, with only a limited quantity of food and oxygen, exposed to the full force of the powder-snow avalanches that were pouring down from the summit rocks.

As the storm raged through the day of the 27th, we abandoned all hope of Mick's survival. Dougal and Doug, who had seen how badly corniced and how narrow was the ridge leading down from the foot of the Hillary Step, felt that it would have been all too easy for him to have walked over the edge in the white-out conditions that must have beset him on his descent. If he had stopped for the night, hoping to get back down to the end of the fixed rope the following morning of the 27th, he could not possibly have moved that day, and there was no way he could have survived two nights at that altitude without food, shelter or oxygen, even if he had dug a snow hole. Mick was dead and every camp was threatened. We had been forced to evacuate Camp 1 on the afternoon of the 26th; its occupants had felt the ice island shift beneath their feet, in its inexorable slide down the Icefall.

I was getting increasingly worried about the safety of the rest of the team. Nick, Ronnie, Ang Phurba and Tut at Camp 5 seemed safe enough, tucked away in the small gully that was guarded by a rock buttress above, but they reported huge powder-snow avalanches pouring in a constant torrent down the Great Central Gully. There was no question of movement either up or down until these ceased.

Camp 4, however, was in a more exposed situation, so I told Adrian Gordon, who was in charge, to abandon the camp and bring down the six Sherpas who were manning it. The Sherpas raced down the fixed ropes and got back to Camp 2 just before dark, but Adrian who had delayed to ensure the camp was left secure, and moved more slowly because he was less experienced, got lost by following the wrong ropes in the dark. Our search party just reached him in time to avert a possible further tragedy. In the night an avalanche flattened much of Camp 2.

It dawned into a brilliant clear still morning. There was no question of mounting a search for Mick or another summit bid. He couldn't possibly be alive. I wanted to clear the mountain, which had a dangerous quantity of snow on it, as quickly as possible. I told the party at Camp 5 to wait for the arrival of Pete, Pertemba and Martin and then to accompany them back to Camp 2. I had decided to abandon everything that they couldn't carry down with them. I was not prepared to take any further risks just to rescue pieces of equipment, however valuable.

That morning of 28 September, they had crawled out of the two battered little tents at Camp 6, and crammed their frozen sleeping bags into their rucksacks. Pete Boardman almost dreaded the return.

I felt isolated from my friends lower down the mountain by a decision and experience I could not share. We looked across the traverse and up the gully to the South Summit, but there was no sign of Mick. We turned and began the long repetitive ritual of clipping and unclipping the piton brake and safety loop and abseiling rope-length after rope-length, 1800m (6000ft) down to the Western Cwm.

'Everest is not a private affair; it belongs to many men.' That afternoon I was in front of a camera, explaining what had happened. But now friends were all around me. Dougal, usually so distant and undemonstrative, had walked out in the midday heat of the Western Cwm to meet me, Doug had tenderly taken off my boots, Chris had reassured me.

The following morning we turned our backs on the South West Face of Everest and headed down the Western Cwm, in a long straggling line of climbers and Sherpas, bowed under monstrous loads of up to 36kg (80lb). I didn't relax until the last man came down the Icefall on 30 September. That night the Sherpas had a party to celebrate the successful outcome of the expedition and the safe return of all their numbers. They lit a huge bonfire and danced round it, late into the night, arms linked, chanting out their songs, swaying in and out, to the brink of the flames and out into the dark, throwing great shadows onto the tents and snow behind us. Plastic jerry cans of chang were passed round; we were offered mugfuls of throat-searing rakshi, tried our hand at dancing and contributed a few noisy and very tuneless chorus songs. There was plenty of laughter and shouting, but there were moments of reflection as well.

I know that I and, I suspect, most other members of the team, would have followed the same course as Mick in similar circumstances. In pressing on alone he took a climber's calculated risk. He balanced in his mind the risks of going on by himself in the face of deteriorating weather, with the knowledge that there were fixed ropes on all the awkward sections and a line of tracks stretching away before him. Although he was travelling more slowly than Pertemba and Pete, he was still making good progress and always had plenty of time before dark to return to Camp

6. Had the weather not deteriorated into white-out conditions so quickly, I am convinced he would have caught up with the others on the South Summit. Sadly, his calculations didn't work out. We were rather like the mourners after the funeral; glad to be alive, getting on with our own lives, the memory of Mick held with sadness and regret, yet accepted as an act that had happened; one of the risks of our climbing game.

Is there a self-centred selfishness in this attitude? For those of us who are happily married and have children, there must be or we should not have carried on our life of climbing aware, as we are, of the risks involved. In our own single-minded drive and love for the mountains, we hope that the fatal accident will never happen to us, and we are frightened to contemplate the cruel long-lasting sorrow suffered by the widows, parents and children – an endless tunnel that for them must never seem to end. Our doubts and sorrow were mixed with a feeling of satisfaction at having taken part in a successful, demanding, yet very happy expedition. Inevitably there had been moments of tension and misunderstanding within the team, but these had

*Mick Burke had come on the expedition as both climber and BBC cameraman. He had worked hard in both roles and was determined to get some film from the summit of Everest.*

been very few and had been quickly dispelled with frank words. Our friendship and respect for each other had been heightened rather than weakened.

In our race to beat the winter winds and cold, we had climbed the mountain in 33 exacting, exhilarating days after arriving at Base Camp. Everyone had stretched himself to his limit.

Each of us had known moments of immense personal fulfilment, of self-revelation, or just simple wonder at the beauty and scale of the mountain itself and the ever-expanding view to be gained from it.

The South West Face of Everest was a major landmark in all our climbing lives, one that had taken up so much of our mental and physical energy in the months of preparation, planning and finally of climbing, but already we were beginning to talk of future objectives in the Karakoram, Garhwal, Nepal, Alaska or Patagonia. There are so many mountains in the world, many of them still unclimbed, all with unclimbed facets, ridges or faces.

There is no question of anticlimax in tackling smaller peaks than Everest, for simply by reducing the size of the team one can maintain the level of challenge that is the essence of climbing. Each problem, whether it be a granite spire in the Karakoram, a great unclimbed snow face in the Nepal Himalaya or a complex ridge in the Garhwal, has its own special mystery and appeal.

One of the joys of mountaineering in this fast-shrinking world is that mountaineers for many generations to come will still be able to discover untrodden corners in the greater mountain ranges of the earth. We, however, shall always feel fortunate and privileged to have been able to unravel the complex problems that were presented by the world's highest and steepest mountain face.

# South West Face – An Afterword

THE SOUTH WEST FACE was left alone until the spring of 1982, the same year that we went for the North East Ridge. A strong Soviet expedition, the first ever to climb outside their own country, chose a challenging new line up the steep buttress to the left of the Central Gully on our route. It was steep and difficult climbing all the way up to their exit on the West Ridge at a height of 8300m (27,230ft) and the remaining 500m (1640ft) up the West Ridge proved to be surprisingly hard. Their achievement in putting 11 climbers on the summit in four separate ascents is particularly impressive and this remains unrepeated and technically the hardest route on Everest.

In the winter of 1985–86 the South Koreans made an unsuccessful attempt on our South West Face route, reaching a height of 7700m (25,250ft) halfway up the Central Gully. They were no more successful the following winter. In the spring of 1987 a 23-strong Czechoslovakian expedition reached the Rock Band but was driven back by bad weather and then in the autumn of 1988 four more Czech climbers set out with the boldest project of all – to climb the South West Face, alpine-style and therefore, inevitably, without oxygen.

Josef Just, Dusan Becik, Peter Bojik and Jaroslav Jasko set out from Camp 2 in the Western Cwm at 3 am on 14 October. They were travelling very light with just a tent inner lining, two 40-m (130-ft) ropes, two sleeping bags (presumably doubles), cooking gear and food for three days. They made good progress on the first day, reaching the foot of the Rock Band, but it took most of the following day to climb the gully and ramp through the Rock Band to camp somewhere near the site of our Camp 6. Their progress was now very much slower and Becik was feeling the effects of altitude. They completed the long traverse across the Upper Snowfield but didn't manage to reach the top of the gully leading up to the col by the South Summit. This was their third night above 8000m (26,250ft) and they were bivouacking at around 8500m (28,000ft). They reached the South Summit the

High on the South West Face of Everest with the Western Cwm bottom right and the West Ridge of Nuptse from right to top left.

following morning, but only Just felt capable of going for the top. The others waited for him and Just radioed down to their base camp at 1.40 pm that he was on top of Everest. He called again at 4 pm that he had rejoined the others and that they were starting down from the South Summit. The final call was at 5.30 pm, when he reported that they were at 8300m (27,230ft) but that all of them were suffering from high-altitude sickness and had blurred vision. They never got back to the South Col and it can only be surmised that one of them slipped and pulled the others off with him. It was blowing hard at the time and the weather was deteriorating.

It was inevitable that a team would try the route in alpine-style, but the tragedy emphasizes the problems of climbing alpine-style at altitude. Messner had pulled it off, climbing the traditional North Ridge route, solo, during the monsoon of 1980. But he had been aware of the dangers of spending too many nights above 8000m (26,250ft). He reached the top with just two bivouacs, the first at 7800m (25,600ft) and the second at 8200m (26,900ft) – about the same height as the first bivouac of the Czechs! He summitted and returned to the same bivvy and then got all the way down the next day. Even so it was a close run thing – he was desperately tired and, had the weather broken, or had there been the high winds experienced by the Czechs, the outcome might well have been different. The lesson however is that more than one night above 8000 metres is dangerous and a night at over 8500m (28,000ft), after two bivouacs above 8000 metres, particularly so.

The Koreans returned yet again in the winter of 1988–89 without success. In the spring of 1989 the talented French climber Marc Batard made a solo attempt, reaching a height of 7800m (25,600ft) before being driven back by high winds. In light of the fate of the Czechs, one can't help wondering if he wasn't lucky to have turned back when he did. He went on the next autumn to make the fastest ascent of Everest by the South Col route in just 22 hours and 30 minutes. This record was broken only in 1998 by Kaji Sherpa, who made the ascent in 20 hours and 24 minutes. Remarkable athletic achievements though these are, it must be remembered that there were tracks all the way and fixed ropes on the difficult sections.

There was a Basque expedition in autumn 1990 which reached a height of 8300m (27,230ft) and then in the winter of 1991–92 a large Japanese expedition spent 12 weeks on the face but was beaten by the high winds and cold. A Ukrainian expedition reached the Rock Band in the autumn of 1992, hoping to make a direttissima ascent, but was overtaken by the winter winds.

Finally, in December 1993, a very compact Japanese expedition led by Kuniaki Yagihara made the first winter ascent and arguably the only completely successful repeat ascent of the South West Face. It was a remarkably fast achievement, just three weeks from setting out from Base Camp, and placed six members on the summit in three separate ascents.

There have been no other attempts since, though climbers have talked of a direttissima, climbing the Rock Band direct and then making a push straight up to the summit. There have, therefore, been ten attempts to repeat the South West Face, of which two have been successful.

All of these climbs were made after I returned to Everest in the spring of 1982 to attempt the true North East Ridge all the way from the Raphu La. The traditional route on the north side of Everest joins the North East Ridge from the North Col, avoiding a long ridgeline leading up to a series of serrated pinnacles. The original idea had come from Al Rouse, one of the most talented British climbers of the late seventies and early eighties. He had joined me with Mike Ward on a reconnaissance of the Kongur massif in Xinjiang in China in 1980 and on the actual expedition to Kongur (7719m/25,325ft) in 1981, when Pete Boardman, Joe Tasker, Al and I made the first ascent. The North East Ridge was obviously a huge challenge and I was fascinated by it. Al and I got on well together, talked about it incessantly on our recce and it seemed logical to invite Joe and Pete to join the team.

In spring 1982 I would be nearly 48 and was conscious that reaching the top of Everest by a long and difficult route as part of a small team without oxygen might well be beyond me, but I couldn't resist the challenge. It was a combination of the quality of the line, the last major unclimbed feature on Everest, the fact that it was Everest, but it was also because I enjoyed the company of these immensely talented young climbers. There was an element perhaps of not wanting to let go, or needing to go on being involved at the cutting edge of climbing.

During the Kongur climb, however, it became increasingly obvious that Pete and Joe did not get on with Al. They came from different climbing backgrounds, almost different tribes of climbers and were very different in temperament. Al was flamboyant, full of ideas, some far-fetched; he was full of stories, some over the top, and yet I liked him and recognized his qualities, both as a brilliant climber and as a warm-hearted friend. But we needed a totally balanced and compatible team if we were to have a hope of success on Everest and so I took the hard decision of dropping Al from the party and inviting Dick Renshaw, who had been Joe's climbing partner on some of his hardest climbs. It was a pragmatic decision that I think was necessary but one that I'll never feel happy about. It was a tribute to Al's character and warmth of spirit that our friendship survived and we even went off on expedition together in 1994, just two years before his death high on K2.

I set out for Everest in 1982 excited, yet full of foreboding.

2

'True, we had seen photographs, paintings, sketches and even models of the North Face and perhaps we did not have the thrill of Bullock and Mallory's first glimpse in 1921, but here, on a windy afternoon in southern Tibet, we were all fulfilling a dream: to visit the northern side of this, the highest mountain.'

# Everest: North East Ridge, 1982
## The Challenge of the Pinnacles

*April 1981–1 March 1982*

# A Worthwhile Objective   by Charles Clarke

'YOU ARE COMING TO EVEREST next year, aren't you?' was how Chris put it. It was the first I knew of it. It was April 1981 and we were spending the weekend at the Glenridding Hotel on the shores of Ullswater in preparation for the 1981 British Mount Kongur expedition to China. While we talked logistics and tested tents, filmed and held a press conference, I sensed that our meeting had two roles. Its overt purpose was to plan our visit to Mount Kongur on the southern border of Xinjiang, China's western province; more surreptitiously, the seeds were sown for the first British expedition to the Tibetan side of Everest for over 40 years.

The highest mountain in the world lies between two Himalayan nations, a giant pyramid astride the frontier of Nepal and Tibet. Its southern flank, bounded by the West Ridge and the South East Ridge, lies in Nepal and has been visited extensively since World War II. The Tibetan side is at present less well known but was explored by British expeditions in the 1920s and 1930s. Between the 3000-m (10,000-ft) East, or Kangshung Face, and the north wall of the mountain lies the North East Ridge, 5km (3 miles) long. Unclimbed, obvious, long and elegant as a route, it was a magnificent virgin line, the only ridge left for a new route on Everest. Thus it remains.

It is often difficult to explain the choice of a route on a mountain. If the peak is unknown or unclimbed, there seems little need to justify the intention to attempt a first ascent. For second and subsequent ascents of peaks above 8000m (26,250ft), such is the scale of the undertaking that the choice becomes of crucial importance. But what influenced us was the simple fact that the Chinese had recently opened selected mountains to foreign expeditions. The north side of Everest was one of them and the North East Ridge was an obvious choice – elegant, unknown, difficult, but possible for a small team determined this time to climb without high-altitude porters and without oxygen. An approach through Tibet would be intriguing, and we would be following routes explored by the British expeditions who came to Everest between the two world wars.

*The '82 expedition was very different from that of '75 – there were just six of us, left to right: myself, Charlie Clarke, Adrian Gordon, Joe Tasker, Pete Boardman and Dick Renshaw.*

'I often feel that the preparations for an expedition are like the description of a first pregnancy – of intense interest and importance to the participants but certainly not unique.'

Our team of six were old friends. Chris Bonington, Peter Boardman, Adrian Gordon and I had been together on the South West Face of Everest, Adrian and I operating at Base Camp, he as an administrator with his fluent Nepali and I as expedition doctor. Chris, Peter, Adrian and I had been together more recently on a first foray into China when Chris and Peter were part of the team which climbed Mount Kongur in Xinjiang Province. This was when I met Joe Tasker, Pete's climbing partner on Changabang, who had also been to Kangchenjunga with Pete and to K2 with Pete and Chris. Spare, with a halo of thinning, dishevelled hair, Joe had a reputation for argument, a brittle veneer that vanished quickly as I grew to know him. Like Peter, he had written two books by the time we set out for Everest, and he had also learned the skills necessary for high-altitude filming. The fourth serious climber in our party was Dick Renshaw, who had climbed Dunagiri with Joe. If Chris was the public persona on this expedition, Dick would be the gentle recluse, ultimately disciplined and dedicated wholly to mountaineering.

I often feel that the preparations for an expedition are like the description of a first pregnancy – of intense interest and importance to the participants but not unique. While Adrian packed in Hong Kong, Chris, Pete and Joe organized the high-altitude equipment in Britain; Dick and I looked after the food. There were no committee meetings. We packed early in January during a weekend when Britain was paralysed under a layer of snow. Somehow we all reached Manchester and I slept on crates outside the warehouse of our generous sponsors, Jardine Matheson, snug in several sleeping bags with the temperature at -12°C (10°F). We were to leave in six weeks.

Everest is, to our generation of climbers, a mountain viewed largely from the south, seen through the haze of the plains of India or from Tiger Hill above Darjeeling. The imperial Survey of India who, under Sir Andrew Waugh, computed in 1852 that Peak XV was, at a little over 8848m (29,028ft), the highest mountain in the world, viewed the mountain from the Nepalese foothills in India. To the Tibetan villager, travelling with his yak to new pastures below the Rongbuk foothills, to the Khamba brigand, hiding from pursuing bands of a local warrior lord, or to the illegal surveyor from India disguised as a monk, the North Face of Everest would, however, be but one of a group of great peaks in the dry, high-altitude, rolling plateau of southern Tibet. Even today the traveller might fail to identify the world's highest mountain from the north until he is well into the Rongbuk Valley.

It was from this direction that the earliest attempts on the mountain were made via the North Col, culminating in 1924 with Norton reaching 8550m (28,050ft) without oxygen and Everest's most famous tragedy: the loss of Mallory and Irvine, last seen near the crest of the North East Ridge at a height above 8500m (28,000ft). Further expeditions in the 1930s via the North Col failed to reach Norton's high point. After World War II, attention switched to the southern approach when Nepal, hitherto more secret than Tibet, opened its borders, and it was by the South East Ridge and the South Col that Everest was at last climbed by Hillary and Tenzing on John Hunt's 1953 expedition. The closure of Tibet by the Chinese helped ensure that the so-called golden age of Himalayan mountaineering which followed was Nepal-based. Accurate Chinese accounts of what had been going on to the north were hard to come by, and I hoped to learn more when we reached Beijing and the offices of the Chinese Mountaineering Association, who supervised foreign expeditions.

In our meeting and at a banquet which followed, we tried to piece together a few missing links in the story of Chinese activity on Everest. In 1960 the first Chinese Chomolungma expedition, led by Mr Shi Zhanchun, climbed the mountain by the North Col route. For the first time yaks were used instead of porters to carry loads to Advanced Base Camp at 6500m (21,300ft). The account of this expedition, whose success was doubted for many years in the Western climbing press, is still hard to follow. This is explained, I believe, by poor translation, accompanied by incomplete photographic corroboration. Looking back nearly 25 years later and having now met the leader, Mr Shi, and others who were on the trip, I find every reason to applaud the very considerable achievements of the party.

During our visit to Beijing we learned for the first time of a second Chinese Chomolungma expedition in 1964 and later checked our interpretation of the facts with Mr Chen, our liaison officer, who had been a team member. This pre-monsoon expedition was the first to set foot on the North East Ridge from the Raphu La and reached about 7000m (23,000ft) before turning back. There was also an unsuccessful attempt by the North Col route. We were told that this expedition was in preparation for one on a larger scale in 1965 – a trip that never took place, probably because of the Cultural Revolution.

The most recent Chinese ascent was in 1975. This expedition was again led by Mr Shi and was a large team accompanied by scientists and a film crew. Nine climbers – seven Tibetan men, one Tibetan woman and one Han Chinese – reached the summit on 27 May 1975, using intermittent oxygen. The ascent was filmed, including the final steps to the summit, by telephoto. Important and unusual scientific work was carried out – for example an electrocardiogram was recorded on the summit. An aluminium survey pole was left on the top and was discovered by Doug Scott and Dougal Haston after the first ascent of the South West Face from Nepal that autumn.

In 1982, ours was the fourth expedition since 1975 on the Chinese side. A joint Sino-Japanese team climbed a new route in the North Face in 1980 and was followed by Reinhold Messner's remarkable solo ascent without oxygen by the North Col route. A large French military expedition attempted the North Col route in the spring of 1981 but failed because of bad weather, reaching a height of 8200m (26,900ft). In the autumn of the same year an American team were the first to attempt the huge Kangshung Face. They succeeded in climbing a steep and difficult rock buttress at the foot of the face, reaching a height of about 7000m (23,000ft) before turning back. I was relieved to discover that there had been no further activity on the long North East Ridge. I had half expected that we would be told gently and in passing that the Chinese climbers went barefoot from the Raphu La to the North East Shoulder on several occasions!

*8 March–4 April 1982*

# From Lhasa to Advanced Base by Charles Clarke

A TURBO-PROP ILYUSHIN roared into the darkness of a warm soggy Chengdu dawn; within an hour we were in daylight, not too far above the ground – a spectacular range of peaks in eastern Tibet, many over 6000m (19,700ft) high. I was unprepared for both the fierceness and scale of the terrain below us. These Tibetan peaks stretched as far as the eye could see on either side of the aircraft, for 45 minutes' flying at 350–400 knots, and were the sharpest range of mountains I had ever seen – towering ridges with knife edges, fluted ice gutters, and spiky summits so thin that it looked as if you could scarcely straddle them. They are, I suppose, 6000–7000m (19,700ft–23,000ft) high; not one of the major peaks has ever been visited.

The rest house at which we were to stay was outside central Lhasa, tucked into a military complex. Across the valley floor, the Potala Palace loomed in the distance like some vast fortress. Militarism persists in Tibet. In 1950 the emergent People's Liberation Army, intent on uniting all the former states of Imperial China, invaded eastern Tibet and defeated a Tibetan army at Chamdo, precipitating the chain of events that culminated in the fourteenth Dalai Lama's flight to India in 1959. Tibet was to become a region with local autonomy. Roads were built, collective farming was introduced on land taken from the monasteries and given to the farming communes. Religion was not actively suppressed but not encouraged by the Chinese. Immigration by Han Chinese workers, officials and soldiers took place on a large scale.

Tibet's troubles were not over, for in 1966 the Cultural Revolution was to cause havoc throughout the land. Bands of Red Guards, most of whom were young Tibetans, destroyed much of the nation's artistic and architectural heritage, which had been preserved by the unchanging order of its clergy and the dry cold climate. Of more than 2000 monasteries and shrines, we were told that fewer than a dozen remained – and we were to see most of them on the journey to Everest.

Passions run high over the rights and wrongs of these unhappy years. Tibet was never, as some suggest, a serene land-locked Himalayan Switzerland, with its

*We flew from Chengdu in western China to Lhasa and half an hour into the flight gazed at this magnificent mountain range, guessing correctly that none of them had been climbed. Chris and I returned 14 years later to find a way to the highest peak in the range and spent the next two years trying to climb it.*

'We left for Xigaze in the icy dawn of the end of winter. The weather was fine but bitterly cold with night temperatures of -12°C (10°F). First we crossed the Tsang Po River and drove up to the Khamba La, a 4800-m (15,750-ft) pass above a magnificent frozen turquoise lake, heading for high mountains and the Kharo La.'

Far left: *A view over Lhasa from the roof of the Jokhang Temple, looking across to Medical Hill.*
Left: *A colossal statue of Maitreya, the future Buddha, in the Jokhang Temple.*

heritage and people cared for lovingly by its Lamas. It was a fierce country, cruel and impoverished, held together by the bonds of a religion which, though once a comforter, had become an oppressive force that had sown the seeds of its own demise.

China is today impressively honest about admitting the difficulties it has had with Tibet, although there are dark areas where detail is sketchy. What was apparent during our three months' stay was that Tibet is still nationally remarkably intact, despite the destruction of many of its monuments, and there is no attempt on the part of the Chinese to regard the country or the people simply as an extension of the central provinces of the People's Republic. Tibet was, and is, an enigma.

Close to the Potala Palace in central Lhasa is the Jokhang Temple. It is the shrine built to commemorate the coming of Princess Wen Cheng from China in the seventh century and houses the golden Buddha encrusted with turquoise, coral and other jewels she brought with her,. Pilgrims walk slowly clockwise round the temple, chanting, '*Om mani padme hum*' (Hail to the jewel in the lotus), spinning prayer wheels and plucking rosaries. To gain advancement along the Path of Enlightenment, a few progress by prostrating themselves along the flagstones. The temple was packed when we visited it, the entrance courtyard black with the grease of prostrating bodies, while a queue, six deep, orderly and mostly silent, wound around the court and disappeared into its inner sanctum. The Jokhang is a place of superlatives and extravagance. In the courtyard were two huge copper vats to provide molten rancid yak butter for about 10,000 lights set in rows upon the floor and tended by a few monks. It was once thought that between a quarter and a third of Tibet's butter production went to fuel the lights of its monasteries.

From the roof of the Jokhang Temple we peered between the golden domes and spires, looking out on multicoloured Lhasa. I had never realized that the shutters would be reds and blues, the dresses carmine, purple, green and brown, the high felt boots richly embroidered. The old town surrounds the temple: whitewashed, two-storey houses with painted sills and lintels, each with a frill of cotton fluttering in the breeze.

Next morning we climbed the steps of the Potala, with Joe filming us. The steps end in a simple entrance some 120m (400ft) above the city. Above it towers the Potala

for another 180m (590ft) – the palace was said to be the tallest building on earth for many centuries. Under the old regime, nobles on horseback would ride up this hill for a limited distance only, in direct proportion to their rank, while for the common people of Lhasa the palace itself was a Forbidden City. Neither were they permitted even to catch a glimpse of their reincarnate deity, the Dalai Lama. A morning's visit does little more than convey a general impression of the place; of the 13 storeys connected by rickety stair ladders; of rows of golden statuettes and of a central shrine somewhere in the depths of the palace, built as a memorial to King Songsten Gampo and his three wives – Chinese, Nepali and Tibetan. This is the oldest remaining part of the Potala, begun in the seventh century. The main structure dates from the seventeenth century, when it was rebuilt.

Our visit was conducted through the gloom of dusty passages, half lit by dim electric bulbs. I felt that though the Potala had indeed been lucky to survive the troubles in Tibet, it was no less lucky to have survived its wiring. The electricity system is a maze of exposed cables and frayed insulation all coated with a layer of dust and grease. Some rather hesitant fire extinguishers lurk in the corners, but if the Potala was to catch fire it would go up in flames like a torch.

We left for Xigaze in the icy dawn of the end of winter. The weather was fine but bitterly cold with night temperatures falling to -12°C (10°F). First we crossed the Tsang Po River and drove up to the Khamba La, a 4800-m (15,750-ft) pass above a magnificent frozen turquoise lake, heading for high mountains and the Kharo La at more than 5200m (17,000ft). We were following, albeit backwards, the road of Younghusband and the invading British 78 years earlier. The Kharo La has the dubious distinction of marking the site of the highest battle ever fought by British troops: a lonely defile flanked by glaciers where hundreds of Tibetans died for four deaths on the invading side.

We drove on, past Gyantse, scene of another British engagement, to a rest house at Xigaze, Tibet's second city, the see of the reincarnate Panchen Lama. It has one of Tibet's most famous monasteries, the Tashilumpo, founded in 1445. This survives, partially rebuilt. Chris and I slipped out of the rest house next morning and walked over to the monastery. We clambered on to the wall of the Tashilumpo like naughty

schoolboys, helped up there by a passing Tibetan, to photograph the golden roofs and the fine long shadows of the early morning. We later paid a more formal visit with a Chinese guide who told us that there were now 6000 monks in residence and that children were, once again, being recruited: we saw several boys, their heads shaven, in monk's robes. There were many pilgrims in the courtyard and once again the fervent activity of worship.

The road to Xegur, the last town on our journey, was memorable only for its monotony, relieved and enlightened by the Sajia Monastery. Sajia, off the main Xegur-Xigaze highway some 400km (250 miles) from Lhasa, was once one of the largest monasteries in Tibet, on the main yak route south. Once there were two monasteries, north and south. Huge and monolithic, the southern shrine survives today, an example of ecclesiastical architecture with a military purpose. After a picnic lunch we entered the inner courtyard through a two-storey portico. Two 6-m (20-ft) grotesque figures faced each other across the entrance – a black demon on the left, a red dragon opposite – beckoning us into the main shrine. Inside, 20 huge tree trunks (in this treeless land) supported the roof and beneath, on low carpeted benches, was seating for 400 monks. Frescoes nearly 12m (40ft) high stretched from floor to ceiling, some from the Yuang Dynasty (fourteenth century). Seven golden Buddhas formed the centrepiece of the shrine, surrounded by hundreds, if not thousands, of vases, presents from China long ago. There is also a fine library housing several thousand books, mostly printed from blocks on hand-pressed paper, but others handwritten and illuminated with gold on thin slivers of wood. Much of the southern monastery has been finely restored (or possibly never damaged). Not so the northern shrine. Now totally destroyed, a photograph taken 50 years ago showed that the structure rose in tiers up the hillside, housing 6000 monks. Nothing remains except here and there a patch of wall with the outline of a battered fresco. We were perhaps moved more by this destruction and pillage than by the splendour of the southern buildings.

Xegur Dzong had once been one of the most spectacular *dzongs* (forts) of Central Asia, a military city clinging to a steep hillside. It is now a small administrative centre with only the walls of the *dzong* remaining. We stayed here two days, still acclimatizing at around 4000m (13,000ft), before starting the final lift to Rongbuk at 5200m (17,000ft).

On 16 March we were up before dawn; blowtorches trained on the trucks' engines, lighting the barracks with spurts of flame in the bitter cold. The engines, as if to surprise us all, did not explode but burst into life and purred, howled or spluttered through the day. We were off, huddled in duvets, masks and boots, most of us in an open truck, which included a party of ten trekkers from our sponsors, Jardine Matheson, with Joe filming out in the front of the jeep. The road to Rongbuk soon left the Friendship Highway from Lhasa–Xigaze–Xegur to Nepal, turned left and headed over a 5000-m (16,400-ft) pass. Here we had our first view of the main Himalayan chain, Makalu, Lhotse, Everest, Nuptse, Gyachung Kang and Cho Oyu.

We stopped to photograph them all. David Newbigging, Jardine's Chairman, who was with the trekking party, asked Peter and Chris to identify the peaks and looked a little uncertain as there was disagreement about which was Everest: 'Well, you should know if anyone does'.

The track climbs gently into the Rongbuk Valley, easier and safer than many Himalayan hill roads. It was late afternoon and the weather cloudy as we entered the wide stony floor below the ruined Rongbuk Monastery. Suddenly, it was there, the massive, sombre pyramid of the North Face of Everest, being the only great peak in view, filling the head of the valley 16km (10 miles) away and 4000m (13,000ft) above us. We had seen photographs, paintings, sketches and even models of the North Face and perhaps we did not have the thrill of Bullock and Mallory's first glimpse in 1921, but here, on a windy afternoon in southern Tibet, we were fulfilling a dream, to visit the northern side of this, the highest mountain. It looked very, very cold.

An hour later, having cut a track through two iced rivers with the help of some local Tibetans (they did it, we watched), and having passed the ruins of Rongbuk, we arrived at a stony plain which was to be our Base Camp at 5200m (17,000ft). It was nearly dark, snowing and the wind howled. We had arrived.

The first night at Base Camp was miserable. Food was long in coming and meagre when it arrived. We were camping on what resembled the outskirts of a municipal rubbish dump and some Tibetan boys who had helped us along the road proved

light fingered in the face of our array of wealth. Mr Chen firmly and sensibly told them off but didn't overdo it. The trekkers had four days to explore with us while we acclimatized and placed a camp on the East Rongbuk Glacier between the prewar expeditions' Camps 1 and 2. So we called it Camp 1½ – (5650m/18,540ft). When the trekkers left we found we had new company, an American North Face expedition led by Lou Whittaker and Jim Wickwire. They were sponsored and accompanied by a brace of wealthy compatriots, Dick Bass and Frank Wells, who were using the trip as a training exercise for a larger project, to be the first men to climb the highest peak in each continent.

Our own plan was simple but we could not carry it out alone: to establish an Advanced Base at about 6500m (21,300ft) on the upper moraines of the East Rongbuk Glacier we needed yaks. We planned to make three ferries, which with the three-day journey up, descent, rest days and bad weather, would take all of a month. Adrian Gordon and I were to organize this while the climbers were to push along the North East Ridge. We sat in the mess tent with Mr Chen and our interpreter, Mr Yu, to have the first of many meetings, each of which had an unhurried formality commencing with tea, biscuits and cigarettes. I liked Mr Chen from the start. In his late forties, with a frostbitten face, efficient, quiet, sensible and determined, he was a man whose attitude to our problems, which were legion, was to solve them rather than to ask

Left: *Pete and Dick at Base Camp plan our route up the North East Ridge.*
Above: *The view of the north side of Everest from Base Camp. The Lho La, leading across to Nepal, is on the right, with the Hornbein Couloir centre right and the Great Couloir centre left. This was the line attempted by the American expedition which arrived shortly after we did.*

us to change our minds. Unexpected changes of plan, although part of any expedition, are anathema to the Chinese and it amused me on many occasions to see his look of resigned anguish as he wrote out methodically in a small notebook the third or fourth alteration to a particular phase of the expedition. Mr Chen also knew his ground in the hills; he had been on the mountain twice and had travelled widely in the Everest region.

The yaks were due on 29 March. In the intervening days we needed to reconnoitre the route to Advanced Base and to become more acclimatized. We left on the 25th as Peter recorded:

THURSDAY 25 MARCH: Base Camp to Camp 1½
We're not ones to rush off in the mornings, despite a faintly big plan. Charlie kindly has sorted out the food. Choosing tent partners – a vegetarian, a snorer

*Our support team of Charlie
Clarke and Adrian Gordon
were in charge of organizing
yaks to ferry our gear from
Base to Advanced Base at
6500m (21,300ft) on the
East Rongbuk Glacier.*

or someone who won't make breakfast? Eventually chose Joe – Dick and Chris
need to get to know each other.

FRIDAY 26 MARCH: To PreWar Camp 2, 6000m (19,700ft)

Our camp is the other side of the Changtse Glacier, wherever that is. Guess how
we're finding the way up here? We're following telephone lines! – Chinese, perhaps French, perhaps Japanese, lying on the ground, occasionally twisted by the
wind around ice cliffs and moraines. This moraine now a broad highway. Find a
lot of stuff – the French must have stopped here and we want to also, since we
are tired. Still snowing lightly. Camp beside a tower of ice like Froggatt
Pinnacle. Feeling the altitude and not feeling very hungry and tonight it's
intensely cold despite wearing all my clothes. Cold, starry and still.

SATURDAY 27 MARCH: PreWar Camp 2 to PreWar Camp 3 (Our Advanced
Base and back)

Find a good spot from where we can contour to the Raphu La. Here we hope
will be our Advanced Base. It seems at the moment the highest, bleakest, most
windswept place on earth. I don't think this is going to be the most comfortable
Advanced Base but at least it's high up. We'll have to wear crampons just to
walk across to the Raphu La, the ground's so icy! A few prewar tins here (the
French camped higher up). But the ridge continues to make a great line…
Decided not to have a brew up here – we scuttle off back down to Camp 2, it
only takes one and a half hours. Chris has his little tape recorder for the BBC
programme and asks for a few comments! He lingers behind to record his own
thoughts in whispered ecclesiastical tones. Back at the camp ahead of Chris we

chat briefly. 'There's no one else like him,' says Dick, 'he's unique – always doing something, even if its projecting plans on the route or writing his diary.'

At Base Camp the yaks had not yet arrived: it was nobody's fault for things move slowly in Tibet.

On 31 March I strolled down the valley with Chris for half an hour to the Rongbuk Nunnery. Perched on the tongue of a huge landslide, its 50 or so dwellings were in ruins, destroyed by man, not rockfalls. A few walls remained with flecks of fresco, but hidden away there was a tiny shrine.

A wooden trap in a sandy floor led in the darkness down a flimsy ladder. With a headlamp, a simple clay Buddha peered at us through the gloom. Around were some cast figures, old prayer flags, coins and carved slates. A butter lamp was still warm, the low vault smoky. This shrine, easily concealed in a cellar, had escaped destruction and was still in use. Chris and I looked down towards the Rongbuk Monastery a mile or so away and decided to go a little further. Within a few minutes we met 13 yaks and five yak herders camped by the stream. They greeted us with smiles, some with the old Tibetan custom of gently pushing forwards their tongues

*Our yak herders looked after their animals carefully, constantly checking to see if they were lame and here making tsampa cakes to supplement their diet. The yaks were part of their family and Charlie and Adrian were adopted too.*

through an open mouth rather than sticking them out like rude children. These were our men and they would meet us next day at Base Camp.

Dusk was approaching so we turned and walked home, more tired than we expected. Chris was relaxed, happy with the team but keen to get moving. We both felt that this expedition, although it might have hidden dangers, contained no personalities in which there lay the seeds of discontent. We knew each other well, knew of our weaknesses, could sniff the signs of irritation or the wish to be alone. There was a fraternal atmosphere, by no means always one of agreement, but one of intuitive understanding. There was much laughter too.

We left in the early afternoon of 2 April for the prewar Camp 1, tucked round the corner at the end of the East Rongbuk Valley. Travelling together seemed a new experience. Joe filmed the yaks on a steep corner, which turns into the East Rongbuk, causing a minor stampede. Peter carried the huge cine tripod and Chris helped with a load of films. An easy walk to the mess of the old French camp site. Peter sat in silent fury with an ice hammer flattening over 200 empty Camping Gaz canisters, the manufacturer's label advertising in vain 'Leave No Litter' in three languages. We sat, cooked and read a while in the heavy military mess tent that was to be home at Advanced Base. We were impressed by our yak herders, a gentle lot who looked after their animals well.

This was my first journey along the Rongbuk moraines to Advanced Base at 6400m (20,100ft). There can be no easier route to this altitude on a great mountain, a

gentle walk along moraine, rather monotonous and, apart from a short Rockfall Alley, entirely safe. Above, to the right, towers the wall of Changtse (7553m/ 24,780ft), a peak opposite the North Face of Everest, rising from the North Col. The northern skyline is of lower peaks, many of them easy and climbed on prewar trips, including Kellas's Peak and Kartaphu. The North East Face of Everest with its crest, the ridge, towered like a huge sail furrowed by couloirs of green ice. The scale had been hard to comprehend from photographs, for this was a country of giant features with ourselves like Lilliputians beneath it. It was about two miles from the Raphu La to the North East Shoulder (8393m/27,536ft) and just under a mile further to the

*The North East Ridge of Everest. We hoped to follow the skyline all the way to the summit from the bottom left corner of the picture. The North Col, on the right, would provide an easier descent. Our Advanced Base is among the rocks, bottom right.*

summit – great distances at these extreme altitudes. We could see the crest almost in its entirety, beginning as snow and looking easy up to 7300m (24,000ft). There were then two steep sections, rock buttresses which looked harder – we thought the Chinese had stopped at the first of these in 1964. Thereafter, 2000m (6,600ft) above us, was a series of jagged pinnacles, rock on the north-eastern side capped by a crest of snow, the corniced head wall of the Kangshung Face of the eastern side of Everest. The Pinnacles looked hard and dangerous.

Adrian and I helped unload the yaks and left for Base Camp. The work had now begun. It was 4 April. Chris takes up the story.

*5 April–28 April 1982*

# Snow Caves

T HE SITE OF ADVANCED BASE was indeed a bleak spot, a tumbled stony moraine at the edge of the glacier. It wasn't a dramatic view. Everest, foreshortened as it was, seemed shapeless and sprawling, hardly the highest mountain in the world, while the peaks on the other side of the glacier, most of them over 7000m (23,000ft), were more like snow-clad hills. It had a polar feel to it and reminded me of pictures I have seen of Antarctic ranges. The weather certainly felt arctic. There was a bitter wind tearing down the glacier and, although it was a bright, sunny day, there was no warmth in the sunlight .

Next day Dick Renshaw and I were keen to reach the Raphu La and investigate the approaches to the North East Ridge. We roped up and put on crampons for the first time on the expedition. I had a feeling of fresh excitement that submerged all my doubts. At 47, was I too old for this? Could I keep up with the other three? Could I reach the summit without using oxygen? But all this rolled away in anticipation of actually setting foot on the North East Ridge. We took with us a few alloy wands to mark the route and started out. We plodded along, breasting a gentle slope that led towards the col. The rocky head of Chomo Lonzo peered over the crest and then, as we reached the col, everything opened out. The slope before us dropped dizzily out of sight. This was no mountain pass and it was hardly surprising that it had never been crossed, for the Kangshung side was steeply glaciated in a series of sérac walls. The Kangshung Glacier itself, 1200m (4000ft) below, was dirty rubble-covered ice seamed with open crevasses.

The peaks on the southern side of the Kangshung Glacier were fiercely dramatic. Chomo Lonzo (7790m/25,558ft) dominated the horizon for it was closer and more rugged than Makalu (8475m/27,805ft), its taller neighbour. Even closer was the shapely summit of Pethangtse (6710m/22,014ft), which led the eye along and up the great eastern ridge of Lhotse (8501m/27,890ft) whose huge and threatening South East Face jutted into wind-driven clouds. But most impressive of all was the back,

*Full of anticipation and feeling well acclimatized, we put on crampons for the first time as we set out on our first recce across the upper East Rongbuk Glacier towards the Raphu La at 6510m (21,358ft).*

'It was a slow painful sequence. It never took less than three hours to make three brews, force down some cereal and perhaps some biscuits and cheese, then crawl out of the warmth of the sleeping bag and grapple with boots and over-boots ready for another day's toil.'

or south-eastern aspect of our ridge which we could just see from the col. The Kangshung Face thrust its way into the cloud base some 1500m (5000ft) above us, in a slope that was crazed with erratic fluting and runnels, sérac walls and naked black rock. The sight was both daunting and immensely exciting. It showed just how serious the North East Ridge was to be, but we hoped to avoid the south-eastern side and follow easier slopes on the north-west.

We set foot for the first time on the North East Ridge that afternoon. From the Raphu La the slope swelled up like the face of a gigantic wave with the occasional cornice breaking at its crest. At first the angle was easy, around 35 degrees, and the snow crisp and hard, giving us a feeling of security as we zigzagged our way across it. I quickly forgot the intimidating aspect of the other side of the ridge in the joy of movement in such superb surroundings. That afternoon we climbed about 200m (650ft), traversing well below the crest to find a spot where we could gain safe access to the slopes leading to it and so find a short cut to the ridge, avoiding the Raphu La.

We had spent a lot of time both back in England and in the early stages of the expedition poring over photographs, discussing tactics. Being a team of four ruled out the use of oxygen as a major part of the plan, for we could never have carried the cylinders, each weighing about 7kg (15lb), up to 7900m (26,000ft) or so. Pete, Joe

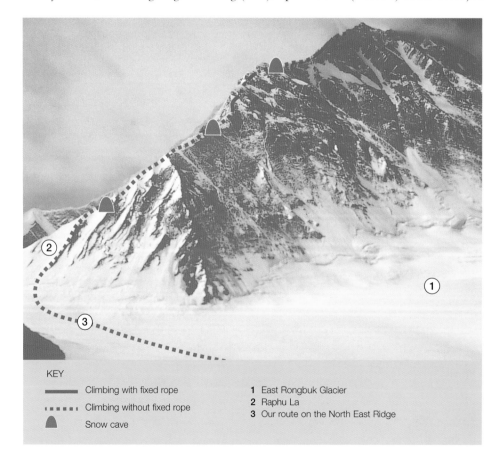

*The North East Ridge of Everest showing our route and the sites of our snow caves.*

KEY

— Climbing with fixed rope

▪▪▪▪▪▪ Climbing without fixed rope

▲ Snow cave

1 East Rongbuk Glacier
2 Raphu La
3 Our route on the North East Ridge

and Dick wanted to climb the mountain without oxygen, though my own attitude was more ambivalent. I wanted to get to the top of Everest and had fairly serious doubts about my ability to do it without the help of oxygen, which was why I had insisted on bringing a stock of cylinders and masks as far as Advanced Base. There was the chance of changing our policy if circumstances suggested it later.

There were two ways we could have tackled the ridge. One was by conventional siege methods with a series of camps linked by fixed ropes until we had a camp close enough to the summit for one or two to make a summit bid. The other way was to climb the mountain alpine-style, which meant packing our rucksacks at the foot of the mountain with about ten days' food, a tent and all the climbing gear and keeping going, camping and bivouacking on the way. Reinhold Messner had used alpine-style tactics in his incredible solo ascent in 1980. He had made a reconnaissance to the North Col but then climbed the mountain in a single push, camping twice on the way up, reaching the summit, getting back to his top camp on the third day and returning to Advanced Base on the fourth. Messner was climbing a known route that was comparatively straightforward. We, however, would be on new ground with the additional problem, which we knew from photographs, that the principal difficulties started at around 7900m (26,000ft) and went on up to 8380m (27,500ft) over a series of pinnacles that barred the way to the upper part of the ridge.

It seemed to make sense to adopt a compromise between the two approaches, establishing a series of camps – we hoped just two – to the foot of the Pinnacles and then to make an alpine-style push from this high base with one or more bivouacs up to the summit. We hoped this would enable us to acclimatize on the route itself, coming down for rests at Base or Advanced Base, until we were ready to make that summit push. We would only be able to use a little fixed rope because of the problems of carrying it, but we were hoping that the lower part of the ridge would be sufficiently straightforward for us to do without this safeguard. In view of the high winds we had already experienced we were hoping to dig snow caves, certainly as far as the Pinnacles – they would be more stable, less noisy and more restful than tents.

So three weeks after reaching Base Camp, rested and acclimatized, we set out over firm crisp snow to establish and stock our first snow cave on the ridge. Digging it out proved much harder than we had anticipated since almost immediately we hit ice. Chipping it away was a laborious process. Only one person at a time could work in the hole and we worked in relays all day. Joe was determined to get everything on film. He crouched outside the hole, asking Pete to shovel the snow straight at him to get a dramatic effect. Pete did so with such energy that the blade of the shovel shot off the end of the handle, hit Joe in the face, nearly knocking him off his precarious footholds and then bounced down the steep slope, coming to rest about 100m (330ft) below. It was characteristic of Pete that with simply a mutter of apology to Joe for nearly decapitating him, he immediately set off to retrieve the shovel, cramponing down steep snow, teetering across some exposed rock and then climbing back up without even pausing to rest.

For two days we divided our labours, two enlarging the cave and exploring the route, two ferrying up loads from Advanced Base.

'You know,' Pete said, 'I really enjoy this business of going up and down the route, slowly getting to know it better. It was like that on Kangch, where we ended up doing the same thing. I find I don't get bored with it. It's getting to know the mountain itself better and better.' I shared his feelings.

Another advantage of a snow hole over tents was that we were always together and could discuss everything. It meant that there was little danger of any kind of schism within the team and that the pairing always remained flexible. There was also an affectionate badinage that helped hold us together and defused tension. It was born from previous trips and mutual respect for each other. Our First Snow Cave was a tight squeeze when all four of us were inside in our sleeping bags but there was a feeling of cocoon-like security while the wind raged unheard outside.

Next morning Pete led off and belayed on an ice axe. 'Chris follows very slowly and so I offer to do the leading so that he can recover in between rope-lengths. Eventually we reach the little rocky ridge running up to Point 7090m (23,260ft) but Chris is depressed at how slow he is going. "I'll do all I can to support you on this climb but..." and I tell him to shut up – we've a long campaign ahead with plenty of time for all of us to fade and recover. He gets a burst of energy and it is all I can do to keep up with him to Point 7090.'

Once on the crest of the ridge it was easy walking, crampons crunching into firm snow, but the very ease of it made the altitude all the more noticeable; we were now over 7100m (23,300ft). I set myself a steady rhythm of 50 steps and then a rest, found

*Calling Advanced Base on the radio outside the First Snow Cave at 6850m (22,475ft). The wind was so high, we found snow caves both safer and more comfortable than tents.*

Overleaf: *Dick, Pete and Joe heading up the ridge towards our Second Snow Cave which was sited at 7256m (23,806ft), just short of where the ridge steepens*

I was able to keep ahead of the others and was childishly pleased about it. I reached Joe and Dick's previous high point where there was a little pile of rope tucked into a hollow in the snow, added some of my load and continued up the slope. By this time the cloud had closed in and the wind was gusting fiercely.

We were now heading for what looked like the first real difficulties on the climb, a steep step in the ridge, and we wanted to get our next snow hole as close as possible to it. We also had to find a bank of snow sufficiently deep in which to dig a cave. We found what we hoped would be a suitable spot in a slight dip in the ridge, dumped the ropes we had carried up and started back down. It had taken us five and a half hours to reach this point. That night I could manage to eat hardly anything. It was Pete's turn to cook and he had made chilli con carne from a freeze-dried packet, spiced up with extra chilli powder and garlic. Normally it was the tastiest of all the freeze-dried food but that night neither of us could force down more than a few mouthfuls. Were we building up a resistance to the uniform bland flavour of freeze-dried food or was it simply the altitude? Whichever it was, we were only absorbing a few hundred calories each day yet were expending several thousand. Fatigue was beginning to set in and it was Joe who suggested that we should carry only light loads up to our high point until we had finished the snow cave.

We had returned unroped the previous day, so now set out independently, each at his own pace, without the worry of delaying one's partner. Dick was away first and I quickly dropped behind, needing many more rests than the previous day, plodding up in a misery of effort. Were the others feeling the same strain? Joe had a racking cough and was sometimes coughing up blood. But he also had that hard, self-contained sense of discipline and never complained. Perhaps he was feeling just as bad as I but had a greater tolerance to suffering and pushed himself, on where I sank into the snow for a rest. Pete, who appeared to have an inexhaustible strength, plodded up the ridge with what to me seemed an effortless ease, and yet he also had his doubts: 'A dullness seems to come over me at altitude. It is so difficult to think about the past or about any aspects of life – beyond the summit, staying alive, little hypochondrias. However much I look around and try to absorb and wonder, try to keep my eyes open, the thought, How much of this climb have we yet to do; will I be able to match up to it? threatens to overwhelm me all the time.'

Pete and Dick arrived first at the site of the Second Snow Cave and probed the hard snow with a ski stick to find a suitable spot. By the time I arrived there half an hour later there was a hole deep enough to crawl into and a cascade of dirty snow, with lumps of ice and grit, being thrown out between Dick's legs. He was like a terrier down a rabbit hole. By mid-afternoon there was just room for two people to work inside.

Pete commented: 'It's cold and bleak and windy outside; Dick's first to voice the obvious fact that there's not enough work for four at a time up here. I suggest that Dick and I stay, but Joe says: "Why you?" Chris sets off down alone; I do a bit of digging but Joe and Dick say I should follow him – "You know what his route-finding

is like." I did promise Wendy I would look after him, and so I rush off down and catch him up as he's leaving the rock rib below Point 7090 and take over the track-finding in the cloud and fresh snowfall. Certainly all the alpine guiding I've done has helped me walk on the snow, without facing inwards with two ice tools all the time, but familiarity with this ground must not breed over relaxation – it's a long bouncy drop down to the glacier.'

*Pete digging out the Second Snow Cave. It was hard slow work since we were cutting our way through ice and rubble and there is always a temptation to stop before it is really big enough.*

That night back in our First Cave, we discussed strategy. I was all for going back down for a rest the next day. Dick, quietly determined, was adamant that we must finish the cave before going down. It made sense and I resigned myself to another day of effort, though that night I could only force down a few mouthfuls of cheesy mashed potato with sweet corn that Pete had prepared.

At least I was bright in the mornings and uncurled myself at about seven when it was still dark, to turn round to get my head at the same end as the entrance. I pushed Pete's slumbering feet up out of the way and shook the pan and stove free from the chill dusting of spindrift that covered everything at the bottom of the snow hole. A struggle with the lighter and soon the stove was melting the snow for the first brew of the morning. It was a slow painful sequence. It never took less than three hours to make three brews, force down some cereal and perhaps some biscuits and cheese, then crawl out of the warmth of the sleeping bag and grapple with boots and overboots ready for another day's toil.

It was a fine windless morning, the best so far, and we got going at half past ten, our earliest so far. I was full of good intentions and away first. I cramponed up the snow just beyond the cave but I had no strength in me and had to use every ounce of will power to make each step. It was not so much a case of breathlessness but rather a heavy lethargy that had taken over my limbs. I confessed my predicament to the others and retreated guiltily. My logic told me that if I were to last the course I would have to nurse myself, yet I hated doing it, hated admitting I no longer had the stamina the others had. That night they rejoined me in the comparative luxury of Advanced Base and the next morning the sun warmed the tent as Charlie and Adrian cosseted us with mugs of tea, while the Second Snow Cave at 7256m (23,806ft) was nearly ready for the next foray.

We were sorry to see Adrian and Charlie leave for Base Camp two days later. It was not just cupboard love. True they looked after us, preparing delicious meals, chiding us for not eating more, collecting ice from the glacier, washing up, but it was their company that was most precious. I could not help thinking of what it must have been like for Pete and Joe on Changabang in 1976, for they had been on their own for three months while climbing its West Wall. There had been no respite from each other's company and the fact that they had come through this had given their relationship a particular strength, though they often bickered with each other like an old married couple. There was a strong element of competition in their relationship, and this was perhaps getting stronger as they expanded their ambitions and talents in writing. Each wanted to write the book describing this expedition.

Dick's relationship with Pete and Joe was slightly different. There was no question of competition, for Dick's ambitions seemed entirely within himself, as a test or perhaps a quest to discover what he could achieve for his own fulfilment. He did not, as they did, need to communicate his experience to a wider audience.

The three rest days went all too quickly. We often gazed up at the ramparts of the North East Ridge, focusing on the two buttresses immediately above the Second Snow Cave. These looked as if they would present the first serious difficulties of the climb. Through the telescope we could see what appeared to be a steep snow gully going through the First Buttress, but the Second Buttress seemed to present a rocky barrier stretching across the full extent of the ridge. We hoped not only to climb the two steps but also to establish a third snow cave on the conspicuous shoulder just below the Pinnacles, which we thought would be the crux of the climb.

On 18 April we were able to install ourselves quickly at the First Snow Cave and settle back into the routine of high-mountain living and load ferrying to the Second Snow Cave. There is always a tendency to declare a snow cave large enough when it barely is and this occasion was no exception. We were tired and cold and longed to creep into our warm sleeping bags. The prized position in any snow cave is obviously as far as possible from the entrance. Not only is this the warmest spot but it also means that no one crawls over you. I suggested that we drew lots, but Dick, with typical selflessness, volunteered to take the uncomfortable door position. I'm afraid the rest of us took no persuading. Joe, still cooking with Dick, was next in line, then me, and Pete was on the inside since it was his turn to cook for us.

One night was enough to tell us that the Second Snow Cave certainly needed more work and that one pair should remain to do this while the other attempted the First Buttress.

'Do you agree with that, Joe?' asked Pete.

'Yeah, but I'm not sure about drawing straws. I think the people who are better at doing snow caves should do the snow caves.'

'I'm inclined to agree to that,' I interjected.

'I'm not saying this because I think I'm better at snow caves, I'd just as soon go on the hill.'

'I know I'm not very practical,' I observed. 'I'm not very good at that sort of thing. Dick's very good at sorting out snow caves because he's practical. I would say, as a suggestion, Dick and Joe are both rather good at it. Pete's very good at charging over the hills and I'm a kind of dead weight to hold him back.'

'Don't you agree, Pete?' checked Joe.

'Yes.'

'I mean, would you prefer to stay here or…'

'No. I'll go with the flow. I'm just feeling guilty that I had such a comfortable night over here.'

And so it was decided. Pete and I were to push the route out, while Joe and Dick improved the snow cave. This was how most of our decision-making took place and it worked well. It was exciting to venture on to new ground next morning and I found the fatigue that had almost overwhelmed me the previous day vanish with the prospect of some real climbing. As always, the distance to the foot of the First Buttress was much farther than we had anticipated. It was up a gentle wave of snow and we did not bother putting on the rope. I was even able to keep ahead of Pete as we plodded over the crisp surface towards a rocky prow that barred our way on the crest of the ridge. A traverse over easy-angled slabby rock led towards a snowfield, which, in turn, led up to the gully, which we hoped would take us through the Buttress at about 7300m (24,000ft). Looked at head-on it seemed very steep.

We continued to climb solo up increasingly steep snow-ice to a small, rocky island. It was time to rope-up but the rock was very compact and there were no cracks for pitons. I ended up putting a deadman snow anchor into the snow just above the island, and Pete started to front point up towards the rocks above. It was a lovely cold, clear day, and I had time to gaze around me. The North Col was far below, the summit of Changtse seemed almost level with us, and we could see over the peaks guarding Everest to the north and east, to the rolling purple hills of the Tibetan plateau, broken by the occasional white cap of some distant snow peak.

Pete's progress was slow. All movement is at that altitude. On reaching the rocks he probed around trying to find a suitable crack for a piton and eventually found one. He then led on the up side of the rocks until the rope had nearly run out. I followed, using my Petzel ascendeur for security. My turn to lead. Once in it, the gully did not seem quite as steep as it had done from below; the average angle was probably around 60 degrees, but there were bulges that were considerably steeper.

My progress was slow, too, but the climbing was enthralling. Fatigue was banished not just by the risk of falling but also by the fascination of breaking new ground, of working out a route, of assessing the security of the deep-packed snow. It took me over an hour to run out 50m (164ft) of rope. To Pete the time crawled, but for me it raced by. I had nearly reached the end, was halfway up the gully and could see a sloping rock ledge to one side of it with some hairline cracks running into it. Just enough for a knife-blade piton. I tapped one in and wondered whether it would hold Pete when he came up. He reached me and led on up the gully. The angle began to relent and he climbed out of sight. Another long pause, a distant hammering and it was my turn to move once more. Pete had gained the top of the First Buttress and had hammered an angle piton as an anchor into a crack beneath a huge boulder just below the crest of the ridge. We crouched in the shelter of the rock and nibbled some chocolate before pulling out on to the ridge itself.

*Climbing the Buttress above the Second Snow Cave. It was steep, slow but enthralling work, involving some real climbing, and this was one of the few places where we fixed some rope.*

Broken rock and ribbons of snow led across towards the Second Buttress. It would have been good to look over the other side of the ridge to the east, but it was now getting late and we were tired. We cached the remaining rope under a rock and started back down. It had been an immensely satisfying day with some real progress to show for it.

Next day, Dick and Joe had found a gangway through the Second Buttress by the time Pete and I caught up with them, but soon it began to snow heavily and it was impossible to pick out the best route to the top of the Shoulder. As usual it was Pete who was keen to push on even so.

'Come on, lads, where's the determination? Really we are going to have to get a grip of this route soon. D-day's not just a build-up on the South Coast, we've got to go on the offensive.'

'That's all very well,' replied Joe, 'but there's a bloody great smoke screen and we can't see where the hell we're going. There's no point pushing on blind.'

Pete comments in his diary: 'The Falkland Islands crisis and all the war books on this expedition, combined with living at close quarters with ex-Sandhurst Chris and ex-Gurkha Adrian, have given a lot of war and battle discussions to this trip – all, it must be said, part of the wide-ranging political conversation.'

But the flurries of snow quickly brought us back to the qualities of the North East Ridge of Everest. As I reached the top of the second fixed rope, they were already returning and by the time I had dumped my load they had vanished in the enveloping snow. There were no tracks, just the glimpse of a flag, which marked the high point of the previous day. The sensation was strange; I could have been coming down Striding Edge in a Lakeland blizzard. There was no point of reference except my own exhaustion, a leaden lethargy that made each physical effort supremely difficult.

To my surprise, I caught up with the others at the top of the first fixed rope. I came upon them suddenly, as I rounded the huge boulder to which the rope was anchored. There was a sense of alarm among them for Pete had just had a narrow escape. He had arrived first and had clipped a karabiner and piton brake on to the fixed rope. He was about to lean back to start the abseil, and had just grasped the rope, when the piton anchoring it pulled out in his hands. Had this happened when he had his full weight on it he would almost certainly have fallen backwards and off the end of the rope to his death. This time we had been very lucky. By the time I joined the others they had put in two deadmen snow anchors and Pete was again ready to descend. At the end of the fixed rope we had to traverse the slabby rocks, now covered in a layer of treacherous snow. Pete, perhaps shaken by what had happened, suggested we needed a fixed rope here but there was none available so Joe simply walked across. Pete followed with uncharacteristic caution, slipping and fumbling. He shouted at Joe heatedly and they had a short slanging match, which seemed to release some of the tension.

That night in the Second Cave we were all tired and subdued. The following morning we had a discussion about what we should do next which verged on the acrimonious. Even Pete wanted a day off since he and I had now been on the go for five days without a rest. We eventually decided to go down for a good rest at Base Camp and then follow my plan on our return, to carry a tent up to the Shoulder at 7850m (25,750ft) and for two of us to sleep up there and dig the third snow cave.

It was a brilliant sunny morning at Advanced Base on 24 April, but the entire mountain was plastered with a fresh fall of snow and we all felt we had made the right decision in coming down. There was a holiday atmosphere as we sorted out our gear and packed light sacks with exposed film to take back down to Base and the luxury of cans of Budweiser brought in from Lhasa and tiny new potatoes boiled in their jackets.

Halfway through the afternoon there was a roar of a truck and the sound of American voices. We knew that the American Everest team were all up on the Rongbuk Glacier. Could these be trekkers? But it was Jim Bridwell, a legendary figure, with many new routes on Yosemite to his credit as well as, more recently, some in Alaska and Patagonia. Jim was part of a small expedition whose object was to ski around Everest. Leader and creator of the project was Ned Gillette, a well-known cross-country skier who had been in the American Olympic team and had written one of the best handbooks on the sport before branching into expeditions. Ned was in constant consultation with their liaison officer, juggling plans and possibilities in an effort to fix their trip from the Lho La, back down the West Rongbuk Glacier, up the East Rongbuk, over the Lhakpa La, which Mallory had crossed 60 years before and then into the Kangshung Valley by the Karpo La. It sounded an interesting trip, during which they would cover much exciting ground. In some ways I envied them, for they were doing something that was well within their powers, yet both Ned and Jim envied us and were already talking of plans to go to Everest, such is the lure of the highest point on earth. We spent the days relaxing at camp, sleeping much and eating well but also wondering about the immediate future. Pete wrote in his diary:

> This mountain is so big, our project so vast, so long, that all our energies are consumed by it and have to be directed towards it. Even Chris has little left over for other things. I find books difficult to read, when on other trips I have always found reading to be a useful distraction. It is even difficult to concentrate on photography, as if it is an energy drain. And now other Everest books, other people's experiences on Everest – their dates, their efforts, their carries have a dwindling relevance as we build up our own experience of the mountain and the pattern of our own attempt becomes increasingly defined.
> I learned a lot on K2 in 1980. Before that I believed nothing could resist if I tried hard enough; but I do want so much to succeed this time… We are a great compact little team, hardly a cross word ever between us. In a way, we all respect, sort of love each other, for we know that when the crunch comes each of us will do the right thing.

While Pete wrote, Dick worked on the swan he was carving. He had brought the mahogany with him and was slowly, patiently chiselling out its gently curved neck Joe either slept through the day or worked on the notes of his film, and I just slept and slept.

The next three days slipped away agreeably. We even had a picnic at the site of the old British Base Camp. A picnic was something our Chinese staff found difficult to understand, it being altogether too frivolous. Lying in the sun, the ubiquitous tape deck rolling, nibbling salami and Stilton, swilling red wine, it was easy to forget, at least for a time, the presence of Everest towering there at the head of the valley. It was concealed by the low moraine ridge on which had stood the memorial to Mallory and Irvine. 'Pass those nuts over, please.'

'More pâté?'

'Want some more wine?'

'I'll borrow *Flesh Wounds* when you've finished it, if I may.'

Charlie flew his kite with the exuberance of a child. A lammergeier circled overhead.

# The Third Foray

T HE HOLIDAYS WERE OVER. On 29 April Pete, plugged into his cassette, was away first. Charlie and Adrian were going to accompany us as far as the foot of the ridge, carrying the big 16mm cine camera so that Joe could get some good close-up shots. It was typical of the thought and work he put into the filming. He had already spent some time with Charlie and Adrian, briefing them both on the working of the camera and also on basic film techniques.

It was a savage return to the mountain. The wind blasted across the Raphu La, sweeping the fresh snow from the ridge and giving us perfect conditions for cramponing, but it was so strong that in the worst gusts we had to stop, crouched, clinging to our ice axes. I could not help feeling discouraged, for I seemed to have gained no benefit at all from our rest. Although I had doubts about my own ability to get to the top, I never had any about the others. I was convinced we had a good chance of success. On my good days I dreamed of getting there myself and on the bad ones wondered at what stage I might have to drop back to a purely supporting role.

The following day, 1 May, was an easy one. It took barely two and a half hours to reach the Second Snow Cave. We had settled on my proposal to move one pair straight up to the top of the Shoulder at 7850m (25,750ft), and for them to camp if necessary while they dug the cave. We sorted out five days' food and fuel, leaving behind much of the freeze-dried meat, which we all found unpalatable. Our standard diet had become a handful of muesli in the morning and cheesy mashed potato at night. We divided the food into two poly bags for Joe and me to carry the next day.

In the morning I got away first as usual. Pete caught up with me at the top of the First Buttress and he and Dick moved steadily together towards the second length of fixed rope. Joe had been filming, but he also passed me. I was determined not to let them get too far ahead, and stayed doggedly behind him.

*The tent Pete and Dick erected on the snow shoulder before digging the Third Snow Cave. They had an appalling night in it, battered by the wind.*

'The sun had a real warmth and everywhere we could hear the sound of running water. The summer had arrived and conditions seemed perfect but had we the strength to return, to climb the Pinnacles and then go for the summit?'

By this time the afternoon cloud had rolled in, filling the great bowl of the Kangshung Face and overflowing on to our side of the ridge in breakers that enveloped us and then dissipated in the tearing wind. It was like the incoming tide, getting imperceptibly deeper until each one of us was enclosed in a world of driving snow. Pete had disappeared from sight around a corner. Joe and Dick were just ahead, Dick having difficulty on a steep little overlapping wall that barred the way. To avoid it, I took a slightly higher line and as a result overtook him. The steps made by Pete and Joe were vanishing under the fresh snow as Dick and I stumbled up over snow-covered rocks probing our way through the mist. Out in front, Pete was thrusting forwards on to new ground:

> At last I can see round the corner, into the col, the rest of the ridge looming through the clouds towards the Pinnacles and what now appears as a promi-nent inset gully, plunging down towards the glacier... No, it's steep round the corner, and I climb straight up. There is no way we can avoid going round the top of this summit. Also there is the spur running up from the Kangshung side. It gives us our only hope for a snow cave. We can't afford to pour all that effort we did last time into hacking a cave out of ice and rock.
>
> Joe arrives. I uncoil a rope and he belays me as I peer over the east side. By a stroke of luck I find the top of the spur coming up the other side, although there is no indication along the edge to tell me where it could be. Enthused, I kick down it. Below the slope goes down quite steeply and then broadens into a shoulder. I get the shovel and dig a bit, yelling back up that it should be fan-tastic for snow caving.

I reached the top of the Shoulder at 7850m (25,750ft), dumped my bag full of food and Gaz cylinders, and peered over the edge to see Pete's boots sticking out of the slope. He had burrowed the entrance passage to the cave. I wished him the best of luck and started back down, to pass Dick a short way below the crest.

Dick complained, 'I don't know what happened on the way up; I just ran out of steam above the top of the Buttresses.'

He started to dig, but became worried by the proximity of the cornice and per-suaded Pete to have a careful look. They decided to abandon excavation for the night and pitch a tent on top of the Shoulder.

While Pete and Dick were getting installed for the night, Joe and I had dropped back to the Second Snow Cave. After a good night's sleep in our now roomy cave, my resolve returned, and I was the first away, carrying my personal gear and a few items of climbing equipment that were still to go up. Joe soon caught up with me and, on the slopes above the Second Buttress, he chose a slightly different route from mine and began to pull away. Soon my progress had slowed to a crawl but at last I reached the crest and flopped down for a rest. Gradually it pervaded my conscious-ness that someone was below me and I glanced back to see Joe coming up behind. He had reached the top about an hour before and, realizing that I was having a struggle, had decided to come back to help me with my rucksack on the final stretch. Unfortunately, because of the slight difference in our routes, he'd missed me. It was too late to let him carry my sack but I felt immensely touched by his kindness. Going back to help someone at that altitude shows a very real concern. We plodded slowly those last few metres up over the rounded snow dome and there below us on the other side of the ridge was a ledge carved out of the snow and the gaping hole dug by Dick and Pete during the day. It was a superb snow cave. The snow was just the right consistency, firm but not too hard. The chamber had an alcove at either end for the cooking stove; it was easy to scoop out snow for making our brews and, being on the lee side of the ridge, was sheltered from spindrift.

We discussed what to do next day and decided that Dick should drop back down to the top of the Second Buttress where we had left some ropes, bring them back up and then enlarge the hole, while the three of us should go to the foot of the Pinnacles and start climbing them.

Next morning dawned fine. The Kangshung Face dropped beneath us in a huge concave bowl. We could see the South Col on the other side of the summit at about the same height as ourselves. From there it was a mere five or six hours to the summit. We, on the other hand, were about 3km (2 miles) from the summit with the jagged Pinnacles between us and the comparatively easy ground of the upper part of the ridge. We could now see the top clearly but this seemed remote, dwarfed by the immediate threat of the Pinnacles. The ridge curved gently and easily to the foot of the first one, a triangle of snow-veined rock, leading to a shapely point. Pete was obviously raring to get at the Pinnacle, so Joe and I tossed for who should hold his rope. I won and Joe set off back to the cave to get a brew on.

Pete started up the bottom snow slope of the Pinnacle. This led to a rocky buttress, split by a shallow ice groove at about 30m (100ft). He hunted around for a crack in which to hammer in a piton anchor, but they were all blind, so he had no choice but to continue up the groove, bridging out on sloping rock holds on either side, looking constantly for a suitable crack. The time crept by and I stamped and shivered, watching Joe wander back along the ridge. The rope crept out through my fingers. It was nearly at an end. No alternative but to tie on another rope. Had Pete slipped, nothing could have saved him and he'd probably pull me off as well.

A deeper ringing tone echoed down. He had at last got in a decent peg, but he didn't stop there. Obviously it was not a good stance. Another couple of pitons and he reached some broken ledges and hammered in a final anchor. It had taken almost three hours. Cold and shivery, I followed, trying to put as little weight as possible on the rope. It had been a fine lead and one that Pete had enjoyed. As I followed, jumaring up the rope, he carried on, unbelayed but towing a rope behind him. I joined him when he paused. He now moved diagonally over quite easy ground and ran out another 30m (100ft). I set off, hammering in an intermediate anchor to make the rope easier to follow. This at last was real climbing. By the time I reached Pete,

the cloud had closed in and it was beginning to snow but he was determined to reach a little notch in the ridge about 30m (100ft) above.

It was to be the turn of Dick and Joe next morning, while Pete and I took it easy, having a leisured breakfast and then following them with a load of ropes and tents. By the time we had emerged from the snow hole, they were only halfway across the easy stretch leading to the Pinnacles. Fresh snow had fallen during the night but they were also tired and moving slowly. Dick had now been up here at 7850m (25,750ft) for three nights, Joe two. As soon as we set off, Pete pulled ahead, reaching the foot of the Pinnacles by the time I was halfway across, while Dick, followed by Joe, was moving very slowly up the fixed rope. They were going no faster than we had the previous day when we had pushed the route out for the first time. It was the insidious effect of altitude, the gradual slowing up caused by sleeping at nearly 8000m (26,250ft) without any oxygen. Plodding in their wake, I certainly felt it. At last I reached the foot of the Pinnacles but could not face the prospect of that long slow toil up the fixed ropes. Hardly thinking, I dumped the tent and ropes on the boulder at its foot and, racked with guilt, fled back down the ridge. At least I could have a meal ready for them when they returned. The ridge jutted steeply above them, looking threatening, even dangerous. The day had started fine but a scum of high grey cloud now blanked out the sun and the very flatness of the light increased the feeling of threat.

Since Dick was first at the high point, and had therefore had the longest rest, it was his pitch:

I hope that Joe will offer to take this pitch as I've been in front up to now. I can't ask him but I console myself with the fact that the pitch after will be his lead. Personal survival; it's hard to think beyond oneself. This self-absorbed suffering must be a cardinal sin.
I select my gear — we are short of deadmen. Hopefully I take some ice screws. Joe is encouraging and we decide on a system of communication. I set off, wary. The steepness becomes alarming. I thrust in both tools. There's a crusty layer which gives a false sense of security, but soon that disappears and I'm left floundering. The trick is to kick a step that will not collapse into the lower one. I sink both arms deep into the snow; gaining little height but quite a lot of horizontal ground and I'm feeling the lack of protection. It's going to be a monster swing if the snow collapses. I become increasingly aware that I might be on a corniced ridge that could collapse. It's a frightening pitch and I have to fight hard.

But the angle began to relent and the snow became firmer. Dick had run out the full length of rope. By this time Pete had caught up with Joe and from the Shoulder

I could watch their slow progress, three tiny dots clinging to the ridge. Pete wondered: 'The surface crust sounds, and is, hollow and underneath it is deep, collapsing and insubstantial. Why didn't Dick even squeal, "Hey, watch me, Joe, this is really unstable and dangerous"? A very cool lead and I (as Joe did) find even following it up a rope very frightening.'

When Dick reached the end of the rope, he managed to find a placement for a deadman, and called down to Joe: 'It's safe, you can come up now.' He was able to sit down and rest while Joe jumared up the fixed rope. On arrival Joe immediately started to set up the cine camera while Dick sorted out the belay so that he could safeguard Joe for the next rope-length. The angle looked easier and the ridge had broadened, giving the promise of firmer snow. It was while doing this that Dick became aware of a strange sensation of numbness spreading down his left arm and leg. At first he thought it was just the cold, but then his left cheek and even the left side of his tongue became numb. He described his symptoms to Joe and they agreed he should go down once Pete arrived up the rope. By the time he got back to the snow cave he felt perfectly normal, even a little shame-faced at having made a fuss and having come back early.

At the high point Joe, belayed by Pete, had started up the next stretch of the ridge. The snow had now improved and he was able to make steady progress, kicking methodically into the snow just below the crest. Another 50m (164ft) of rope and he slotted in a deadman to bring up Pete. Just two pitches on that day. They were still 60m (200ft) short of the top of the First Pinnacle; they dumped the ropes and the tent Pete had carried up and started down.

Back at the Third Snow Cave, I had started melting snow for brews, when Dick crawled in. Diffidently he described what had happened to him, saying that he felt perfectly all right again. Joe and Pete got back about an hour letter, tired, but elated with the progress they had made. I had started a large panful of cheesy potato, by now the only food we could face. By the time they had brushed the snow from their down suits and boots and had crawled into their sleeping bags it was ready. I lifted it off the stove by its handle to pass it over Joe for Pete to have the first spoonful. As I lifted it above Joe, the handle gave way, and the pan toppled into his sleeping bag, covering it in a yellow goo. Joe, ever self-controlled, said nothing at all, just lay back and left me to spoon up the fast-freezing mess. I scraped it back into the pan and

eventually recovered about a quarter of it, which I reheated, but somehow we had lost our appetites.

That night we did not talk much about plans for the next morning. I think we were all too tired. I had been in favour of going back down for a rest, feeling that we were now exhausting ourselves just getting up to the high point and then, as had happened

*Joe and Dick in the Third Snow Cave the morning after Dick experienced a minor stroke at the top of the First Pinnacle. We were all desperately worried and decided to drop back to Base Camp.*

that day, only pushing out two rope-lengths. But Pete and Dick felt that we must at all costs get the route run out farther along the Pinnacles to be sure of crossing them and making an effective bid for the summit on our return.

It was only next morning, 6 May, we finally came to the decision to descend. I left my sleeping bag, all my spare clothes and some camera equipment in the cave. It was a form of demonstration to myself that I was going to return, that I would not give up, though in the back of my mind there were now some very serious doubts.

The slopes below were covered with nearly half a metre of fresh snow, making the descent slow and insecure. Even so, we climbed unroped, picking a way down slowly. Dick stopped halfway down the long easy slope towards the top of the spur at Point 7090 and I quickly caught him up. His crampon had fallen off and he was struggling to push it back on. I crouched in the snow beside him, tried to give him a hand and, holding the crampon, thrust it up against the sole of his overboot. Dick toppled off balance, grabbed me, and pulled me over as well. We rolled over, did a somersault in the soft snow, both clawing at its surface to stop ourselves. What a stupid lunatic way to go, but we came to a stop, laughing nervously. I apologized for my over-eagerness and Dick, struggling with his crampon without further help from me, eventually jamming it back on his boot. We continued down and plodded back towards Advanced Base.

Joe, dedicated as ever to the film, had told Charlie and Adrian to come out and film our return. Charlie commented in his diary: 'And so they're back, shortly after six p.m., captured on celluloid by Adrian and me as budding cameramen. Oh, they came up that slope so slowly. At first we thought something had happened to them because we could see their tracks coming down from the Raphu La into a piece of dead ground and then we waited and waited and waited. The answer was quite clear; they were exhausted and crept in like old men, but rallied a bit, like soldiers, for the last few metres to Advanced Base – which is exactly what we don't want on the film!'

We all had sore throats and that night Charlie made for us his own brand of inhaler, bashing a hole in the lid of a mess tin and pushing through it a length of rubber tubing so that we could breathe in the steam from a brew of honey, lemon and whisky. We looked like a group of opium smokers crouched round the stone table in the middle of the mess tent, as we coughed and hawked and spoke of our adventures of the previous days.

*Back at Advanced Base, Charlie had devised a makeshift inhaler to relieve our painfully sore throats.*

On the way down to Base Camp next day Charlie told me that he was sure that Dick had had a stroke and that it was unlikely he would be able to go back to the ridge. And what about me, I wondered? Had I the strength to make it to the summit? Could I keep up with Pete and Joe?

The sun had a real warmth and everywhere we could hear the sound of running

'You've no bloody idea how much I've been pushing myself… I've never pushed myself

water. The summer had arrived and conditions seemed perfect but had we the strength to return, to climb the Pinnacles and then go for the summit?

As I walked slowly into Base Camp, our Chinese staff came out to greet me, shaking me warmly by the hand. Joe and Pete were in the base tent, reading their mail. For a few moments Everest was forgotten as I skimmed through my letters, digging out first the ones from Wendy so that I could transport myself back to our Lakeland home and fells, then letters from the children and from friends. There were cans of beer, a thermos full of hot water for tea and a bowl full of delicious new potatoes.

Charlie was with Dick, examining him. We were subdued in spite of our pleasure at being back in the comparative warmth and luxury of Base. We were all waiting for Charlie's verdict but instinctively avoided talking about it. The atmosphere was charged with foreboding, but I did not want to rush into any rash decisions which we might regret later, and therefore suggested that we waited till the morning before we discussed anything.

Charlie completed the examination of Dick in his tent, told him that he had had a mild stroke and that he would have to consider seriously whether or not he should return to altitude. Dick did not sleep much that night as he tried to determine what he should do. He had felt wonderfully fit on the way down from Advanced Base. He seemed to have absolute confidence in his own and the team's ability to complete the climb and passionately wanted to be part of this. Charlie had very little sleep that night either, for he was worried that he had not spelt out sufficiently clearly the seriousness of what had happened to Dick. He was up early the following morning and went over to Dick's tent.

'I've been thinking it over, Dick. I'm afraid I've got to tell you not to go back up again. You've got to think of what would happen if you did have another stroke. If you were paralysed, it wouldn't just be your life at risk, it'd be the others as well, because they'd have to get you down. I'm sorry.'

'How likely is it to happen again?'

'It's difficult to say. But it is a distinct possibility. I don't think it's a risk you're justified in taking, if only for the sake of the others.'

Dick was silent for a long time. There were so many implications. Would he ever be able to return to the high peaks of the Himalaya? How could he adjust to a life without mountaineering? He then agreed with Charlie that this was the only possible course. Charlie suggested to Dick that it might be easier for him if he went for a walk after breakfast while the rest of us were told. Charlie's voice slipped into that unemotional, slightly clinical tone of all doctors as he explained the position.

so hard, never felt so out of control. I know my own limits and I've reached them'

'I'm afraid I've got yet another bombshell,' I told them. 'I've been thinking about it ever since we got back down to Base Camp and, the more I go into it, the more I realize I just can't keep up with Joe and Pete. Quite honesty I'm not at all sure I could even get back up to our high point.' I went on to suggest that Charlie, Adrian and I could usefully establish a line of retreat for them down to the North Col. Pete and Joe immediately tried to reassure me that they were all shattered and all I needed was rest, they were just as tired as I was.

'You've no bloody idea how much I've been pushing myself!' I exploded, almost tearful in the violence of my own emotion. 'I've never pushed myself so hard, never felt so out of control. I'm sorry. I know my own limits and I've reached them.'

It was halfway through the morning when Dick came into the tent. He had shaved off his beard, it was as if he was already in a different world. We all stopped talking. What could one possibly say? I just muttered, 'We're terribly sorry, Dick.'

He could not hold back his tears. It was not only Everest, or a matter of leaving the close companionship of our little group; it was his entire life that was altered. Dick was not interested in fame or money but he loved the mountains, needed to stretch himself to his own limits – and now all that seemed closed to him. But he quickly got hold of himself.

'I'll be all right. It's just getting used to it that's difficult.'

We talked around it and then I asked him whether he wanted to stay on at Base Camp, but he replied that there seemed no point. And so it was decided that Dick should set out for Lhasa in a few days' time, just before we returned to the climb. This would enable Charlie to keep him under observation a little longer and Dick to rest before his journey. We talked around the problem a while and then trailed back to our tents to read, write diaries or worry.

Pete observed: 'Lying in my tent you can tell exactly who is who; Chris, from the snuffle breathing, Joe from his groans. He's on his way over the gravel towards our windy bog. But Joe returns and arouses Charlie and they go and inspect his stool. I think 'Oh no; blood in his stool; ulcer. Chris is out too, and Dick. I'll have to solo the North Col route, damn it! Feel worried the whole trip is falling apart.' Charlie wrote in his diary:

And Joe, poor Joe. What on earth is going on? Dull, central abdominal pain, tarry black stool which can only mean blood. The easiest conclusion is an ulcer, but he had a very bloody throat with a hard black crust right across the pharynx. I suppose this could have seeped down and caused the problem. We'll have to wait to see the outcome but clearly he cannot go anywhere with a bleeding bowel. I've told him he mustn't go up unless he's really better.

And so we bathe our wounds and hope for a reasonable enough recovery to get three up high and I suppose two on the summit. One would do. Trying to look at it all objectively, I do not think we have a hope in hell. The days required to kill the Pinnacles, added to the summit ridge, cannot be less than six and this is simply too long without oxygen. I think:

Pete could do it.

Joe probably could, but is ropey.

Chris has said he doesn't think he can and I'm sure he's right.

Dick can't because of illness.

This leaves two alternatives, either go for it, as Pete would like – or abandon it and go for the Col route as a threesome. The first seems the purer – for two to climb as far as they can on the ridge – and I expect that is what will happen on the day.'

Resting in the sun at Base Camp. I had already decided I was not strong enough to make another attempt.

I was more optimistic than Charlie, feeling that Joe and Pete had a very good chance of completing the Pinnacles. They had only to make a height gain of about 300m (1000ft) over a distance of around 400m (1300ft). With the knowledge that they could drop down to the North Col on the other side and would not have to return over the Pinnacles, they could surely make the traverse in a couple of days. We could even see what looked like an easy line of traversing ledges that bypassed the Final Pinnacle.

I was less sanguine about their chances of reaching the summit, since it did seem that they would need at least one night, maybe two, on the Pinnacles before they reached the final section of the ridge. It was reasonably easy but there was a lot of it – 1.5 km (1 mile) in horizontal distance and 450m (1500ft) of vertical height to gain. But even if they only managed to climb the Pinnacles, this would have been a comparative success, for they would have crossed the unclimbed part of the ridge.

And what of my feelings? I was not depressed by my own failure. Now that I had finally decided to drop back into a support role I felt a vast release of tension and looked forward to our trip to the North Col as something which seemed a useful contribution to the expedition, was within my capabilities, and a goal in itself.

Dick borrowed a telephoto lens so that he could go for one last walk and get some fresh pictures of Everest from around the ruined nunnery. It was a lovely clear morning, the sky a far-flung vault of blue with Everest towering at the head of the valley with its characteristic cloud-banner blowing out from its summit. Dick felt as well and fit as he had ever done on the expedition as he strode down the jeep track. The ruined nunnery was just a short way up a slope and for the first time that morning he had to climb uphill. His strength suddenly drained from him and he slowed down to little more than a crawl. He sat down on a rock; his vision became distorted, his heart pounded; he could hardly breathe. On the previous occasion he had not been frightened because he had not really known what was happening. Now he did. These were the symptoms of another stroke.

It took Dick a quarter of an hour before his heart returned to normal and he could see clearly enough to walk back to camp and have another word with Charlie. There was now no question of him lingering at Base Camp any longer, nor travelling unaccompanied. Charlie would have to go with him at least as far as Chengdu.

'You will come straight back, of course,' I exhorted Charlie.

We broke up and wandered to our tents. Pete nudged Charlie. 'Thought you were going home, didn't you, you bugger!'

On the morning of 10 May, we all shook hands with Dick, slightly embarrassed, emotion pent up and inhibited, and then silently watched as the jeep bumped over the shingle road in the washed-out grey of the early dawn.

In the big base tent the tiny size of our team really hit us. We missed Dick's strength and Charlie's caring cheerfulness. On a more material level, it was Charlie who baked the bread, who cooked the delicious fresh vegetable broths we had so enjoyed at Advanced Base. We were a sombre bunch, but, at the same time, felt we could now start planning positively for the future. Joe and Pete were poring over photographs of the upper part of the ridge, calculating heights and distances. There was a hidden level of communication between them from which, inevitably, I now felt excluded. And yet they never made me feel unwelcome. There was no resentment in their manner, nor was it recorded in their diaries. Joe in a letter to his partner Maria, merely stated:

> Chris is feeling a bit slow on the mountain… There is a big job for Pete and me to do but hopefully it could go well next time we go back up and if fortune, weather and spirit favour us we could be up the mountain in a few days from when we start…

We celebrated Joe's 34th birthday on the evening of 12 May, our last night at Base Camp. Our cook had risen to the occasion, baking a birthday cake and preparing a lavish feast. We decided to open one of our bottles of champagne but in the rarefied atmosphere the pressure difference was so great that most of the contents jetted out in a great streamer of foam, leaving little more than a few teaspoonfuls of wine. We opened another bottle, this time holding a plastic bucket ready to catch the exploding bubbles. It was a happy boozy night with Joe in fine form, wryly funny, Pete gentle and very boyish, Adrian quiet and serious but with a twinkle of humour. 'Adrian's climbing career is rising like a phoenix,' said Pete. 'At this rate he'll be the first Englishman since the war to reach the North Col.' I had a feeling of immense affection for all three of my companions.

That night, in his tent, Pete wrote: 'A great birthday for Joe…whatever may happen on this trip, we'll be able to say we've had some good times.'

*15 May – 21 May 1982*

# They Walked Out of Our Lives

T HE 15TH DAWNED CLEAR though windy at Advanced Base. Pete and Joe fussed around with final preparations, packing their rucksacks and putting in a few last-minute goodies. Then suddenly they were ready, crampons on, rope tied, set to go. I think we were all trying to underplay the moment.

'See you in a few days.'

'We'll call you tonight at six o'clock.'

'Good luck.'

And then they were off, plodding up the little ice slope immediately beyond the camp, through flurries of wind-driven snow. They were planning to move straight through to the Second Snow Cave, to avoid spending longer than absolutely necess-sary at altitude. This would mean they would reach the Third Cave on their second day, and then on the third they hoped to traverse the Pinnacles and reach the North Ridge. If they could do this they would be in a very good position to make their bid for the summit on the fourth or fifth day. To have any chance of success they had to keep to this schedule, for they could not afford to spend more than two nights above 8250m (27,100ft) before going for the summit.

Adrian and I were hoping to find a way up to the North Col that same day. We left shortly after the others, roping up for the glacier which sloped in a series of gentle waves, but the great wall at the end of the valley loomed even steeper. I had thought of 'just nipping up to the North Col', but now began to realize that I had under-estimated things. Adrian's climbing experience was strictly limited and he had done practically no ice climbing. But he, like me, was glad to be doing something positive again, though commenting phlegmatically on the North Col in his diary: 'The first time I set eyes on it, I thought, I'm bloody glad I'm not going up there. But now here I am.'

There appeared to be a choice of three routes up to the Col, none of them im-mediately appealing for an inexperienced climber. We eventually decided on the left-

*On 15 May Joe and Pete set out from Advanced Base for their final attempt to cross the unclimbed section of the ridge and push on to the summit.*

'It was another perfect day, cloudless, almost windless, a pleasure to be out. I staggered over to the mess tent and for the first time that morning, peered through the telescope. I started at the snow Shoulder, behind which hid the Third Snow Cave. No sign of them there, so I swung the telescope along the crest of the ridge leading to the First Pinnacle. Still no sign. Could they have overslept?'

hand route Mr Chen had recommended and the one Reinhold Messner had used when he climbed the mountain solo. It was uninterrupted by séracs or crevasses but it looked rather steep for Adrian. By this time the day had galloped away and it was time to return to Advanced Base for our scheduled radio call to Pete and Joe who had made good fast time to the Second Snow Cave and told us they felt they were going well.

I told them we would try to reach the North Col the next day. But once more I was being over-optimistic. Our left-hand line led up to the bergschrund, with a long stride on to a steep wall of crusty snow. Not the easy slog I had promised Adrian. I saw a better route to the right, which we reached by tiptoeing beneath a shattered sérac wall. Adrian was none too happy. But once on easier ground he was able to take over the lead and I was content for him to do the trail breaking as he was undoubtedly going more strongly than I was. We had now reached the area of sérac walls on the upper part of the face. I had observed what seemed to be a gangway between two of them which would lead to the final slopes just below the Col. What I could not have observed was the huge moat-like crevasse which once more brought us up short.

But it was time for our evening call again. This time we had the radio with us and we retreated with some relief from the crevasse so we could have a direct line of

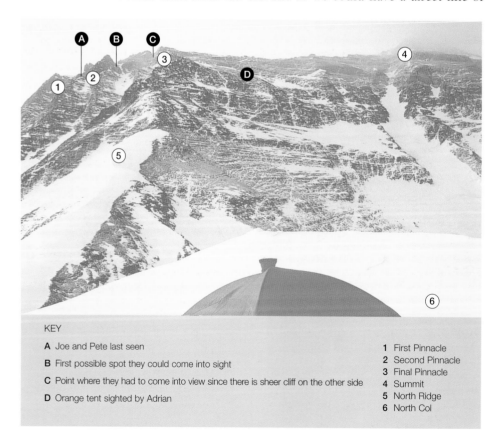

*The view that Adrian and I had from our tent on the North Col when we were watching for Pete and Joe.*

KEY

A Joe and Pete last seen
B First possible spot they could come into sight
C Point where they had to come into view since there is sheer cliff on the other side
D Orange tent sighted by Adrian

1 First Pinnacle
2 Second Pinnacle
3 Final Pinnacle
4 Summit
5 North Ridge
6 North Col

sight with the crest of the North East Ridge.

'Hello Snow Cave Three, this is Chris just below the North Col, can you hear me? Over.'

There was no reply. We tried again a few minutes later and Pete's voice came through, telling us that they had reached the Third Snow Cave in good time and would be going for the

Pinnacles the next morning. I replied that we had not managed to reach the North Col that day, that we would be having a rest day tomorrow, and would move up to the North Col on the 18th, ready to receive them if they came down that way. We arranged to have a radio call at three o'clock the following afternoon and then again at six. A hurried 'good luck' for the morrow and the radio was dead.

We dumped all the gear we had carried up on the lip of the crevasse, marked it with an alloy wand and started down. We were both very tired and Adrian, who had never been on snow as steep as this without the reassurance of a fixed rope, was understandably nervous. We trailed slowly back to the camp, reaching it in the dark. It had been a 14-hour day and we were both exhausted. That night we were too tired to cook any food. We just melted some snow for tea, and collapsed into our sleeping bags.

It was always difficult getting up before the sun warmed the tent, which happened at about nine. Even then, I lay for a long time in a stupor before thirst and hunger drove me out of the warmth of my sleeping bag. It was another perfect day, cloudless, almost windless, a pleasure to be out. I staggered over to the mess tent and for the first time that morning, peered through the telescope. I started at the snow Shoulder, behind which hid the Third Snow Cave. No sign of them there, so I swung the telescope along the crest of the ridge leading to the First Pinnacle. Still no sign. Could they have overslept? And then I saw them, two small distinct figures, at the high point they had previously reached on the First Pinnacle. To get there they must either have travelled very fast, or perhaps had even set out before dawn. They certainly knew that they had to cover a lot of ground that day, for to have a good chance of reaching the summit they had to reach Point 8393 that evening.

The image through the telescope was so sharp that I could actually see their limbs. For the rest of the day, either Adrian or I watched through the telescope as Pete and Joe slowly made their way along the ridge. But now their progress had slowed down. They were on new and presumably difficult ground. We assumed they were leaving a fixed rope behind them for they had with them about 300m (1000ft) of rope. Their slowness was not surprising. They were now at around 8250m (27,100ft) above sea level. They must have had around 15kg (33lb) each on their

backs, with their sleeping bags, tent, stove, food, fuel and climbing gear. It was difficult to tell how hard the climbing was but I suspect it was harder than they had
anticipated. I wondered if anyone had ever climbed to that standard at that height
before. They were now higher than all but five peaks in the world.

We spent the day cooking, drinking and eating, but constantly going back to the
telescope to gaze up at those tiny figures. I longed for three o'clock, so that we could
turn on the sound, have some kind of contact with them, hear how they were, what
the climbing was like – but most of all just to hear them. It was five to three. I
opened the radio and started calling.

'Hello climbing team, hello climbing team, this is Advanced Base, do you read
me? Over?'

The set crackled in my hand, but it was just some distant voices speaking Chinese.
The Pinnacles, etched black against the sky, were stark and jagged. I tried again. It
was now past three but there was still no reply. I was not unduly worried. Perhaps
their set had failed, but more likely they were so engrossed in the climbing they
either forgot to open up or just did not have time. I could clearly see one figure on
the ridge, outlined against the sky, halfway between the crest of the First Pinnacle
and the black tooth of the Second. The other figure was just below the skyline,
moving very slowly.

We now called on the half hour through the rest of the afternoon but there was
no reply. At nine that evening, the sun already hidden behind Everest, we looked up
at them for the last time and called them yet again on the radio. One figure was silhouetted in the fading light on the small col immediately below the Second
Pinnacle, while the other figure was still moving to join him.

They had been on the go for 14 hours. It was only 20 minutes or so before dark,
so they had to find somewhere to spend the night at the foot of the Second Pinnacle,
either a snow cave, or more likely a small ledge cut out of the snow on which they
could pitch the tent. But what was it like up there? The ridge was obviously narrow
and the slopes on either side seemed steep, but there was plenty of snow on the eastern side. The only problem, perhaps, could be that it was too soft and insubstantial.

We had our evening meal, looked up at the ridge, whose black serrated edge
could be seen clearly against the inky blue of the clear star-studded sky. There was
no twinkling of a light and presumably they were camped or holed up on the other
side. I slept deeply that night but next morning I immediately went over to look
through the telescope.

There was no sign of them. Perhaps they were already on their way down. It was
another brilliant clear day and the absence of a snow plume from the summit indicated that there was little wind to trouble them. We knew that they would be out
of sight on the other side of the ridge for 100m (330ft) or so, since on the north side
the way was barred by the sheer rocky buttresses of the Second Pinnacle. I had a
feeling that they would try to get back on to the north as quickly as possible, both
because the snow on the east would probably be insecure and also to have some kind

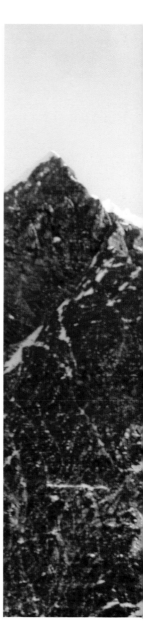

*Our last glimpse of Pete or Joe just before dusk on the evening of 17 May. The tiny figure is discernible to the left of the Second Pinnacle (second from left in the picture). They had been on the go for over 14 hours that day and progress had been painfully slow.*

or contact with us, even if their radio was no longer working. There also seemed to be interconnecting ledges across rocky slopes on this side.

At this stage we were not unduly worried. We leisurely packed our rucksacks, had one last brew, and then, leaving a note for Charlie to let him know what was happening, set off for the North Col. This time we retraced our descent route and made steady, uneventful progress. I had brought with me a pair of binoculars and every ten minutes or so I gazed up at the ridge, hoping to see Joe and Pete. From the slopes leading up to the North Col we had an excellent view. Beyond the Second Pinnacle there was a small col. The crest of the ridge then levelled out for what, I estimated, were about three rope-lengths, before dropping away to the col beneath the Final Pinnacle. We knew from photographs that they then had to come on to this side of the ridge. But there was nothing. Just rock and snow and ice.

I could not stop myself praying that they were all right. I found myself crying in the intensity of an anxiety that had crept up on me almost unawares. I chided myself. Nothing to worry about yet. They're just on the other side of the ridge.

We were now on the ramp leading up to the centre of the North Col. Our steps from two days ago were covered with wind-blown snow and again I was very happy to let Adrian do the trail breaking. It was six in the evening before we reached our previous high point. I took a tentative look at the narrow arête of snow. It looked feasible, but steep and frightening, something to be attempted in the morning when we'd be feeling fresh.

'Come on, Adrian, we'll stop here for the night. It's safe enough with this crevasse between us and the slope.'

I started digging a platform beside the crevasse. Adrian was appalled at the exposure of our perch but I tried to reassure him that it was perfectly safe. 'Once in the tent you can forget the drop.'

It was a wonderful dusk, the sky cloudless, with hardly a breath of wind. To one side the North East Ridge was black and massive, while below us the East Rongbuk Glacier swept away in a vast white highway.

The following morning we struck the tent and I set out along the fragile crest of a fin-like arête, which we hoped would bypass the crevasse. As so often happens, it was easier than it looked, and although it steepened into a nearly vertical drop into the huge crevasse below us, I had the security of the rope paid out by Adrian.

*Adrian and I reached the North Col on 19 May. We spent the next three days gazing up at the North East Ridge, hoping that our friends would appear.*

Cutting big bucket steps, I worked my way down, then shouted to Adrian to anchor the rope so that he could follow. We now had the rope in position for our return. Soon we had both cautiously abseiled down it and were able to break out on to an easy ramp we had seen from below. Once more I was pleased for Adrian to take the lead on straightforward ground. As we went up, we were still searching the ridge every few minutes but there was still no sign. Although we were getting anxious, we could not help enjoying the sensation of being on new ground, of finding our way up to the North Col. There were intriguing reminders of our predecessors. An old cable-laid nylon rope hung from a huge overhanging boss of snow. Could it have been left by the Chinese in 1975? Farther up, by a formidable narrow ice chimney, projected a butane gas cylinder, French 1981 vintage, no doubt. This route seemed too hard for us and we continued up the ramp to the foot of an acutely angled snow slope that seemed to lead to the crest of the ridge. Once again I went into the lead, kicking my way up the steep but secure snow, until suddenly my head poked over the crest. I had reached the North Col.

It was a sharp knife edge, dropping away steeply on the other side with the fresh vista of Pumo Ri, shapely and elegant, in the near distance and behind it the great bulk of Cho Oyu. I moved cautiously along the knife edge to where it broadened into an easy slope and buried a deadman snow anchor. While Adrian jumared up the rope I was able to look around. The ridge opened out into a wide dome just above the lowest point of the Col. It would provide both a good camp site and an excellent viewpoint of the North East Ridge. In the concentration and very real joy of climbing that final pitch to the Col, there had been no room for my growing worry about Pete and Joe, but now it came creeping back. I got out the binoculars and searched the line of ridge again but to no avail.

But what of the Americans in the Great Gully of the North Face? I started searching for them and picked out a collection of tents, tiny coloured boxes, clinging beneath a sheer sérac wall. There was no sign of movement, but a line of tracks wound sinuously across the slope, taking a route round the huge icefall that barred the Great Gully at about half height. There was another camp, tucked below a rocky overhand just near the side of the couloir, and I could just discern some more tracks. Surely they also would be going for the summit in such perfect weather.

Just after Adrian arrived we saw two tiny figures descending the fixed ropes on the American route. Could they be Pete and Joe, who had somehow got across on to the North Face without us seeing them? But this was clutching at straws. Our logic quickly told us that these were Americans, perhaps on their way down from a successful summit bid. We dug out a platform for the tent and spent the rest of the day taking it in turns to examine the North East Ridge. It was now 19 May and I was very worried. Pete and Joe had been out of sight for two nights and almost two days. From this viewpoint we could see just how short a distance they would have had to cover before we could expect them to come into sight on our side of the ridge after turning the Second Pinnacle.

That afternoon, Adrian picked out some movement at Advanced Base. Could it be them? Could they somehow have retreated all the way down without us seeing them? But no. There were three figures. It could be the American skiers, or perhaps it was Charlie who had come up with some Tibetans. We opened up on the radio at six o'clock. There was no reply from Pete or Joe, but Charlie, reassuring and cheerful, came on the air. I immediately told him of my fears. Charlie recalls:

> At 6 p.m. on the 19th I had a crackly radio link with the Col. I was about to berate Chris about the mess but his message was anxious, high pitched, almost unintelligible. They had not seen them… "I am concerned…" "I share your concern", I replied. I share your concern…my world of elation was quick-frozen, replaced, not yet by sorrow or pain, but by a curious reality. I was in a high camp, with two Tibetans for the night. Three miles away on the North East Ridge something had happened or was happening. Two miles away on the North Col Chris and Adrian were safe. We were 6000 miles away from home.

*We left Adrian to wait at Advanced Base in the forlorn hope that Pete and Joe might miraculously reappear, while Charlie and I set out up the Kangshung Valley to investigate the other side of the ridge.*

I did not sleep well that night and as soon as it was light enough I was gazing up anxiously through the binoculars. Another perfect day but still no sign of Pete and Joe. We opened up on the radio on the hour throughout the day, but with little hope of a reply since it was unlikely that we should hear them unless they were in direct line of sight. I now searched not only the crest but also the glacier at its foot, just in case they had fallen. That night Adrian went outside for one last look up at the ridge and called, 'Chris, come and have a look at this. I think I can see something. It could be a tent.'

He handed me the binoculars.

'It's about a third of the way along the ridge, above and beyond the Pinnacles, just below the crest. Look, there are three slight bumps. Go down from the left-hand one. There's a bit of a gully, and there it is, on a kind of ledge. It's just a little orange blob. It could be a tent, couldn't it?'

It was certainly on the line from the Final Pinnacle on to the North Face. Then why hadn't we seen them? They would have been in view, moving slowly, for a long time. But that little orange blob was a slender strand of hope. I pushed logical doubts aside. That could be Pete and Joe. Perhaps they had reached the top and were on their way down. They could be with us tomorrow. Neither Adrian nor I slept that night. I imagined what they would have to say, what they had done, how they would look, convincing myself that it was undoubtedly their tent and that they were on their way down. The night crept away so very slowly. We had arranged a call to Charlie at eight and I expressed my hope.

But as the light on the North Face improved and we gazed at the distant little blob, our hopes dwindled. There was no sign of movement. It was the wrong colour, being orange when the outer of the Sumitomo tent was a deep red and its inner a bright yellow. It was also the wrong shape, looking more square than domed. It was perhaps a box tent abandoned by the French the previous year. The weather had been so clear and our viewpoint so good that surely we should have seen them if they had reached the end of the Pinnacles? Our hopes vanished and despair set in. They had now been out of sight for four days – four days to cover a distance of about three rope-lengths at the least, eight or so at the very most. Four nights above 8250m (27,100ft). If their progress had been so slow, surely they would have decided to retreat. We had already seen the effects of spending four nights at 7850m (25,755ft).

The only explanation must be that a catastrophe had occurred. What if one of them had fallen and was injured? Surely the other would have retrace his steps to signal us for help, particularly since we assumed they had left a line of fixed rope behind them? It would have meant retreating only two or three rope-lengths. Or could both of them have fallen sick or be so incapacitated by exhaustion that neither could move? This seemed unlikely. They were well acclimatized, and though perhaps tired from our long siege, they knew how to pace themselves and had been at these altitudes without oxygen before on Kangchenjunga and K2. One of them could perhaps have collapsed, but not two. That left a grim interpretation – that they were both dead. Either one had fallen, pulling off the other, or perhaps one of those fragile ice flutings had collapsed, sweeping both of them down the huge Kangshung Face. I could remember its immense scale, just how steep the upper part of the ridge had seemed, and how insubstantial and dangerous Dick had found that pitch on the First Pinnacle.

I talked it over with Adrian and then at midday with Charlie. There seemed nothing to gain by staying on the North Col. We left the tent in place, anchored to a snow shovel and its valance securely wedged down with snow. We also left the radio, the cooking gear, all the remaining food and a note welcoming them back and telling them what we had done.

We held ourselves tightly in control. Although I had very little hope of their survival, I could not bring myself to admit it. Besides, we were still on the mountain and needed all our concentration to return safely to Advanced Base. By the time we reached the sérac wall where I had left a fixed rope, the clouds had engulfed us and the wind was beginning to whip stinging snowflakes into our faces. Adrian, who wears glasses, was almost blinded as they misted up. He was also feeling the debilitating effects of spending three nights at around 7000m (23,000ft). We were both very, very tired as we stumbled down the slope, thankful for the marker wands we had placed to guide us down.

Back on the glacier we could begin to relax, and then, having reached the rocky moraine, we were able to take off the rope and walk down in our own time. I pulled ahead, forcing myself over the broken rocks covered in fresh snow, to get back to the camp. At last it was in sight and Charlie was coming towards me.

'They've had it. I'm sure they've had it,' I muttered.

'I know.'

We held each other and wept.

# A Fruitless Search

IT WAS ALL SO FAMILIAR. Adrian sat quietly in his usual corner. Charlie cut some bread. The big kettle bubbled on top of three Gaz stoves, the pressure cooker hissed quietly, the canvas of the big green tent rattled in the wind. Books, gloves, karabiners, cine equipment, packages of food were piled on the boxes round the cluttered stone table. Some of the gear belonged to Pete and Joe. We had to decide what to do and the very urgency of this demand was a therapy in itself, helping us to control our grief.

In front of us was the file of pictures so meticulously collected by Pete before the expedition, some of them from the prewar expeditions, others taken by the Americans who had attempted the Kangshung Face the previous year. The stark black and white pictures emphasized the ferocious steepness of those snow flutings on the East Face. We thrashed over the possibilities and arguments that we had all been grappling with in the last few days.

'You know, when you look at that face,' I said, 'it's just great clusters of snow plastered on to very steep rock so that the whole lot could come away. If they did fall, it wouldn't have been 100 metres, it'd be nearer 1000. It's horrendously steep.'

'But it is just possible, isn't it, Chris, that they could have survived in some huge slide of snow, and could somehow have got all the way down on to the Kangshung Glacier?' said Charlie.

'It'd be a one in a million chance,' I replied. 'I just can't believe they could have survived a fall on that, and even if they did, just look how steep the bottom is. They'd never get down it.'

'But it's still just possible,' persisted Charlie. 'Look at Messner on Nanga Parbat. There've been other instances as well when people have fallen and got down into another valley. However unlikely it is I think we must go up the Kangshung Valley.'

'I agree,' I said, 'but we've also got to keep this side under observation, just in case they do get back this way. Someone's going to have to sit it out here as well.'

'I don't mind doing that,' volunteered Adrian.

*Pethangtse (6710m/ 22,014ft) at the head of the Kangshung Glacier. Charlie and I walked up the valley to a point where we could look up at the other side of the North East Ridge.*

'You know, I suppose we should really go back up the ridge itself and try to reach their high point.

'Come on, Chris, be realistic,' said Charlie. 'I don't think Adrian or I could make it, and for that matter, could you? And anyway, would we see anything?'

'Yeah, but even if you managed to get all the way to the Second Pinnacle, how much would you see? Would it confirm anything?' asked Adrian.

'I suppose if we found a broken rope at their high point, that'd be some kind of confirmation. But at least we'd know they weren't there, that they hadn't collapsed from exhaustion or were sick. But quite honestly, I don't see how they could be. I could believe that one of them might be sick, but not both of them. They'd have such a short distance to get back into sight, and they should have had a fixed rope as well. I'm afraid the only real explanation is that they've both fallen. The trouble is as well that, unless we actually reached their high point, we'd learn no more than we know now. And you're right; quite honestly I don't think I could make it again up to the Pinnacles.'

'Well then, it's the Kangshung Valley,' said Charlie.

'I agree. I think we'll see more from there with the telescope than we ever would on the ridge itself.'

Next morning Charlie and I set off, leaving Adrian to his solitary vigil. On the way back to Base Camp I wanted to make a diversion to the American camp, to tell them of our fears and to ask them to keep an eye out for our two friends. There was just a chance that they might see something from high on the North Ridge during a summit bid. But they nursed a grief of their own. Marty Hoey had fallen to her death a few days before. They had decided however to make one more bid for the summit and they promised to keep an eye out for Joe and Pete if they did manage to reach the crest of the ridge.

It was dark by the time I got back and Charlie had already told Mr Chen. There was no criticism, no questioning, only sympathy and offers of help. Next morning we made our plans in detail. Mr Yu, our interpreter, was going to accompany us when we took the truck round to the Kharta Valley. In the meantime Mr Chen was going to organize our flights back to Hong Kong, reassuring us that in no circumstances would our fears about Pete and Joe be revealed prematurely to the press.

On 24 May we drove the 160km (100 miles) on bumpy dirt roads to the Kharta Valley. It was now summer, and the fields were lush with newly sprouting barley. We were following the broad valley that drains the Rongbuk Glacier, the Dzakar Chhu which curls round to the east into the great Arun River and flows through the Himalaya into Nepal. The village of Kharta is described as a leafy paradise in the early Everest books, such a contrast from Rongbuk that several expeditions seem to have been lured this way because of its beauty. Now the terrain has changed with the woods thin and many fields barren, the result of ruthless deforestation for fuel. We paused at the Kharta Commune Headquarters – a soulless, corrugated courtyard in a wind- swept valley. Where were the hedges of rhododendrons, where were the

Previous page: *The Raphu La is bottom right, the summit of Everest top left and Pinnacles are clearly visible to the right of the summit. There was no sign of Pete or Joe.*

flowers? Trees had been demolished here on a huge scale. We bought potatoes, arranged porters for the next day and drove on 10km (6 miles) up the Kharta Valley.

Suddenly, around a corner we saw some familiar tents. The American ski team were pitched on a grassy bank by the Kharta stream. Ned and Jim greeted us wildly at first — they had become great friends — then we told them tersely of our fears. They asked questions, voiced their sympathy, and offered to keep us company in our search, even though it would mean retracing their steps. We were delighted. Not only would it mean that we should have someone with us who knew the way but, more important, they would be able to help in the remote event of a rescue.

We set out the following day, accompanied by three cheerful Tibetans who were going to act as guides and porters. The terrain was so different from the Rongbuk side. On the valley floor azaleas were in bud, rhododendrons already in flower, while alpine flowers were beginning to bloom in the meadows beneath the Langma La.

On the second day we crossed the pass, getting a glimpse of the huge snowclad Kangshung Face of Everest for a few minutes through the clouds. We descended to the glacier past frozen lakes and then over hillsides covered in coarse tussocky grass and azaleas. To the south, the walls of Chomo Lonzo and Pethangtse fell precipitously to the valley floor, huge spires looming out of the mists. Sometimes we caught glimpses of Everest some 16km (10 miles) up the valley.

On the third night we arrived at the head of the valley. Tension was mounting within me. Would the fog clear during the night? Would we see anything? I didn't know whether to dread seeing no trace at all, or to be confronted with irrefutable evidence of what had happened. In the pallid pre-dawn of 28 May, the fog had cleared and the Kangshung Face was now clearly visible at the head of the valley.

We mounted the telescope on a tripod and took turns to stare through it. I could pick out the Shoulder where we had dug the Third Snow Cave, the First Pinnacle and the col below the Second Pinnacle where, 11 days before, I had seen that small figure outlined against the darkening sky. Near-vertical ice flutings dropped away below the pinnacles, sheer runnels swept clear of snow. Below were the tiers of séracs, icefalls and finally rock buttresses, which form the 3000-m (10,000-ft) high face. Nothing moved other than the occasional avalanche. There was no sign of Pete and Joe. We walked back quietly, often apart, wrapped in thought. There was little to say. The faint hope we had lived with for over two weeks was now gone.

*Charlie had chosen a large slate from near the 1924 memorial and during the evenings had picked and chiselled away at a simple epitaph to Pete and Joe.*

Three days later Charlie and I were back at Base Camp. Adrian had arrived from Advanced Base: he had no news. There remained the final act. As in 1924, the Tibetans built a cairn upon a hill near Base Camp. We placed the tablet with Charlie's inscription and stood silently, tearful in the wind. Next day we left to bring our bad news home.

# North East Ridge – an Afterword

It is especially hard to accept the death of friends when they just vanish. It's even harder for those closest to the deceased – the partners, parents and children. Hilary Boardman and Maria Coffey made a pilgrimage to the North side of Everest just a few months after they heard of the tragedy. Their journey (described by Maria in her book, *Fragile Edge*, helped them accept what might have happened. There were still so many questions to answer and most important of all no tangible sign of the men they had loved, no possibility of the ceremony of burial, that provides some kind of solace and conclusion.

In 1984 I received a letter from an American climber called Donald Goodman. He had just come back from an expedition on the traditional North East Ridge and on the crest of the ridge at a height of around 8290m (27,200ft) had looked across at the Pinnacles and noticed something red that was sticking out of the snow just short of the final Pinnacle. He took a photograph but the definition of the red object is not very clear. I blew the negative up as much as I could, and it looked like part of a rucksack sticking out of the snow but I couldn't be sure. The question immediately occurred to me – could the body of Pete or Joe be under the sack, concealed by the snow. They certainly had got that far, just short of the final barrier presented by the third and last Pinnacle, but what had happened remained a mystery.

The next attempt on the North East Ridge was in the spring of 1985, the same time that I returned to Everest to climb it by the South Col Route. It was a 19-strong British expedition led by Mal Duff and they reached a height of around 8150m (26,740ft) near the top of the First Pinnacle. They came across two tents, two harnesses, a jumar, a figure of eight and two ski poles at the foot of the First Pinnacle. I can't remember if Dick Renshaw and I left our harnesses there when we came down from our ascent, but it seems unlikely which implies that they belonged to Pete and Joe and that they were trying to reduce weight to an absolute minimum. At the end of the expedition, Rick Allen, strongest member of the team, made one last attempt on the Pinnacle, climbing solo. He found the cartridge-loading cine camera that Joe was using, hanging from a piton with some coils of fixing rope at his high point – another indication that Pete and Joe were trying to reduce weight to the minimum and that perhaps the altitude was really beginning to hurt.

The following spring another large British expedition led by Brummie Stokes, Regimental Sergeant Major of the 21st Special Air Service Regiment, made an attempt. The team was made up from members of the SAS and civilian climbers including Mo Anthoine, Bill Barker and the legendary Joe Brown. They took a more direct line on to the ridge by what came to be known as Bill's Buttress, leading directly up to what had been our Second Snow cave in 1982. This saved time and effort but they were rebuffed by high winds on the First Pinnacle. In 1987 Doug Scott made an attempt with a small team, closer in size to our own in 1982. They suffered appalling weather and got half way up the First Pinnacle.

The following year, during the monsoon, Brummie Stokes returned with another big team. Harry Taylor and Russell Brice succeeded in crossing the Pinnacles, bivouacking just short of the Final Pinnacle, before completing the crossing and dropping back down to the North Col. They were travelling light with just one small bottle of oxygen for emergencies and were too tired to go for the summit. They saw no signs of Pete or Joe, but this is hardly surprising since the ridge was plastered in fresh monsoon snow and the weather was bad though, being the monsoon, comparatively mild. They did comment on how difficult and time consuming was the knife-edge ridge connecting the Pinnacles.

I had been unable to resist the challenge presented by the North East Ridge, particularly in the light of the number of failed attempts, and had put in an application for the spring of 1989. But once Taylor and Brice had completed the crossing of the Pinnacles, there seemed little point in creating the large expedition using fixed rope and oxygen that I felt one would need to get all the way to the top. I therefore withdrew my application and must confess was relieved to do so. My heart had never really been in the venture.

In the spring of 1992 a Japanese expedition with four members from Kazakhstan attempted the complete ascent. They succeeded in crossing the Pinnacles, putting a line of fixed rope all the way across, but did not have the strength to complete the climb to the summit. They did, however, come across a body, partly buried in the snow, beyond the Second Pinnacle. Both from the clothing and the features it was positively identified as that of Pete Boardman. There was no sign of Joe though at this stage I thought that the red object sighted by Donald Goodman in 1984 was farther along the ridge and therefore could possibly be where Joe had died.

In 1995 the complete ridge was finally climbed by a strong Japanese expedition supported by Sherpa high-altitude porters using oxygen and over 4000m (13,000ft) of fixed rope. They also came across a body, which they described as being just on top of the Second Pinnacle. At first it was surmised that this was Joe Tasker, but after carefully comparing the written descriptions and the photographs provided by each expedition, I became convinced that this was the same as the original sighting and therefore that of Pete. In addition to Pete's body there was a tangle of rope, nylon tape and the remains of what could be a red tent exposed a few yards to the right. I still thought however that the picture taken by Goodman showed something farther along the ridge.

While working on this book I started examining all the evidence once again, met up with Russell Brice on a visit he had to England, and e-mailed Kazbek Valiev, a Kazak climber who summitted Everest as a member of the Russian South West Buttress Expedition. He hadn't been with the '92 Expedition but was able to talk to Yuri Moiseyev one of that team and very kindly sent me a marked-up photograph that showed the spot where they came across Peter's body. I examined all the pictures again and it became increasingly obvious that this was undoubtedly the same spot as shown in both the Japanese pictures and that of Goodman. And so we can be certain that there has been just one sighting and that was of Peter.

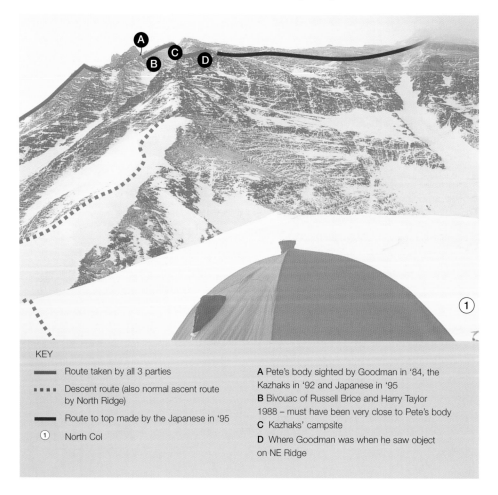

*This diagram shows the routes of subsequent expeditions and the sightings of Pete's body.*

KEY

——— Route taken by all 3 parties

▪▪▪▪ Descent route (also normal ascent route by North Ridge)

——— Route to top made by the Japanese in '95

① North Col

**A** Pete's body sighted by Goodman in '84, the Kazhaks in '92 and Japanese in '95
**B** Bivouac of Russell Brice and Harry Taylor 1988 – must have been very close to Pete's body
**C** Kazhaks' campsite
**D** Where Goodman was when he saw object on NE Ridge

And so, what did happen on those fatal days after our last sighting on 17 December 1982? Pete and Joe had moved quickly and strongly up to the top of the First Pinnacle, having reached the Third Snow Cave in just two days. They had also reported feeling fit and well on their last radio call to us on the evening of the 16th. We spotted them at the top of the First Pinnacle at around 9 am that morning, which implied an early pre-dawn start. Their progress on new ground as they crossed the ridge linking the First and Second Pinnacles was painfully slow and they took 12 hours to cover a relatively short distance. Was this because of bad snow conditions or the effects of altitude? Probably it was a combination of the two. Russell Brice and Harry Taylor also took a long time over this section.

We can't tell how far they got that night, once they had moved out of sight behind the Second Pinnacle. Did they stop just beyond that point, struggle on the next day, perhaps had a second bivouac where Pete's body was found? We shall probably never know. And what of Joe – is he buried in the snow near Pete? Did he have a fall? It couldn't have been down the Rongbuk side – we'd have seen him, but perhaps it could have been down the Kangshung Face. But what of the tangle of ropes in the Japanese photograph? That implies they still had their ropes and that therefore they were still together. Perhaps both were so exhausted or suffering from high altitude sickness that they perished during the night and perhaps Joe is under or within the remains of that red tent spotted by the Japanese?

The irony is that they were only just out of sight from where we watched for them from the North Col. They had covered the most difficult ground and had they been able to struggle on just a few more metres, it would have been easy going all the way back down to us. We'll probably never know what happened. These days very few expeditions attempt the harder routes on Everest, so Pete and Joe may be left in peace high in their mountain eyrie. I hope so.

But back in 1983 we knew nothing of this. We had only the memory of that tiny figure silhouetted against the sky and then disappearing from sight behind the Second Pinnacle. I had just returned from a wonderful little expedition with a local climbing friend, Jim Fotheringham. We had made the first ascent of the West Summit of Shivling in the Gangotri Himalaya. We had climbed it alpine-style, taking five days up a complex route up its south-west face and arête and one day down the other side. It had been a bold, exciting ascent with a high level of risk. I was beginning to regret a promise I had made spontaneously to Wendy immediately after getting back from the North East Ridge – never to go back to Everest.

3

'…all I had to do was put one foot in front of the other for that last stretch to the highest point on earth. And suddenly I was there, everything on all sides dropping away below me. I hugged Pertemba who crouched beside me. The summit is the size of a pool table. We could all move around on it without fear of being pushed over the edge.'

# Everest: South East Ridge, 1985
## A Personal Resolution

# A Promise Broken

'MY NAME IS ARNE NAESS. I do hope you don't mind me ringing you. I wonder if I could come and see you? I'm organizing an expedition to Nepal and would appreciate your advice.'

He had a slight foreign accent but his English was fluent. I often get enquiries about expeditioning.

'Of course. When do you want to come up?'

'How about next week? What day would suit you best?'

'What about Monday? Could you make it in the afternoon, say, just after lunch? I'm working flat out on a book at the moment and try to do my writing in the mornings.'

'That's fine. Have you got an airport near you?'

'Not really. Newcastle's the nearest, but that's sixty miles away on the other side of the Pennines; but the train service isn't bad. It takes just under four hours to Carlisle.'

'I'll check and get back to you.'

He phoned again, an hour later.

'You've an airfield just by Carlisle. I'm chartering a plane. I'll be with you at two o'clock on Monday.'

I was impressed .

And that was how I became involved with the shipping magnate and mountaineer who was planning to lead the first Norwegian expedition to Everest in 1985. My role was equipment and planning adviser, but in the immediate aftermath of Pete and Joe's death in 1982 I could not contemplate returning to Everest and had promised Wendy I would never go back. So I told Arne that I would not be joining the expedition. In the following year he played me like a fly-fisherman would a salmon, teasing me with questions about Sherpas or equipment and then mentioning that I could always change my mind. I remained firm into 1983, but after trips to

*Fixing rope on the Lhotse Face above Camp 3, Bjørn Myrer-Lund is in the foreground, with Sundare and Ang Rita crossing the snow slope below. The rocks of the Geneva Spur are to the far left, and the pinnacles top right are on the summit ridge of Lhotse.*

'It is the wives of climbers who are the courageous ones, who have to cope with real stress, who have to sit back and wait, and all too often break the news to wives of the ones who don't come back.'

Shivling in India and Mount Vinson in Antarctica my mountaineering enthusiasm was rekindled and I was wavering. Here was a chance of reaching the highest point on earth being handed to me on a silver platter – Sherpas, oxygen, the easiest route by the South East Ridge and South Col, the chance of indulging my penchant for organization, without the ultimate responsibility of leadership. I just couldn't resist.

How could I tell Wendy? Inevitably she was deeply upset and yet I suspect she always half-knew that I'd go back. It is the wives of climbers who are the courageous ones, who have to cope with real stress, who have to sit back and wait, and all too often break the news to wives of the ones who don't come back. I had no excuse except the strength of my need to return to Everest. There were no recriminations, except from my two sons who were indignant.

'But you promised. You can't go back. What about Mum?'

Wendy, having accepted it, gave me total support and concentrated on getting me fit for the climb.

Pertemba, looking hardly a day older than when he had been with us ten years earlier, was waiting at Kathmandu airport. I had, of course, recommended him as sirdar. Pertemba had told Arne he would be happy to take on the job but that he had promised his wife Dawa that he would not go through the Everest Icefall again. As the main job of the sirdar is administrative, it was agreed he could do this at Base Camp and a climbing sirdar would be appointed to take charge on the mountain. We flew to Luglha by helicopter over the paths I had walked in the past.

Luglha had certainly changed since 1975. There were many more buildings, most of them so-called hotels, though they were really just hostels with dormitory accommodation. You could even get hot showers, though these were no more than an empty tin with holes punched in the bottom, set in the roof of a hut, through which a Sherpa lad would pour buckets of hot water. The men now wore western clothes, but the Sherpanis still wore their traditional dress and apron. There was certainly more money around. This was reflected in the difficulty we had getting porters to carry our gear to Base Camp. We were using more yaks than we had done in the past and Pertemba was having a hard job finding enough of these. Our gear was going up the valley in a trickle. Gone were the big porter trains of the seventies.

I could remember Namche Bazar as it had been in 1961, a collection of houses

*The Norwegian team with the South Face of Nuptse and the summit of Everest behind. In front from left to right, Kjell Torgeir Stokke, Arne Naess, myself and Odd Eliassen; middle row, Bjørn Myrer-Lund, Pertemba, Håvard Nesheim, Christian Larsson and Ralph Høibakk; at the back, Ola Einang and Stein Aasheim.*

clinging in a little crescent to a basin-like valley above the Dudh Kosi. We had been given a meal at the police post and had had to eat traditionally without knives or forks, shovelling the rice and dahl into our mouths with our fingers. It was very different now, packed with new hotels, some of which really merited the title. The most lavish belonged to Pasang Kami, my sirdar on the 1970 Annapurna South Face expedition. Fine-boned and now wearing horn-rimmed glasses, he had always been more an organizer than a climber. He was one of the most successful Sherpa businessmen and, besides part-owning a trekking company with Pertemba, had built a three-storey hotel with a penthouse restaurant. It even had electric light, an innovation that had come with a small hydro-electric scheme for Namche Bazar.

At the bridge over the Dudh Kosi I sought out the tea-house of Ang Phurba, the Sherpa with whom I had climbed on those memorable final days of our 1972 expedition. He was sitting on the porch with his youngest child, a rosy-cheeked baby. We exchanged news of the expeditions we had been on in the intervening years. His wife offered me some chang. It hardly tastes alcoholic but its effects are insidious.

We spent a week acclimatizing at Pheriche and two further nights were planned at Lobuche. But I was now impatient to reach Base Camp and begin assessing a route through the Icefall so, with Arne's blessing, I went ahead to join the Sherpas, who, I found, had already constructed our kitchen shelter. The following morning, I left early with Pema Dorje, our climbing sirdar, to find a vantage point from which to view the Icefall. We scrambled up the broken rocks at the foot of Khumbutse, the peak immediately above Base Camp, to the crest of a small spur, until we were looking down on to the lower part of the Icefall and could see across to its centre. It was completely lacking in snow, very different from the two previous occasions on which I had been there, when many of the crevasses had been hidden by the monsoon snows and even the sérac walls and towers had been softened by the depth of their cover. Now it was bare, gleaming in the early morning sun, seamed with the black lines of crevasses and pebbled with a chaos of icy talus slopes, the debris of collapsed walls and towers.

'Have you ever seen it as bare as this?' I asked Pema Dorje.

'Never. It looks very dangerous,' was the reply.

The others were beginning to arrive. It was the first time the entire expedition of ten climbers and 28 Sherpas had been together in one place and Arne gave a welcoming speech aimed particularly at the Sherpas, expressing his appreciation of their quality and the work they were going to do for us. He was certainly right in telling them that they were the strongest team that had ever been assembled. Quite apart from Pertemba, who had now been twice to the summit, and Pema Dorje who

*Everest Base Camp, with the strings of prayer flags stretching out from the altar and the Khumbu Icefall lurking immediately behind. The West Shoulder of Everest is on the left and the West Ridge of Nuptse on the right.*

*On the way to Tengpoche I called on Ang Phurba who had been with me in 1972 and 1975. He has invested most of his earnings in a lodge and this supplements his income during the tourist season.*

had been once, Sundhare had the record, having reached the top on three previous occasions. In his late twenties, his first expedition had been with us to the South-West Face in 1975 when he had reached Camp 5. He appeared to be very westernized, loved pop music and disco dancing and cultivated the fashions of a smart young man about Kathmandu, with a trendy shoulder-length hairstyle and tight jeans. Ang Rita had perhaps achieved even more, having reached the summit twice without oxygen. He was very different from Sundhare. Stolid and very much a farmer, one felt he had a firmer hold on his own heritage and background. Three other members of the Sherpa team had been to the summit of Everest once before and over half the team had reached the South Col.

After Arne's speech the Sherpas conducted their *puja*, lighting a fire of juniper wood on the chorten of piled stones they had built in front of the camp. It was 15 March and on the following day we planned to venture into the Icefall.

There are many rituals associated with climbing Everest, and their very familiarity was a reassurance, a series of signposts towards the summit. I enjoyed waking in the dark of the pre-dawn in my own little tent, then going across to the cook's shelter which was so much warmer and cosier than the mess tent. The cooking stoves, which had been lit by one of the cook boys, were standing on a table of piled stones in the middle of the shelter, roaring away under the big detchies. Ang Tendi, our chief cook, was still in his sleeping bag, curled up on a mattress on top of some boxes at the end of the shelter. Ang Nima, one of the cook boys, poured me a mug of tea and I sat on a box.

'What are the Sherpas having?'

'Dhal bhatt, you want some?'

'Yes, please.'

Ang Nima ladled out a plateful of rice covered with dhal in which swam big red chillies. I nursed the hot plate as other Sherpas trooped in one by one. Soon the shelter was packed with Sherpas and the three other climbers going into the Icefall that day.

There were no commands. The Sherpas drifted out, picked up the loads which had been allocated to them the previous evening, and then, pausing at the chorten on which a fire was smouldering, muttered a prayer, tossed on it a handful of rice or tsampa, and plodded off in the dim light towards the Icefall. I, too, always uttered the prayer that everyone would return safely from the Icefall that day.

We nibbled away at the route through the Icefall, the climbers divided into two teams taking alternate days. It was nerve-racking yet invigorating, trying to pick out a safe route through this maze of ice. We were also starting to work as a team, not just the climbers, but also with the Sherpas, who took their full share in route finding. Each day we pushed the route out a little farther but it was taking too long. A week had gone by and we still hadn't broken through into the Western Cwm. It was the morning of 22 March and I was having breakfast in the Sherpa kitchen when Pertemba came in, dressed for the hill.

'Instinctively I chose the narrow passage behind it. It seemed to give what could have

'I think I'll have a look at the Icefall today', he said.

I certainly didn't mind. Apart from anything else it meant that I was not the only one to have broken a promise to his wife! Pertemba wanted to get things moving and to see for himself why we hadn't pushed the route through to Camp 1. But I don't think that was the only reason. At Base Camp, as so often happens, petty misunderstandings were causing tension. It was all about money and food – it nearly always is.

Arne and Christian Larsson, our Base Camp manager, were used to doing business in the world of shipping with firm contracts which were honoured to the letter, every dollar accounted for. Business in Sherpa country is different. The Sherpas had opted to be paid a ration allowance so that all their food could be bought locally but then, almost inevitably, they had yearned for the chocolates, sweets and biscuits that the climbers were eating.

It all came to a head over a load of fresh oranges. The trekkers who had come in with us to Base Camp had chartered a helicopter to take them back to Kathmandu from Pheriche and Arne had used it to bring in the oranges. Ang Tendi asked if the Sherpas could have some but was told they were reserved for the climbers. It was the only time I had anything approaching a row with Arne.

'It's inevitable they're going to want to share in the goodies,' I pointed out. 'You always want something all the more if you're not allowed to have it. It's human nature.'

'It cost me a great deal of money getting those oranges in', he replied. 'The Sherpas said they wanted to buy their own food and we've already paid out a hell of a lot for it. They should stick by their agreements. Anyway, if we shared out the oranges amongst everyone at Base Camp, there'd hardly be enough to go round.'

'But can't you see? We're going to depend on the Sherpas' enthusiasm to get us up this mountain. What on earth are a few oranges compared to keeping them happy? It's worth making concessions at this stage when it could make all the difference between success and failure later on.'

In the end Arne agreed to share out the oranges and, once the concession had been made, very few Sherpas bothered with them. We ended up throwing most of the oranges away after they had become rotten. As the expedition progressed, Arne and Christian became much more relaxed in their dealings with the Sherpas and consequently their relationship with them got better and better.

That morning Pertemba wanted to escape from all these niggles and grapple with the much more tangible problems of the Icefall. The worst section was near the top.

*Sherpas carrying ladders, ropes and anchors into the Icefall to help make a route which can never be completely safe but can at least be climbed quickly in the danger areas.*

been little more than psychological protection from the threatening wall above'

A tottering cliff of ice about 70m (230ft) high barred our route. The only way to bypass it was through a canyon filled with ice blocks spawned from the sérac walls. About halfway along a huge fin of ice protruded. Instinctively I chose the narrow passage behind it. It seemed to give what could have been little more than psychological protection from the threatening wall above.

The passage was shoulder-width and about 5m (16ft) long. I had walked a dozen paces or so beyond when I heard a sharp crack, followed by a dull heavy crunch. Glancing behind me I saw that the fin, for no apparent reason, had broken off at its base and, like a vice, had closed the passage I had just walked through. It needed little imagination to visualize what would have happened had this occurred just ten seconds earlier.

Pertemba's drive took us into the Western Cwm and Arne deployed his team to establish camps. Camp 2 halfway up the cwm would be our Advanced Base. I was

*Left: A huge crevasse in the middle of the Icefall. It is in constant movement, with new crevasses opening, ice towers tumbling and sérac walls collapsing. Right: Arne Naess was a good leader, consulting with his team but prepared to make firm decisions. Overleaf: Climbers and Sherpas in the Western Cwm, one of the highest and most beautiful mountain valleys in the world.*

enjoying supervising the flow of supplies up the mountain. Although at times I found it frustrating not being able immediately to implement my own ideas, I could be very much more relaxed than I had been on previous trips.

My Apple IIc had stood up amazingly well to the dust and glacier grit, to temperatures ranging between -10°C (14°F) at night and the mid-eighties inside the tent during the day, all of which computers tend to hate. It had been bumped on the back of a yak as far as Base Camp and then carried by a porter up through the Icefall. I could only operate it during the day when the temperature rose above freezing and the power of the sun could charge the battery through the solar panel. It was to achieve a record of its own when I took it up to Camp 2 at 6400m (20,100ft), as I suspect this is the highest on the earth's surface that a computer has ever been used.

Once the three out in front had reached the middle of the Lhotse Face where we planned to establish Camp 3, the only people available to replace them were Odd Eliassen, Bjørn Myrer-Lund and myself. I was beginning to look forward to being in the lead. It would be our job to make the route to the South Col.

Walking below the South West Face, and now looking across towards it, brought many memories. Most amazing of all, though, was the site of our old Camp 4. The super-boxes, specially designed by Hamish MacInnes, were still there, faded into a brown yellow. No doubt they were stuffed with ice, but they clung to the snow slope below the little rock spur we had feared would give all too little protection from the avalanches coming down from the walls above. The site had been better than we had thought, and the boxes themselves had more than justified their weight.

The Sherpas were pulling far ahead. Odd was with them. Bjørn and I went more

slowly, pulling up the fixed ropes over endless slopes of ice, broken only by steeper bulges. The average angle was little more than 40 degrees, but the ice was so hard that it must have been intimidating to lead. I glanced up to see Odd and the Sherpas now on their way down. They had pushed beyond the high point of the others and found a site for Camp 3 on a wide shelf, sheltered by a sérac wall. We were at a height of around 7400m (24,275ft)

*I joined Bjørn Myrer-Lund to help make the route from Camp 3 to the South Col. The South West Face, very bare of snow, is in the background on the left.*

The following morning it was Bjørn and I who set out with Ang Rita and Sundhare to establish Camp 3. We were quickly left behind by the two Sherpas as we slogged up the ropes, weighed down with our personal gear, much heavier loads than the previous day. One advantage of this was that by the time we reached the camp the Sherpas had erected both tents. All we had to do was crawl inside and light the stove for our first brew.

That night we slept on oxygen. On the South West Face in 1975, we had only started using oxygen at Camp 5, at about 7700m (25,270ft), but since we had plenty of oxygen bottles and the Sherpa-power to carry them, it seemed to make sense to start using it at Camp 3 as Bjørn and I wanted to avoid burning ourselves out in this push to the South Col. Snuggled in my sleeping bag, the hiss of the oxygen was reassuring as I woke from time to time through the long night.

I started cooking just after dawn, but we were slow in getting away and had extra brews as we waited for the sun to creep over the shoulder of Everest and give us the benefit of its warmth. I poked my head out of our tent and saw the Sherpas just emerging from theirs. Time to move. Bjørn and I were using oxygen that day, but the Sherpas weren't. Consequently they were ready first, shouldering rucksacks filled with rope and climbing hardware. I was still struggling with my oxygen system. The straps of the mask were the wrong length. I couldn't fasten one of the buckles, lost my temper and hurled the mask into the snow. Bjørn seemed quietly amused. By the time I had got myself organized the others had vanished round the corner of the sérac. The oxygen didn't seem to be doing anything at all for me.

I soon arrived at a steep little step. They hadn't bothered to put a fixed rope on it. I climbed it clumsily, my goggles misting up, and the snout of the oxygen mask making it impossible to glance down and see where I was kicking my cramponed boots. Why the hell hadn't they put a rope here? I cursed them, cursed the mountain, cursed the whole expedition. Sundhare and Ang Rita were no more than little dots on the other side of a sweep of ice leading to the distinctive broken limestone rocks known as the Yellow Band and Bjørn was already halfway across the ice slope on his way to join them.

'Come on, Bonington; get a grip. You're behaving like a small child,' I told myself.

I was going so badly there seemed little point in trying to catch up with the others. Sundhare and Ang Rita were obviously capable of fixing the route and Bjørn would soon be with them. They had run the rope out almost horizontally across the slope towards the lowest point of the barrier formed by the Yellow Band. It looked as if it could do with a few intermediate anchor points, and that the approach to the traverse needed some fixed rope. I decided I might just as well spend the rest of the day doing this. I'd be conserving my energy yet doing something useful. I immediately felt better, dropped back down to the camp and collected some more ice pitons and rope, dumped the oxygen gear that had been so cumbersome, and returned to the fray in a much better humour.

I have always enjoyed putting in fixed ropes; there's an element of craft to it, getting the rope to just the right tension and placing the anchors so that it is easy to transfer from one rope-length to the next. I was enjoying myself. Meanwhile I could see that the others were making good progress, slowly climbing up alongside the Geneva Spur.

After a couple of hours I returned to the tents to prepare tea for Bjørn and the Sherpas when they came back. They had fixed about 300m (1000ft) of rope, most of it salvaged from the many old ropes left embedded in the snow and ice. Sundhare had done most of the leading and it is in this that one major change since 1975 can be seen. Then, most of the Sherpas had still been essentially load-carriers, but today an increasing number of them are becoming first-rate mountaineers, accustomed on some expeditions to guiding their clients up the mountain. The Lhotse Face was familiar territory to Sundhare and Ang Rita. Not only were they much faster than we were, they knew the way from previous experience.

Next day, Bjørn and I had the shits and with the best will in the world could not uphold the honour of Norway by pushing the route out to the South Col. Bjørn tried, but met Sundhare and Ang Rita on the way back. The following morning at Camp 2 Arne called a meeting to discuss the composition of the summit teams, the Sherpas listening and occasionally adding their comments. The excitement was infectious. I was already suffering from an acute attack of summititis, but I was impatient to get back to Base Camp or lower to recuperate for my own bid. Before I left Base Camp for three days at Pheriche, Pertemba came over.

'You know, Chris, I'd really like to go to the top with you,' he said. It meant a great deal to me.

*April 1985*

# Fulfilment

T HERE ARE MANY PARALLELS between climbing a mountain and fighting a war.
This is perhaps why the vocabulary is very similar – assault, siege, logistics. The
dangers of climbing the higher Himalayan peaks are probably greater than those
encountered in most wartime battles, yet the essence and spirit of climbing is
very different. The climber doesn't fight anyone or, for that matter, anything. He is
working with, and through, the natural forces. He doesn't fight the storm; he works
his way through it, perhaps shelters from it. But a climb, particularly one using set
camps and a support team, needs planning that is very similar to a successful military assault. It doesn't matter how talented the lead climbers are. If their supplies
don't reach them, they are going to be forced to retreat, just as a brilliant military
advance can be halted through lack of fuel or ammunition.

We were now like troops at the start line for a big offensive, programmed to move
from one holding area to the next. It was 18 April. Ralph Høibakk, Håvard Nesheim
and Ola Einang were at Camp 3 and would move up to the South Col, while Ang
Rita and Pema Dorje would go straight through from Camp 2 to join them at the
top camp. Odd, Bjørn, Pertemba and I were moving up to Camp 2 that same day to
come in behind them for the second summit bid.

The 19th was to be summit day for Ralph, Håvard and Ola. We made a leisurely
start from Advanced Base, having just to reach Camp 3, halfway up the Lhotse Face.
I walked steadily but slowly, soon dropping behind the others, but I didn't mind,
feeling that I was keeping up a steady rhythm, of pushing up the jumar clamp, kicking crampon points into the hard ice and of measuring the slow progress upwards
against landmarks that had become all too familiar – a rock sticking out of the ice,
the foot of the Geneva Spur. A plume of cloud was flying from the summit pyramid;
gusts like whirlwinds picked up flurries of spindrift and chased them across the face.

I was just short of the camp and noticed a figure coming down the fixed ropes
from above. It could only be one of the summit team. Had they made it? As the

*The summit at last. From
left to right, Bjørn having a
pee, Odd crouching, Dawa
Nuru, Pertemba getting
out the T-shirt that Pete
Boardman had worn on the
summit in 1975, and Ang
Lhakpa flying the Nepalese
flag from his ice axe.*

'We plodded up the crest of the ridge, our shadows cast far into Nepal.
Ever steepening, sometimes rock, mostly snow, it was much harder than
I had imagined. It seemed to go on for ever.'

*Camp 4 on the South Col with the tent roped down against the high winds. Some of the empty oxygen bottles and debris which litter the world's bleakest rubbish tip date back to 1953, but efforts are now being made to clear them up.*

figure came closer, moving slowly, ponderously even though it was downhill, the face hidden by oxygen mask and goggles, I somehow didn't think he had. It would not have mattered how tired he was, he'd have waved, there would be more spring in his step. I reached the tents first. The approaching figure staggered those last metres, sank into the snow and pulled off his mask. It was Ralph Høibakk.

'How did it go?' asked Odd

'We didn't make it.'

They had set out at four that morning and made steady progress with Ralph breaking trail for most of the way. He had reached the South Summit 40 minutes in front of the others

'The wind wasn't too bad when I got there and I was tempted to go for the top, but we'd agreed we'd all go together. So I waited. But the wind got worse and worse. By the time the others arrived it was hurricane force. The Sherpas wanted to turn back and so we did too.'

They had been so close. Now we were in line to make the first ascent of the expedition. That didn't mean very much to me – I'd be the seventh Briton to reach the top of Everest – but Bjørn and Odd had the chance of being the first Scandinavians to get there.

The following morning we climbed the fixed rope to the South Col. It was less windy than the previous day and there wasn't a cloud in the sky. I handled the ropes with care. Sundhare and Ang Rita had done a good job, but some of the old ropes we were using were frayed and knotted in great clusters at the anchor points.

It was a surprisingly long walk from the top of the Geneva Spur to the South Col, over slaty rocks that resembled tiles on a roof. Looking back down the Western Cwm, I was level with the summit of Nuptse. The Col itself was far more extensive than I had ever imagined, a wild flattish expanse the size of a football field, covered with the same slaty rock I had just crossed, and littered with the debris of previous expeditions; the skeletons of tents, oxygen bottles, old food boxes in little clusters – ugly memorials to the ambitions of our predecessors. The final slopes of Everest rose on the other side, in not so much a ridge as a face of snow and broken rocks that looked steep and inhospitable. Three tents, moored down by cradles of climbing ropes, were pitched near the centre of the Col. The Sherpas, Dawa Nuru and Ang Lhakpa, had come up from Camp 2 that same day and were going for the summit with us. Neither of them had been to the top before.

Pertemba was already ensconced in our tent, with the gas stove going. Inside, with the stove and the heat from the afternoon sun, it was quite warm. I lay on my sleeping bag, sipping tea and savouring the knowledge that I was on the threshold of fulfilment. It was good to be sharing a tent with Pertemba.

It was 1.30 a.m. when we set out across the flatness of the col, crampons slipping and catching on the stones underfoot, and then on to a bulge of hard, smooth ice that slowly increased in angle as we approached the ridge. Each of us followed the pool of light cast by our head torch. Pertemba was out in front. He had been here before. I was bringing up the rear and it wasn't long before the gap between me and the person in front increased. We were now on a snow slope, a tongue reaching up into the broken rocks that guarded the base of the ridge. At the top of the snow was rock – crumbling steps, easy scrambling but unnerving in the dark with all the impedimenta of high-altitude gear.

I was tired already; not out of breath but just listless, finding it progressively harder to force one foot in front of the other. Three hundred metres (1000ft), an hour and a half went by. I was so tired. I had dropped behind, the lights of the others becoming ever more distant weakening glimmers. They had stopped for a rest but, as I caught up, they started once again. I slumped into the snow and involuntarily muttered, almost cried, 'I'll never make it.'

Odd heard me. 'You'll do it, Chris. Just get on your feet. I'll stay behind you.'

And on it went, broken rock, hard snow, then deep soft snow, which Pertemba ploughed through, allowing me to keep up, as I could plod up the well-formed steps made so laboriously by the people in front. The stars were beginning to vanish in the grey of dawn and the mountains, most of them below us, assumed dark silhouettes. The crest of the ridge, still above us, lightened and then the soaring peak of the South Summit was touched with gold as the sun crept over the horizon.

By the time we reached the crest, the site of Hillary and Tenzing's top camp in 1953, all the peaks around us were lit by the sun's low-flung rays. The Kangshung Glacier, still in shadow, stretched far beneath us. The Kangshung Face itself was a great sweep of snow set at what seemed an easy angle. Just beneath us some fixed rope protruded, a relic of the American expedition that climbed the East Face in 1983. Across the face was the serrated crest of the North East Ridge. I could pick out the shoulder where we had had our Third Snow Cave and the snow-plastered teeth of the Pinnacles where we had last seen Pete and Joe in 1982.

*Overleaf: Odd and Bjørn on the South East Shoulder, with Makalu, fifth highest mountain in the world, in the middle distance and Kangchenjunga, third highest, 130km (80 miles) away on the left horizon. The huge unclimbed South Face of Lhotse is to the right.*

We were at 8300m (27,230ft) and it was five in the morning. Time to change our cylinders. There was still some oxygen in the old bottle but this could be used as a reserve on our return. We set out again, the Europeans and Pertemba with full cylinders, but Dawa Nuru and Ang Lhakpa with the same ones which they had used from the South Col. They would have to nurse their flow rate very carefully.

We plodded up the crest of the ridge, our shadows cast far into Nepal. Ever steepening, sometimes rock, mostly snow, it was much harder than I had imagined. It seemed to go on for ever. Glancing behind me, the black rocky summit of Lhotse still seemed higher than we were. A last swell of snow, with the wind gusting hard, threatening to blow us from our perch, and we were on the South Summit. We gathered on the corniced col just beneath it. This was where Doug and Dougal had bivouacked on their way back down from the top in 1975. The gully they had climbed dropped steeply into the South West Face.

There was a pause. Pertemba had broken trail all the way so far but the ridge between the South Summit and the Hillary Step looked formidable, a fragile drop on either side. Odd was worried about our oxygen supply. It had been three hours since we had changed bottles and he questioned whether we had enough to get back. The others had been climbing with a flow rate of three litres per minute, but I had found that this had not been enough. I had frequently turned mine on to four and so would have even less than they. But I knew I wanted to go on and at this stage was prepared to risk anything to get to the top.

Pertemba said decisively, 'We go on.'

Ang Lhakpa got out the rope, 20m (65ft) between six of us. Bjørn took the initiative. He tied one end round his waist and pushed out in front, trailing the rope behind him, more of a token than anything else, as we followed. The going to the foot of the Step was more spectacular than difficult, but the Step itself was steep.

Odd took a belay and Bjørn started up, wallowing in the deep soft snow, getting an occasional foothold on the rock wall to the left. Pertemba followed, digging out an old fixed rope left by a previous expedition. The Step was about 20m (65ft) high and Bjørn anchored the rope around a rock bollard near its top. The others followed, using the rope as a handrail.

I was last, but Dawa Nuru waved me past. I gathered he had run out of oxygen. I struggled up the Step, panting, breathless, apprehensive and then I felt what was almost the physical presence of Doug Scott. I could see his long straggly hair, the wire-rimmed glasses and could sense his reassurance and encouragement. It was as if he was pushing me on. Les, my father-in-law, was there as well. He has a quiet wisdom and great compassion. He had thrown the I Ching just before I left home and had predicted my success. This was something that had given me renewed confidence whenever I doubted my ability to make it.

Doug and Les got me to the top of the Hillary Step. The others had now vanished round the corner and I seemed to have the mountain to myself. The angle eased and all I had to do was put one foot in front of the other for that last stretch to the

*Descending Everest just below the South Summit, with the Kangshung Glacier below. I always dread the descent — it can be the most dangerous part of a climb when you are tired, moving faster than on the ascent and perhaps losing concentration.*

highest point on earth. And suddenly I was there, everything on all sides dropping away below me. I hugged Pertemba who crouched beside me. The summit is the size of a pool table. We could all move around on it without fear of being pushed over the edge. Odd and Bjørn, who were raising and photographing the Norwegian flag, came over and embraced me.

Then there was time to look around us. From west through north to east lay the Tibetan plateau, a rolling ocean of brown hills with the occasional white cap. To the east rose Kangchenjunga, a huge snowy mass, first climbed by George Band and Joe Brown in 1955, and to the west the great chain of the Himalaya, with Shisha Pangma,

*We met Arne and his team on the Lhotse Face as they moved up towards the South Col and we made our way back to Base Camp. They too were to reach the summit.*

China's 8000-m (26,250-ft) peak, dominating the horizon. Doug, Alex McIntyre and Roger Baxter-Jones had climbed its huge South Face in 1982. Immediately below us, just the other side of the Western Cwm, was Nuptse, looking stunted, the very reverse of that view I had enjoyed 24 years earlier, when Everest had seemed so un-attainable. To the south was a white carpet of cloud covering the foothills and plains of India. We were indeed on top of the world.

At that moment another figure appeared, moving slowly and painfully. It was Dawa Nuru. He hadn't turned back; he was coming to the summit without oxygen. There was no longer any sign of the Chinese maypole that Doug and Dougal had found in 1975. It had finally been blown away some years earlier. There were, however, some paper prayer flags embedded in the snow which must have been left there the previous autumn.

Pertemba had brought with him the Mynedd T-shirt that Pete Boardman had worn to the summit of Everest in 1975. It had been to given him by Hilary, Pete's widow. We lingered for another 20 minutes or so before starting the descent.

There was no room for elation; the steepness of the drop ensured that. I concen-trated on every step down, now full of apprehension. The others caught me up and passed me. I was feeling progressively more tired. I sat down every few paces, beyond thought. But almost imperceptibly I was losing height. I reached the top of the snow slope that stretched down to the Col, cramponed down it cautiously, zigzagging from side to side, then noticed what looked like another tent in the middle of the slope. I veered towards it without thinking and, as I came closer, realized that it was a woman sitting very upright in the snow, fair hair blowing in the wind, teeth bared in a fixed grimace. I didn't go any closer but looked away and hurried past. I guessed that it was the body of Hannelore Schmatz, the wife of the leader of the 1979 German expedition. She had reached the summit but had died from exhaustion on the South East Ridge on the way down. Sundhare had been with her. She had died higher on the mountain but her body must have been carried down to its present exposed position by an avalanche.

Pertemba and I spent the night on the South Col while the others hurried down to bring the news of our success. Next morning we too descended to hugs and congratulations and I made what I vowed was my final trip through the Everest Icefall.

These days an ascent by the South Col route is almost routine, but nonetheless our expedition achieved a large number of records of varying merit; we eventually put 17 on the summit, the largest number of any single expedition; it was also the earliest pre-monsoon ascent; the first Scandinavian ascent; Sundhare now had the personal record for the number of ascents of the mountain, having climbed it four times; and Ang Rita had climbed it three times without oxygen; I had the dubious honour of being the oldest person, by ten days, to climb Everest, a record I held for all of nine days when Dick Bass took it from me. Being 55 years old, I suspect he might hold the record for a long time. He also achieved his ambition of being the first man to climb the highest point of every continent.

As I walked back towards Luglha, I had a sense of profound contentment. I hadn't achieved any records. I was the seventh Briton and the 173rd person to reach the summit of Everest. I had had a great deal of help from the Sherpas, as we all had. But standing on that highest point of earth had meant a great deal. Gratification of ego? Without a doubt. But it was so much more than that, though I still find it difficult to define exactly what that drive was. It is as difficult as finding a precise definition of why one climbs.

There was certainly very little physical pleasure at the time – none of the elation I find in rock climbing on a sunny day near to sea level where the air is rich in oxygen, when there is strength in one's limbs, and a joy in being poised on tiny holds over the abyss, moving with precision from one hold to the next. There is none of that on Everest. There had been little questing into the unknown or even the challenge of picking out a route. I had been content to follow, indeed only capable of following, the others to the top. But there had been the awareness of the mountains, slowly dropping away around me, the summit of Everest caught in the

*Safely back down at Base Camp, we can relax and celebrate at last. Kneeling, Pertemba and Ang Lhakpa, standing, Bjørn, Dawa Nuru, myself and Odd.*

first golden glow of the rising sun, the North East Ridge, with all its memories, glimpsed through a gap in the cornice, winding, convoluted, threatening in its steep flutings and jagged towers, now far below me.

It was a focal point in a climbing life, a gathering of so many ambitions and memories that had climaxed in a burst of grief and yet relief, when I reached the summit of Everest.

# Conclusion

I'VE OFTEN BEEN ASKED, 'Isn't everything an anticlimax after reaching the top of Everest?' The answer is an emphatic no. Yes, reaching the top was very important to me – I don't think I realized just how important until I finally made it. Reaching the top is the natural culmination of any climb. After hours, days or even months striving on a ridge or face, with a view that is limited by the mountain in front of you, there is an extraordinary sense of elation when you can look all around you. That sense is particularly strong on Everest when mountains like Lhotse, which seem so huge from below, are dwarfed as you look down upon them. But what climbing Everest did was free me to concentrate on the kind of climbing I've always enjoyed, which is going off with small groups of friends to unclimbed peaks, ideally in wild unexplored areas like Tibet or Greenland. In 2000 I took my eldest son Daniel, my brother Gerald and nephew James to the top of the unclimbed Danga II (6200m/20,341ft), near Kangchenjunga, to share with them the joy of finding our way up somewhere that no one had ever been. We could see Everest some 130km (80 miles) to the west, dominating all around it. Ours had been a modest climb, little more than a long walk to a dome-like summit, but my emotion in sharing that experience with my closest family was if anything more intense than my feelings on top of Everest.

I was lucky to climb Everest when I did. Our expedition was one of the last to have the Western Cwm to itself. There was an American expedition, who made pleasant neighbours at Base Camp, attempting the West Ridge from the Lho La, and a British expedition led by Mal Duff were on the other side of the mountain attempting the North East Ridge. It was shortly after this that the Nepalese authorities increased the peak fee to $100,000 and limited the number of climbers allowed to go above Base Camp to seven. Initially they maintained the rule of only one expedition to each route, but very quickly began to relax it – you can't blame them. Nepal is one of the poorest countries in the world and Everest is their major

*Memories flooded in as I stood on the summit of Everest with Ang Lhakpa, too bemused to take off my mask and goggles for the photograph.*

asset. The number of expeditions at Base Camp increased rapidly in the years that followed and soon there could be up to 20 different expeditions, several hundred people, camped on the Khumbu Glacier and up to 50 climbers on the South Col poised for a summit bid.

Dick Bass's ascent as part of our Norwegian expedition was arguably the first guided ascent, and it was to open up not only the challenge of collecting the highest tops of the seven continents but also the business of commercial expeditions. These have expanded over the years until today the majority of expeditions on Everest are commercial, offering places to fee-paying clients. It seems a natural development, since guiding has been a part of the climbing scene from the very beginning of the sport, when Victorian gentlemen hired local chamois hunters or crystal collectors to take them into the high parts of the Alps. Indeed, during the nineteenth century it was considered irresponsible to go without a guide. There are some big differences however. In the Alps a guide has effective control of his client, he can put him on a short rope, arrest his fall if he slips and give him immediate and direct guidance and support.

Above 8000m (26,250ft) it's different. The guide is often in as bad a way as the client and anyway it would be too expensive to organize an expedition on a one-to-one or even a one-to-two guiding basis. A system has therefore evolved where there are just one or perhaps two 'guides', though they are not necessarily accredited by any of the national guiding bodies, with six or so Sherpas who fix the route most of the way from the South Col to the summit and then supervise the clients as well as they can. The clients are cosseted all the way to the top camp, their tents erected, meals cooked for them, and all but their personal gear carried by Sherpas. Most of the commercial operators, certainly the better ones, ensure that their clients have some mountaineering experience, ideally the ascent of a lower 8000-m (26,250-ft)peak and at least Denali or perhaps Aconcagua. Most of the clients, however, lack the depth of mountain experience to cope with a crisis, such as the storm that hit Everest in 1996. On that occasion eight died, including two of the top high-altitude guides of the time, Rob Hall and Scott Fischer.

Having so many people from different expeditions on one route at the same time leads to other problems. The sense of loyalty and friendship that one can hope exists in a single expedition sadly does not necessarily extend to the rest of the expeditions on the mountain. There have been cases where climbers have not only used the fixed ropes put up by others without asking but also the tents and even the food and oxygen stored in those tents. There have also been incidents when other climbers, hell bent for the summit, have ignored people in trouble or with injuries.

Solutions aren't easy. At one extreme, the outstanding Swiss climber Erhard Loretan has suggested that the use of bottled oxygen on Everest should be banned. This certainly would act as a drastic filter to limit numbers, since comparatively few are capable of getting to the top without its use. I certainly couldn't have done.

Such a rule would undoubtedly also put an end to guided climbing, something that would be applauded by quite a few climbers who abhor the concept of people with limited mountaineering background being able to buy their way on to the highest point on earth. I believe, however, that one needs to have a broader perspective.

There is nothing wrong with guided climbing in the Himalaya as long as this new industry is properly regulated. Anyone guiding in the European Alps must be fully accredited and therefore trained. Yet in a much more dangerous high-altitude environment anyone can at present take on the role of guide. A professional alpine guide is not necessarily capable of performing in the Himalaya, where not only are there problems of altitude but also different tactics and strategy are called for. The guiding qualification recognized by the International Federation of Mountain Guides certainly provides a sound base but needs an additional training course and qualification for guiding at altitude.

There is also a real need for a system of qualification for Sherpa mountain guides. Commercial expeditions have provided a whole new source of relatively highly paid employment for the Sherpas. A recognized qualification would not only ensure that anyone taking on the role was qualified to do so, but would also raise their status from being just high-altitude porters.

All this may be a far cry from the freedom of a bunch of mates going for a mountain, but once one accepts the principle of guided climbing in the Himalaya, there needs to be a clear and fair contract between client and guide. There are some excellent guiding operations providing effective support and care for their clients but there are also some real cowboys.

Having defended their right to exist, I have to admit that, however well run the guided expedition is, the client must inevitably lose something from the experience. Jon Krakauer, in his book *Into Thin Air*, described his experience in the disastrous storm of 1996 that claimed eight lives high on the mountain. He was an experienced mountaineer who joined Rob Hall's guided team and he describes how he quickly lost all sense of initiative on an expedition where not only was everything done for you but also the guides positively discouraged initiative – since this could be unpredictable and perhaps even dangerous. But for the person who desperately wants to stand on the top of Everest but hasn't the time or experience to organize their own expedition, this is the only way he or she can achieve that dream. It is very easy to dismiss the client as someone who has just paid their way to the top of the mountain. This is an oversimplification of the case. Even with the very best of support, it is still a huge physical and mental challenge to reach the top and for all who achieve it, plenty more fail.

By January 2002 around 1500 people had reached the summit of Everest while, an interesting comparison, only two, Jacques Piccard and Don Walsh have been to the deepest depth of the Ocean, the Challenger Deep in the Marianas Trench, which, at 11,033m (36,194ft), is more than 2000 metres deeper than Everest is high.

Numbers have increased dramatically in the last few years with an all-time record in 2001 of 182 reaching the summit. Most of these have been guided ascents and are in large part due to the improved strategies and techniques introduced by the guides. The vast majority of the ascents are made in the pre-monsoon season and almost all by the traditional South Col and North Col routes, with the highest number on the south side.

There are very few ascents being made of the other more challenging routes on Everest. The last new route on the mountain was in 1996, when a Russian expedition made an impressive ascent of the North North East Face, between the North East Ridge and the North Col route. There are now almost as many routes on Everest as there are on Mont Blanc and the few remaining unclimbed lines are either very hard or very dangerous. There is the direct line up the Kangshung Face to the right of the American line that tops out at about 8300m (27,230ft) on the South East Ridge, but it would be suicidally dangerous. Then there's the Fantasy Ridge, to the right of the Kangshung Face, joining the North East Ridge at the site of our Third Snow Cave at just over 8000m (26,250ft) with a long way to go to the summit. Perhaps the most worthy line that still awaits a serious attempt is the South West Face Direct, taking the Rock Band up its sheer centre and then going straight for the summit – this would be taking extreme technical climbing above the 8200m (26,900ft) mark. Another interesting challenge that quite a few climbers have investigated is the Everest Horseshoe, up the West Ridge, over the top to the South Col, and then over Lhotse to finish along the serrated and very long ridge of Nuptse – quite a challenge. I'd say it was impossible without supplementary oxygen, since the climbers would be spending a long time above or around the 8000-m (26,250-ft) mark, so that would involve setting up a series of food and oxygen dumps along the route.

With the exhaustion of obvious new routes the same syndrome as has occurred in the Alps has now happened on Everest – the development of other firsts that are not necessarily linked to climbing. The Japanese mountaineer Yuichiro Miura started it by skiing down Everest from the South Col in 1970, though to be more accurate he fell most of the way, having lost control at an early stage. Fortunately he lived to tell the tale. Others have since repeated this from progressively higher points until Davo Karnicar, a Slovenian, succeeded in skiing all the way from the summit down the South East Ridge back to Base Camp in just five hours. He didn't take his skis off during the descent, skiing the Hillary Step and the narrow corniced ridge linking it with the South Summit. In the spring of 2001 the Frenchman Marco Siffredi made the first complete snowboard descent of the mountain down the traditional North Ridge all the way to Advanced Base.

Everest is no longer a mysterious place. The route into the north side has been improved so that tourist buses can get all the way in to Base Camp where there is a proposal to build a lodge. It is opposed by many but the proponents of the scheme point out that as several hundred people camp there each season the presence of a permanent lodge would be less unsightly, easier to keep clean, and it could be powered by the ecologically friendly recycling of human waste into methane. On the south side, all human waste is carried out from the Khumbu Glacier and the campsite, also home to several hundred each season, is comparatively clean. I am told that Advanced Base Camp on the north side is now clear of rubbish and kept clean by the more responsible of the commercial expeditions. The South Col is also very much cleaner than it was and efforts have been made to cover the bodies of dead climbers with stones.

I envy Mallory and the other members of the 1921 expedition when they were the first Westerners ever to approach Mount Everest. The experience of Ed Hillary and Sherpa Tenzing when they first found their way up the mountain was unrepeatable, as was that of Tom Hornbein and Willy Unsoeld, who reached the top after climbing the couloir up the North Face and then made the first traverse of the mountain to drop down to the South Col. I have a sense of nostalgia about the time that I walked into our Nuptse Base Camp in 1961 when Namche Bazar was tiny and the weekly market sold local wares to the people from the surrounding villages. But you can't hold people or places in a time warp. I do believe the development of the Everest region has brought more benefits than disadvantages to the people living around the mountain. Everest, like Mont Blanc before, has become a tourist mountain, a honey pot increasingly available to a wide range of people. I don't begrudge them – to do so would be elitist. I even welcome it, for the very nature of the honey pot is to concentrate activity around it and, as a result, leave the less well known but no less attractive areas clear for others to explore. On my own doorstep in the English Lake District, which has over 20 million visitors a year, you can still wander across the fells on a public holiday hardly seeing a soul. In the Himalaya, a hundred times as big with a tiny fraction of that number of visitors, this is even more the case.

Everest filled my horizons for 15 important years of my life, from the age of 35 to 50. There were other mountains, other adventures – Brammah, Changabang, the Ogre, K2 and Kongur – but that highest point was always there, sometimes in the background, but often the focus of my being. Everest has that special magic. I can think of very few climbers who could resist an invitation to Everest. It's why so many flock to it today – not just 'because it is there', but because it's the highest, the ultimate point, Chomolungma, Goddess Mother of the World. Our reasons for going there are mixed – a challenge that can be exploratory, spiritual, athletic, egotistical or downright commercial. It encompasses the full range of human emotions. I've experienced the extremes of joy and exhilaration, the depths of despair on that mountain. I've pushed myself to limits I didn't think I had in me. I've gazed out over a vista that grows wider and more wonderful as one gains height on the mountain, until at last comes that final reward, the 360-degree panorama when you at last reach the top of the world.

# Climbing Record

Symbols: *first ascent **first winter ascent ***first British ascent. Words in *italics* indicate the name of a particular climb.

1951  *Ash Tree Gully* Dinas Bach (Tom Blackburn) – first climb; *Hope* Idwal Slabs (Charles Verender) – first lead.

1952  *Chimney Route* Clogwyn Du'r Arddu (Dave Pullin); *Rana Temporia* Quinag* (Tony Moulam) – first new route, a VS.

1953  *Agag's Groove* Buachaille Etive Mor** (Hamish MacInnes, Kerr McPhaill, John Hammond, G. McIntosh) – first winter climb; *Crowberry Ridge Direct** and *Raven's Gully* Buachaille Etive Mor** (Hamish MacInnes); *Hangover* Clogwyn y Grochan (Geoff Francis) – first 'Brown' route.

1954  *Surplomb* Clogwyn y Grochan (Steve Lane) – second ascent.

1955  *Macavity* Avon Gorge *(Geoff Francis) – first new route on Avon's Main Wall.

1957  First alpine season: South East Face of Aig. du Tacul* (Hamish MacInnes). *Steger route* Cattinacio and *Yellow Edge* and *Demuth route* Tre Cime (Jim Swallow); North Wall Direct of Cima Una*** (German climber). *Malbogies* Avon Gorge* (Geoff Francis, Henry Rogers).

1958  *Bonatti Pillar* of Petit Dru*** (Hamish MacInnes, Don Whillans and Paul Ross, with Walter Phillip and Richard Blach); West Face of Petites Jorasses*** (Ronnie Wathen).

1959  *Comici/Dimai, Brandler/Hasse*** and *Cassin/Ratti* routes Tre Cime (Gunn Clark); *Woubits* (Jim O'Neill) and *Mostest* (Jim Swallow) Clogwyn Du'r Arddu – second ascents.

1960  Annapurna 2* by West Ridge Nepal (Dick Grant and Ang Nyima) – expedition led by Col. James Roberts; *King Cobra* Skye* (Tom Patey).

1961  Nuptse* by South Face Nepal (part of second summit team with Jim Swallow, Ang Pemba and Les Brown – first pair: Dennis Davis and Tashi) – expedition led by Joe Walmsley; Central Pillar of Frêney, Mt Blanc* (Don Whillans, Ian Clough and Jan Djuglosz)

1962  *Trango* Castell Cidwm* (Joe Brown); *Ichabod* Scafell (Mike Thompson) – second ascent; *Schmid/Krebs route* Karwendal*** (Don Whillans); *Walker Spur* of Grandes Jorasses (Ian Clough); North Wall of the Eiger*** (Ian Clough)

1963  Central Tower of Paine* by West Face Chile (Don Whillans) – expedition led by Barrie Page.

1964  North Face of Pointe Migot* and West Ridge of Aig. de Lepiney* (Tom Patey, Joe Brown and Robin Ford); *Andrich/Fae route* on Civetta (Jim McCarthy); *Medlar* (Martin Boysen) and *Totalitarian* (Mike Thompson) Raven Crag, Thirlmere.

1965  *Coronation Street* Cheddar* (Tony Greenbank); *The Holy Ghost* Scafell* (Mike Thompson); West Face of the Cardinal* (Tom Patey); West Face Direct of Aig. du Plan* (Lito Tejada Flores); North-East Ridge of Dent du Midi * (Rusty Baillie and John Harlin); Right-hand Pillar of Brouillard, Mt Blanc* (Rusty Baillie, John Harlin and Brian Robertson).

1966  North Face Direct of the Eiger* – in supporting role; Old Man of Hoy Orkneys* (Tom Patey and Rusty Baillie).

1968  North Face of Aig. d'Argentière (Dougal Haston) – in winter.

1969  *March Hare's Gully* Applecross** (Tom Patey); *Great Gully* of Garbh Bheinn** (Tom Patey and Don Whillans).

1970  South Face of Annapurna Nepal* – leader of expedition – summit reached by Dougal Haston and Don Whillans.

1971  East Face of Moose's Tooth Alaska – attempt with Jim McCarthy, Tom Frost and Sandy Bill curtailed by bad weather; *White Wizard* Scafell* (Nick Estcourt).

1972  South West Face of Everest Nepal – leader of expedition curtailed by cold and high wind; Great Gully of Grandes Jorasses (Dougal Haston with Mick Burke and Bev Clarke in support) attempt in winter.

1973  Brammah* by the South Ridge India (Nick Estcourt) – joint leader of expedition with Balwant Sandhu.

1974  Changabang* by East Ridge India (Martin Boysen, Doug Scott, Dougal Haston, Tashi and Balwant Sandhu) – joint leader of expedition with Sandhu.

1975  North Face Direct of Aig. du Triolet** (Dougal Haston); South West Face of Everest Nepal* – leader of expedition – summit reached by Dougal Haston and Doug Scott, Pete Boardman, Pertemba and possibly Mick Burke.

1976  North Face of Pt.20,309
Kishtwar, India (Ronnie
Richards) – attempt gaining
two-thirds height; East Ridge of
Mt Cook and Symes Ridge of Mt
Tasman New Zealand (Nick
Banks, Keith Woodford and Bob
Cunningham).

1977  The Ogre* by the South Face
Pakistan (Nick Estcourt) and the
West Ridge (Doug Scott) – the
South Face climb ended at the
West Summit. Clive Rowland
and Mo Anthoine took part in
the West Ridge ascent to the
foot of the summit tower.

1978  West Ridge of K2 Pakistan –
leader of expedition curtailed
after death of Nick Estcourt in
an avalanche below Camp 2.

1980  Pts 6200m* and 5400* Kongur
Group, China (Al Rouse and
Mike Ward) – climbed during a
reconnaissance expedition.

1981  Kongur* by the West Ridge
China (Al Rouse, Pete
Boardman and Joe Tasker) –
expedition led by Mike Ward.

1982  North East Ridge of Everest
Tibet – leader of expedition
curtailed after disappearance of
Pete Boardman and Joe Tasker.

1983  Orion Face of Ben Nevis (Stuart
Fife); South West Summit of
Shivling* by the South East
Ridge India (Jim Fotheringham);
Mt Vinson Antarctica***(Dick
Bass, Tae Maeda, Yuichiro Miura,
Steve Marts, Rick Ridgeway
and Frank Wells) – soloed final
section prior to ascent by the
others. Expedition led jointly
by Bass and Wells.

1984  West Ridge of Karun Koh
Pakistan (Ikram Khan, Maqsood
Ahmed and Al Rouse) – leader
of expedition curtailed by bad
weather; Cruel Sister Pavey Ark
(Jim Loxham) – first E3 lead.

1985  South East Ridge of Everest
Nepal (Odd Eliassen, Bjørn
Myrer-Lund, Pertemba, Ang
Lhakpa and Dawa Nuru) –
expedition led by Arne Naess.

1986  North East Pillar of Norliga
Skagastozstind Norway (Odd
Eliassen); Athanor Goat Crag
(Dave Absalom) – first 6a lead.
Yellow Edge Avon Gorge (Steve
Berry); South Pillar of Grosse
Drusenturm Rätikon and North
East Diedre of Brenta Alta (Jim
Fotheringham).

1987  South West Buttress of
Menlungtse West Tibet – leader
of expedition curtailed by bad
weather.

1988  Menlungtse West* by the West
Ridge and Face Tibet – leader of
expedition – summit reached by
Andy Fanshawe and Alan
Hinkes.

1991  Lemon Mountains Greenland –
as climbing leader with Robin
Knox-Johnston (Jim Lowther,
Perry Crickmere, James Burdett).

1992  Panch Chuli II Kumaon, India
West Ridge*, with Graham Little
on Indian/British Kumaon
Expedition – joint leader with
Harish Kapadia.

1993  Chisel*, Ivory Tower*, Needle*
Lemon Mountains, Greenland
(Jim Lowther, Graham Little,
Rob Ferguson).

1993  Elbrus and North East Ridge
of Ushba, Caucasus. (Louise
Wilson, Gerry Wilson, Jim
Fotheringham, Jim Curran,
Richard Else, Vocha Gorbach,
Sasha Vasko).

1994  Rangrik Rang* Kinnaur, India –
Indian/British expedition with
Harish Kapadia.

1995  Drangnag-Ri* Rowaling, India
(Høibakk, Myrer-Lund, Pema
Dorge, Lhakpu Gyalu).

1996  Sepu Kangri Tibet –
reconnaissance with Charles
Clarke.

1997  Sepu Kangri Tibet – expedition
defeated by heavy snowfall.

1998  Sepu Kangri Tibet – Scott Muir
and Vic Saunders reach West
Shoulder; Seamo Uylmitok*
Graham Little.

2000  Danga II* (6200m) with son
Daniel, brother Gerald, nephew
James and Furtenjee Sherpa.

2000  The Colossus* by South East
Ridge; Junction Peak * by East
Ridge; The Blade * by South
Ridge, from head of Kangikitsoq
Fjord (South Greenland) with
Rob Ferguson, Jim Lowther
and John Porter.

2001  Arganglas International
Expedition 2001 to Ladakh,
Abale Peak* (6360m) with Muni,
Shroff, Sherpa Samgyal; Amale
Peak* with Captain Lingwal,
Dam and Sherpa Wangchuk;
Yamandaka* (6218m) with Mark
Richey, Mark Wilford.

# Glossary

**A**

**abseil** method of descending a rock face by sliding down a rope, usually doubled so that the rope can be pulled down afterwards.

**acclimatization** process of physiological adaptation to living and climbing at high altitude.

**aid climbing** using equipment such as pitons, ice screws, bolts directly to assist progress; also called artificial climbing.

**alpine-style** climbing at high altitude in one continuous push from the foot to top of the mountain, carrying minimum gear, bivouacking en route as necessary, but not returning to base to restock, nor using fixed camps or fixed ropes.

**anchor** the point to which a fixed abseil or belay rope is anchored; either a natural feature or a piton, bolt or nut.

**arête** a sharp ridge of rock or snow.

**B**

**belay** a method of safeguarding a climbing partner from falling by tying oneself to a firm anchor from which one can pay out or take in the rope. A lead climber may safeguard himself with a running belay (runner) by putting in a piton, nut or, in earlier days, placing a rope loop over a natural rock spike or round a chockstone, then letting his rope run through a karabiner (or sling and karabiner) attached to it.

**bergschrund** the gap or crevasse between the glacier proper and the upper snows of a face.

**bivouac** to spend a night in the open or in a snow hole on a mountain, or in a minimal bivvy sack or tent, as opposed to a proper tent or fixed camp.

**bolt** an anchor point hammered into a hole drilled in the rock, which expands to create a friction grip.

**bouldering** exercising or training by climbing boulders that require a high level of technical expertise.

**C**

**chang** Sherpa beer brewed from rice or sometimes millet.

**chimney** a fissure in the rock or ice wide enough to climb up on the inside.

**chockstones** stones found wedged in a crack or placed there specially to hold a running belay, or belay, the natural precursors of manufactured wedges and nuts.

**climbing roped** climbers rope together on difficult or dangerous ground for safety, and can either all move together or move one at a time, leaving other member(s) of the team constantly belayed.

**col** a pass or dip in a ridge, usually between two peaks.

**cornice** an overhanging mass of snow projecting over the edge of a ridge, formed by prevailing winds.

**couloir** an open gully.

**crampons** steel spiked frames which can be fitted to boots to give a grip on ice and firm snow slopes.

**crevasse** a crack in a glacier surface which can be both wide and very deep, made by the movement of the glacier over the irregular shapes in its bed, or by bends in its course.

**cwm** a deep, rounded hollow at the head or side of a valley, formed by glacial action.

**D**

**deadman** small alloy plate which is dug into the snow to act like a fluke anchor, digging deeper the harder it is pulled.

**descendeur** alloy device used for belaying and abseiling.

**E**

**étrier** portable rope and metal or webbing loop ladders of a few rungs used in aid climbing.

**F**

**face** a steep aspect of a mountain between two ridges.

**fixed ropes** on prolonged climbs up steep ground the lead climber, having run out the full length of rope, ties it to an appropriate anchor, and subsequently all climbers move independently up and down the fixed rope, clipped on to it, using it either as a safety line or, on very steep ground, for direct progress. The rope is left in place for the duration of the climb.

**front pointing** climbing straight up steep snow or ice by means of kicking in the front points of crampons and supporting balance with an ice axe, or, on steep ground, using the picks of an ice axe and ice hammer in either hand

**G**

**gendarme** a rock pinnacle obtruding from a ridge, often surrounded by snow.

**H**

**headwall** steep rock barrier at the head of a valley.

**I**

**icefall** where a glacier falls steeply and creates a series of crevasses and pinnacles of ice.

**J**

**jumar clamps** devices that lock on to fixed rope to support a climber's weight when subject to downward force, but which can be slid up the rope as a method of climbing, or jumaring, it.

**K**

**karabiners** oval metal snap-links used for, among other things, attaching rope to an anchor.

**L**

**la** pass (Tibetan).

**M**

**monsoon** the monsoon reaches the Himalaya and climbing is impossible by the middle of June, so expeditions are made in the pre-monsoon season (mid-May to mid-June) or the post-monsoon season (mid-September to mid-October). The Karakoram is not affected by the monsoon in this way.

**moraine** accumulation of stones and debris carried down by a glacier.

**N**

**névé** permanent snow at the head of a glacier.

**nuts** originally were nuts (of nuts and bolts) with the thread drilled out, but progressed to alloy wedges. Used in cracks to support belays.

**O**

**oedema** a high-altitude illness in which water accumulates in the brain (cerebral oedema) or the lungs (pulmonary oedema). Immediate and swift descent is imperative for survival.

**off-width** cracks too wide to fist jam, too narrow to take more than an arm and leg. Difficult to protect.

**P**

**pitch** section of climbing between two stances or belay points.

**piton** a metal peg hammered into a rock crack to support a belay.

**powder-snow avalanche** caused by freshly fallen snow on steep surfaces before it has had time either to thaw or freeze; one of the most spectacular and dangerous avalanche conditions.

**protection** the number and quality of running belays used to make a pitch safer and psychologically easier to lead.

**prussiking** a method of directly ascending a rope with the aid of prussik knots, or friction hitches, with foot loops.

**R**

**rakshi** Sherpa spirit usually distilled from rice.

**runner (running belay)** an intermediate anchor point between the lead climber and the main belay, when the rope runs through a karabiner attached to this anchor, thus reducing the distance a leader would fall.

**S**

**sérac** wall, pinnacle or tower of ice, often unstable and dangerous.

**siege-style** the method by which the 8000-m (26,250-ft) summits were first climbed. It involves establishing fixed camps up a mountain, connected by fixed ropes. These camps are stocked by porters and/or climbers who move up in relays, taking turns out in front making the route and establishing the next camp, then returning to Base Camp to rest while another team moves up to continue from the new high point. The use of supplementary oxygen on the higher 8000-m peaks and using large porter teams are other regular features of siege-style climbing.

**Sherpas** an ethnic group of Tibetan stock, living in the Everest region, who have obtained an effective monopoly of high-altitude portering in Nepal.

**sirdar** head Sherpa on an expedition.

**sling** a loop of rope or nylon tape used for belays or in abseiling.

**spindrift** loose powder snow carried by wind or small avalanche.

**spur** rock or snow rib on the side of a mountain.

**stance** place where a climber makes his belay, ideally somewhere comfortable to stand or sit.

**step** vertical or short steep rise in a gully or ridge.

**T**

**top rope** a rope secured from above.

**traverse** to move horizontally or diagonally across a rock or snow slope. Also the ascent and descent of a mountain by different routes.

**tsampa** barley flour, a staple of Sherpa diet.

**U**

**undercut** low horizontal crack or pocket with a lip on its upper surface around which a hold or pinch grip can be attained.

**W**

**wedge** made from wood and used for hammering into wide cracks for belays or runners.

**white-out** condition of driving snow and mist with a snow background, which makes it impossible to judge distance or distinguish between solid ground and space.

**windslab avalanche** occurs when a snow layer formed by wind-compacted snow settles insecurely on top of old snow and descends in enormous blocks, or slabs.

# Index

# Acknowledgements

## Picture credits

All photographs are from the Chris Bonington
Picture Library. Credits for individual photographers
are listed below.

t top; b bottom; c centre; l left; r right

Stein Aasheim: 214; Peter Boardman: 5l, 77, 91, 128–29,
131, 149, 168, 181, 186; Chris Bonington: 2, 4l, 5r, 9, 10,
11, 12, 16, 19, 21, 22, 25, 30, 31, 32, 33t, 33b, 34, 36, 41,
44–45, 46l; 46–47c, 48–49, 53, 55, 56, 57, 58, 59, 65,
68–69, 70, 76, 78, 82, 84, 86–87, 94, 95, 97, 99, 100, 105,
110–11, 132, 137, 142, 150l, 150r, 151l, 152–53, 156, 158,
159, 163, 170–71, 172, 175, 178–79, 184–85, 187, 188,
197, 199, 200, 202, 205, 209, 217, 218, 219, 220, 221, 223,
224, 225, 226–27, 228, 229, 231, 232, 234–35, 237, 238,
239, 241; Charles Clarke: 189; Dennis Davis: 8; Jim
Duff: 79, 80–81; Nick Estcourt: 23, 35, 46r, 47l, 47r, 51,
61, 73, 75, 88, 114, 139; Tom Frost: 13; Adrian Gordon:
145, 157, 160–61, 193, 195; John Michael Jardine: 151r,
154; George Lowe: 206–7; Dick Renshaw: 166–67;
Ronnie Richards: 92–93; Doug Scott: 85, 103, 107, 113,
119, 122–23, 126–127; Pertemba Sherpa: 133; Ken
Wilson: 7, 43; Dr Keiichi Yamada: 4r, 26–27

Photos used as bases for maps: 14 Peter Ganner; 20,
42 and 62 Dr Keiichi Yamada; 164 Adrian Gordon; 196
and 212 Chris Bonington

## Author's acknowledgements

Writing and assembling this book has been very
much a team effort. My first thanks go to my fellow
team members and all the others who helped make
my four expeditions to Everest possible. Some of
them contributed directly to the books, either
writing original pieces or allowing me to use their
diaries. These are acknowledged in the text.

Putting the book together has also been a team
effort. Margaret Body was my editor for all four
books and has done a wonderful job in helping me
to condense them into their present form and in
editing my link pieces. My great appreciation and
thanks to Frances Daltrey who runs my picture
library and has not only dug out all the relevant
pictures but also cleared permissions and has
constantly checked the text against pictures. Jinny
Johnson has done a wonderful job in putting the
whole book together and integrating the pictures
and text, while Clive Hayball has worked on the
actual layout of the pages to give them a fine crisp
appearance. Susan Haynes has managed the entire
project and Ion Trewin had the original idea.
Vivienne Schuster, my agent, has looked after all
the contracts, Alison Lancaster, who looks after
my accounts, has managed my finances at this end,
while Margaret Trinder, my secretary, has taken
innumerable calls and organized my life around and
outside the project. Finally and central to it all, my
wife Wendy has given me her love, support and a
host of good advice. My deep appreciation to them
all – a great team effort.

256

10   9   8   7   6   5   4   3   2   1

Text copyright © Sir Christian Bonington, 1973 and 2002
Extracts from *Everest The Hard Way* © British Everest Expedition/Barclays Bank
International, 1976
Extracts from *Everest The Unclimbed Ridge* © Jardine Matheson Holdings
Limited, 1983
Design and layout copyright © Weidenfeld & Nicolson 2002

This edition published in 2003 by Ragged Mountain Press
a division of The Mc Graw-Hill companies

First published in the United Kingdom in 2002
by Weidenfeld & Nicolson

Some of the text in this book first appeared in *Everest South West Face*, Hodder &
Stoughton, 1973, *Everest The Hard Way*, Hodder & Stoughton, 1976 and *Everest The
Unclimbed Ridge*, Hodder & Stoughton, 1983

A CIP catalogue record for this book is available from the Library of Congress

ISBN  0-07-141424-X


Printed and bound in Italy